The Complete Book of
Bible Activities

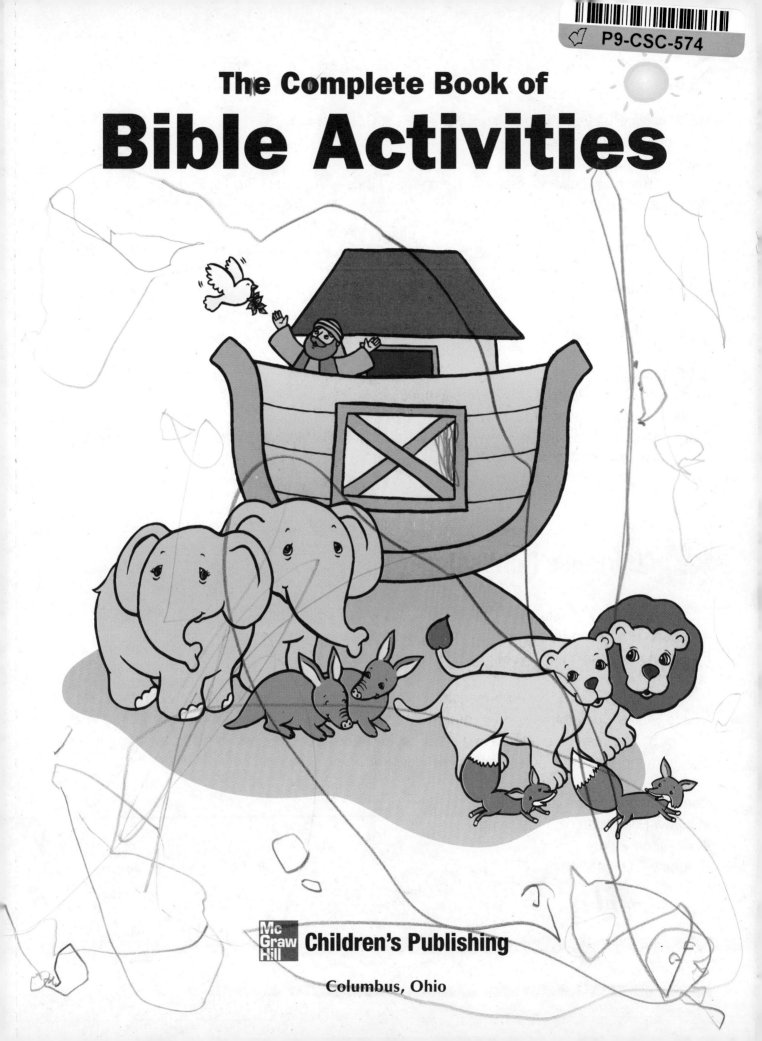

McGraw Hill Children's Publishing

Columbus, Ohio

Credits:

McGraw-Hill Children's Publishing Editorial/Art & Design Team
Vincent F. Douglas, *President*
Tracey E. Dils, *Publisher*
Jennifer Blashkiw Pawley, Teresa A. Domnauer, Lindsay A. Mizer; *Project Editors*
Robert Sanford, *Art Director*

Authors:

William Schlegl
Linda Standke
Sonja Turner

Also Thanks to:

MaryAnne Nestor, *Interior Design and Production*
Bobbie Houser, *Interior Production*
Julie Anderson, Anthony Carpenter, Gary Hoover, Shauna Mooney Kawasaki, Deb Kirkeeide,
Barb Lorseyedi; *Interior Illustration*

 **Children's Publishing**

Send all inquiries to:
McGraw-Hill Children's Publishing
8787 Orion Place
Columbus, OH 43240-4027

ISBN 1-56189-383-8

4 5 6 7 8 9 10 POH 07 06 05 04 03

The McGraw-Hill Companies

Table of Contents

Language Arts

Section 1, Language Arts

God is With You

⭐ Joshua struggled just like we do at times. What were God's comforting words to him? We can use these words in our lives today. Fill in the missing vowels using the code to read the Bible verse.

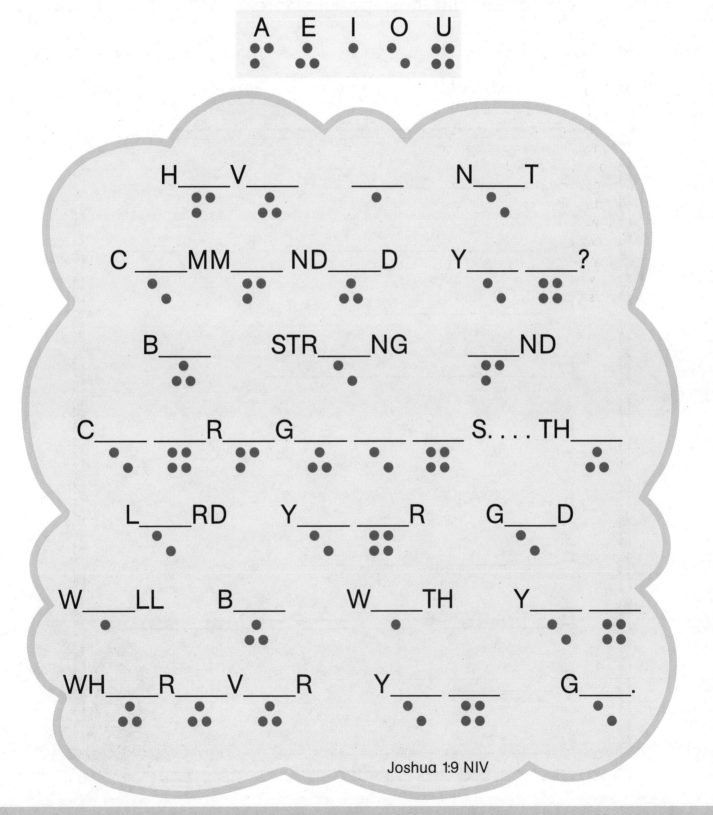

Joshua 1:9 NIV

vowels

Gimme an "E"

⭐ Several people mentioned in the Bible have names that begin with the letter **E**. Some of the names have several **E**'s in them. The names are listed below. Fit them into the correct lines below. Use a Bible dictionary to discover who these people were.

Ebenezer	Enos	Eli	Ephesians	Elijah
Esther	Elizabeth	Eve	Elisha	Eunice

E ___ ___ ___ ___ e

E ___ ___ ___ ___ ___ e ___ ___

E ___ ___ ___

E ___ ___ ___ ___ ___

E ___ e ___ e ___ e ___

E ___ e

E ___ ___ ___ e ___

E ___ ___ e ___ ___ ___ ___ ___

E ___ ___

E ___ ___ ___ ___ ___ ___

Silly Sarah

⭐ Look at how silly Sarah dressed today. Fill in the blanks with the missing short vowels to spell what she is wearing.

1. b____g s____ngl____ss____s

2. s____lly n____cklace

3. y____llow r____bb____n

4. dr____ss w____th f____t c____ts

5. ch____ckered s____cks

Mary Remembers

⭐ Say the sounds of **ar**, **er**, **ir**, **or**, and **ur**. Then read the story.

Mary will always remember Jesus' birth and the events that followed. After Jesus was born, a bright star shone in the dark sky above the stable. Shepherds followed the star and were the first to see baby Jesus, who lay still, not stirring, curled in the arms of his mother. Mary lay Jesus in the manger and covered him with furs. Later, wise doctors called magi came from far away bringing gifts: a bag of gold, a jug of incense, and a jar of myrrh. Mary was amazed at all that occurred.

⭐ List the words from the story that have these letters.

ar	er	ir
_____	_____	_____
_____	_____	_____
_____	_____	_____
_____	_____	**or**
_____	_____	_____
_____	_____	**ur**
	_____	_____
		_____

M-m-m . . . Good

Name_____

⭐ Do you know any people from the Bible whose names begin with the letter **M**? The clues below provide information about some of them. Write their names on the lines below. Can you think of any others?

Clues

I am an archangel.
(Jude 9)

I was thrown into a fiery furnace and survived.
(Daniel 3:26–27)

I was a disciple of Jesus.
(Matthew 10:2–3)

I was a prophet and wrote the last book in the Old Testament.

My sister and I were friends of Jesus. (There will be two names.)
(John 11:1)

My mother made a papyrus basket to put me in.
(Exodus 2:1–10)

_____
(amhicle)

_____
(hhemsac)

_____
(thwemat)

_____
(iaahclm)

_____
(htaarm)

_____
(ramy)

_____
(smseo)

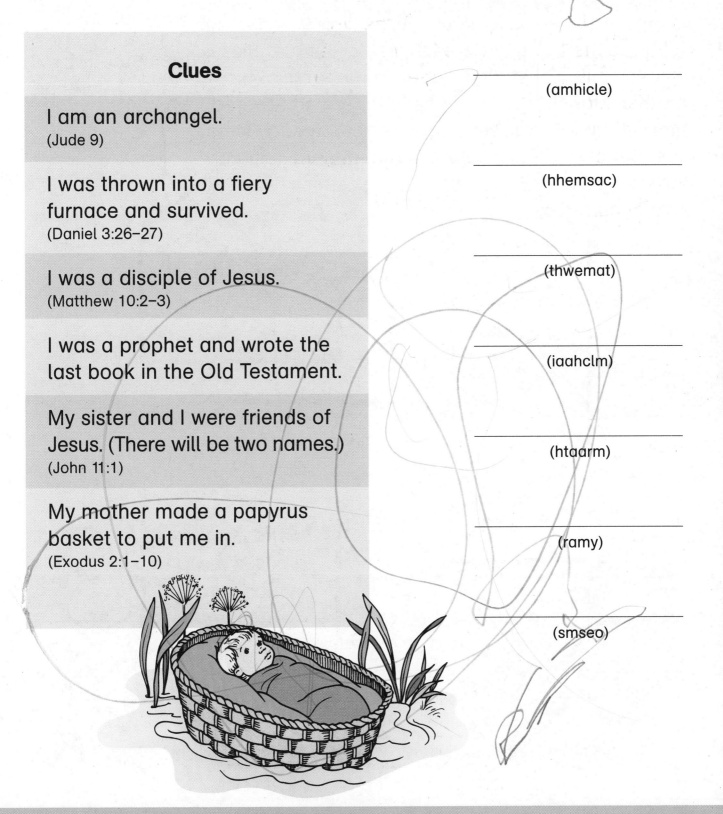

consonants

⭐ Can you list the six people below whose names begin with the letter **S**? Read the Bible verses if you are stumped. Write each name in the section under the correct description.

The Names

Genesis 5:32	Luke 2:34–35	1 Samuel 3:1–4
Luke 6:15	1 Samuel 11:15	Acts 5:1–10

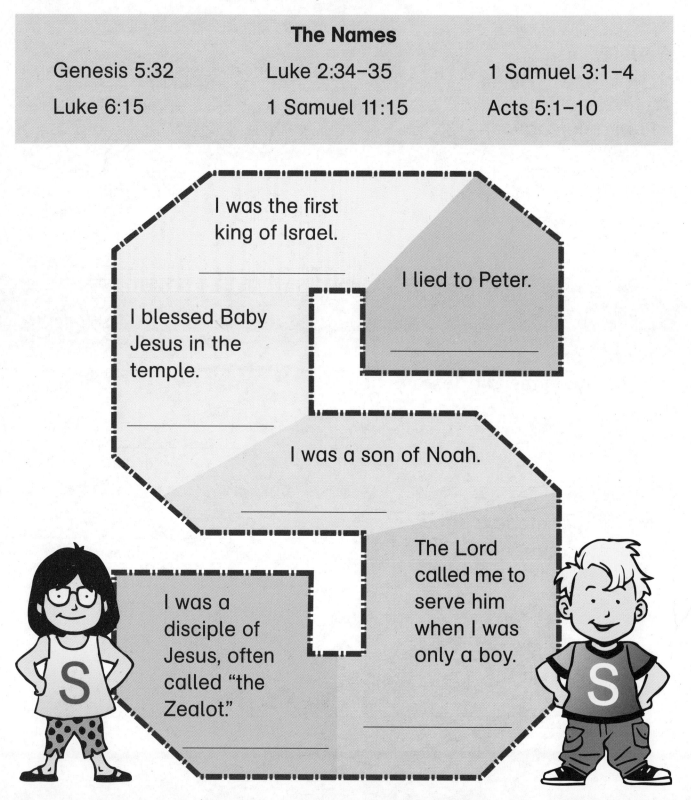

I was the first king of Israel.

_____

I lied to Peter.

_____

I blessed Baby Jesus in the temple.

_____

I was a son of Noah.

_____

I was a disciple of Jesus, often called "the Zealot."

_____

The Lord called me to serve him when I was only a boy.

_____

A Gift from God

Name_____

⭐ Every day is a beautifully wrapped gift from God—just look around you. Write the missing blend for each word. Then color the bow the correct color.

bl	**tr**	**pr**	**st**	**fl**	**cl**	**dr**
(red)	(green)	(blue)	(yellow)	(orange)	(pink)	(purple)

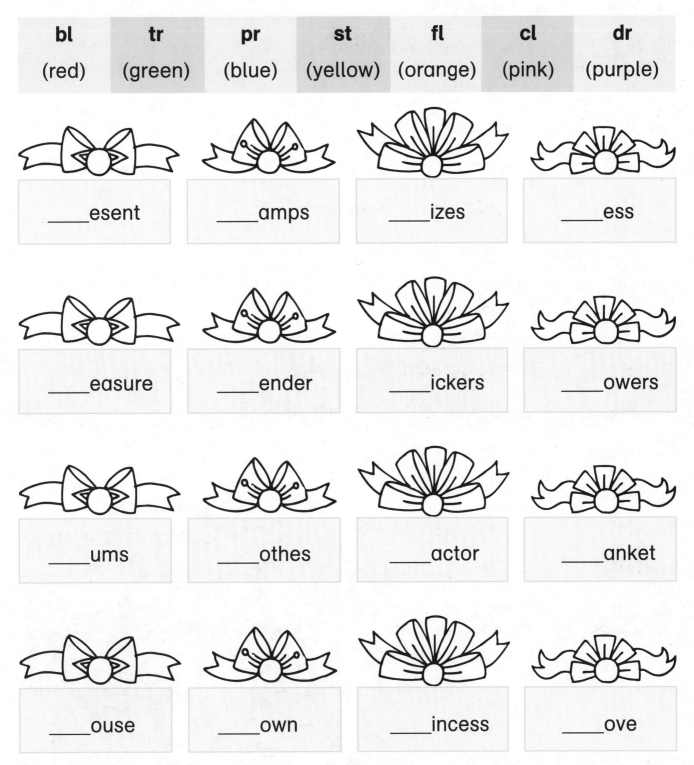

____esent

____amps

____izes

____ess

____easure

____ender

____ickers

____owers

____ums

____othes

____actor

____anket

____ouse

____own

____incess

____ove

initial consonant blends

Seeing Doubles

Name_____

⭐ Use the clues to write the correct double consonants (**ff**, **ss**, **ll**, or **zz**) at the end of each word.

1. che____ ____ = a game

2. hi____ ____ = a small mountain

3. le____ ____ = not more

4. hi____ ____ = snake noise

5. cu____ ____ = bottom of sleeve

6. fi____ ____ = bubbles in a drink

7. se____ ____ = opposite of buy

8. gu____ ____ = a sea bird

9. me____ ____ = clutter

10. ye____ ____ = to scream

11. gla____ ____ = holds something to drink

12. du____ ____ = not sharp

13. sni____ ____ = to smell

14. we____ ____ = not sick

15. bu____ ____ = bee's sound

16. dre____ ____ = gown

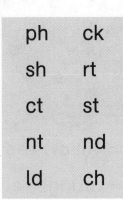

Jesus Fed 5,000

Name_____

⭐ Write the missing consonant blend.

ph	ck
sh	rt
ct	st
nt	nd
ld	ch

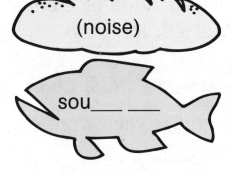

(noise)

sou___ ___

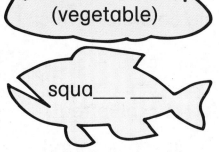

(vegetable)

squa___ ___

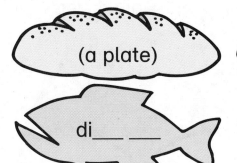

(a plate)

di___ ___

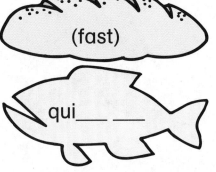

(fast)

qui___ ___

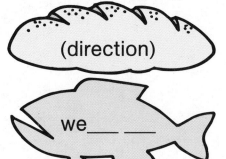

(direction)

we___ ___

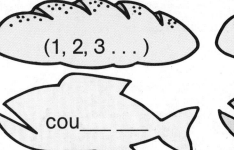

(1, 2, 3 . . .)

cou___ ___

(hairless)

ba___ ___

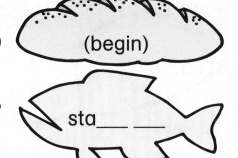

(begin)

sta___ ___

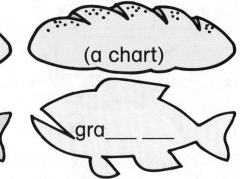

(save)

colle___ ___

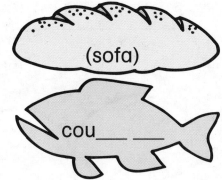

(a chart)

gra___ ___

(sofa)

cou___ ___

final consonant blends

Ernest the Elephant

Ernest kept busy on the ark learning the words below. Can you help him? Write the final consonant blend for each word. Color each toe by blending the colors shown on Ernest's Color Chart.

Ernest's Color Chart

ft = blue/red **nd** = yellow/brown **nt** = yellow/red

lt = purple/red **nk** = yellow/green **pt** = orange/red

mp = pink/orange **ld** = purple/brown **st** = black/red

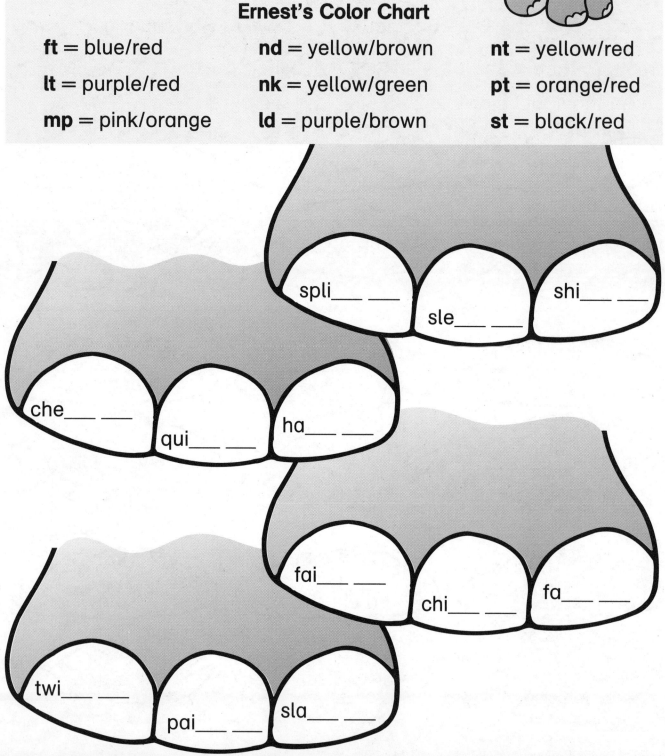

spli___ ___

sle___ ___

shi___ ___

che___ ___

qui___ ___

ha___ ___

fai___ ___

chi___ ___

fa___ ___

twi___ ___

pai___ ___

sla___ ___

Show and Tell

⭐ Say the **sh** sound. Read the story. Then circle each **sh** in the story.

Shannon's teacher, Mrs. Sheldon, had things to share. She had just come back from the seashore. "Look at the shiny seashell," she said. "I also have a scallop shell. God made them both."

After she shared with the children, she thanked God for sharing his creation. Then she put the shells on the shelf.

"I'm thankful I didn't see a shark with sharp teeth at the seashore," said Mrs. Sheldon.

⭐ Write the **sh** words in the puzzle.

Across

1.

4.

3.

5.

Down

1.

2.

4.

consonant digraphs

Paul in Chains

⭐ Say the **ch** sound. Read the story. Then circle each **ch** in the story.

The church was still as the children sat in their chairs listening to the story of Paul in prison. The teacher told them that God chose Paul to show charity to the Gentiles by telling them about the champion of the world, Jesus. For preaching the gospel, Paul was thrown in a chilly cell and locked in chains. Even in chains, Paul was cheerful and suffered gladly. He continued to spread the good news from his prison cell.

⭐ Write a **ch** word from the story for each picture.

_____   _____   _____

Don't Be Afraid!

Name_____

⭐ Say the **th** sound. Read the story. Then circle each **th** in the story.

Elizabeth loved Jesus. Every night she said her prayers with her mother and father. She thanked God for her parents, who both loved her very much. She also thanked God for her brother and her three best friends. Sometimes she prayed that God would help her with her math and other homework.

One night while Elizabeth lay in bed, it began to thunder. She was afraid until she remembered that God was always with her, watching over her. She whispered, "Thank you, God," and fell asleep.

⭐ Circle the **th** words in the wordsearch below.

father
mother
thunder
both
brother
three
other
with
math
that
thanked

t	b	t	h	o	t	h	e	r
h	s	a	t	h	a	t	t	b
u	w	t	h	o	y	b	h	r
n	n	b	c	t	d	o	a	o
d	w	i	t	h	j	t	n	t
e	e	g	i	a	k	h	k	h
r	w	u	s	t	h	r	e	e
m	a	t	h	b	n	a	d	r
b	m	o	t	h	e	r	k	p
t	u	r	f	a	t	h	e	r

consonant digraphs

A Zoo Surprise

⭐ Say the **ph** and **gh** sounds aloud. (They both sound like "f.") Read the story. Then circle each **ph** and **gh** in the story.

Phil went to the zoo. He saw a pheasant sitting in a tree. Then, he took a photo of a dolphin swimming in a pool. Next, he saw a tough gorilla pound its chest. Later, an elephant walked up to Phil. This did not upset Phil. He knew the elephant was a phony. The elephant said, "Would you like my autograph?" Phil just laughed.

⭐ Draw pictures of these.

pheasant	dolphin
elephant	Phil

Bible Nouns

⭐ Color each Bible blue if the word in it is a noun. Put an **X** on each word that is not a noun.

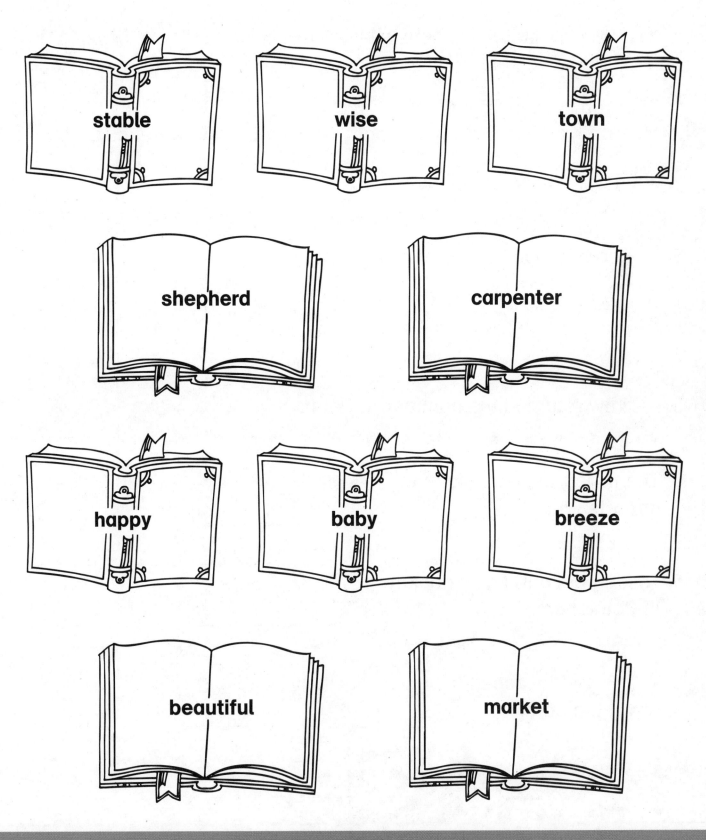

stable

wise

town

shepherd

carpenter

happy

baby

breeze

beautiful

market

Ready, Set, Go!

Name_____

Underline each noun. Then, in the boxes, draw the symbol for each noun in the order it appears in the sentence.

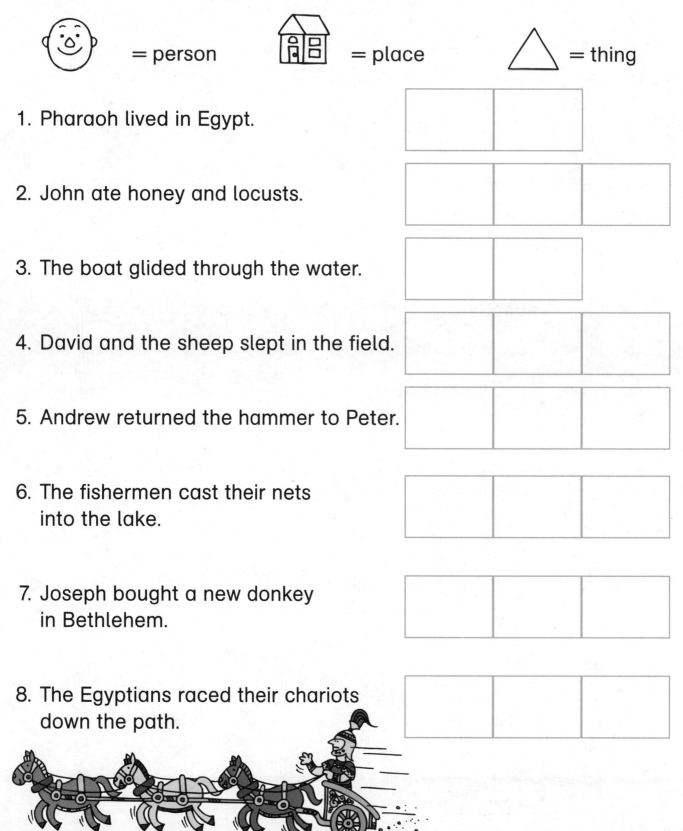

😊 = person   🏠 = place   △ = thing

1. Pharaoh lived in Egypt.

2. John ate honey and locusts.

3. The boat glided through the water.

4. David and the sheep slept in the field.

5. Andrew returned the hammer to Peter.

6. The fishermen cast their nets into the lake.

7. Joseph bought a new donkey in Bethlehem.

8. The Egyptians raced their chariots down the path.

Reflections

⭐ Mirrors are like copy machines. Write the plural for each noun. Then draw each reflection in the mirror.

fox

mouse

watch

leaf

lady

child

ball

bunny

tooth

Summer Vacation

⭐ Circle the proper nouns in each sentence.

1. The students in Mr. Hoover's Bible class at Grace School had visited many places during their summer vacation.

2. In June, Robbie visited his sister Kate in Georgia.

3. When he was in Atlanta, he went to the Bible Olympics at Fulton County Stadium.

4. Marco had fun at God's Kingdom Bible Camp in Sunnydale, Florida.

5. His family also went to the Kennedy Space Center.

6. Carla enjoyed a ride on the cable car in San Francisco.

7. Her Aunt Gloria's living room window overlooked the Golden Gate Bridge.

8. Last Thursday, Carmen brought her pictures of the Grand Canyon to show us.

A Day at the Zoo

⭐ Read this story and fill in each blank using a pronoun from the Word Bank. Some of the words will be used more than once.

Word Bank

it	him	she	their	they	we
you	them	his	her	its	

Nick was having a great time. _____ parents had brought

_____ to the zoo for the day. Together, _____ wanted to

see the new reptile display. Nick thought it was cool the way God had

made snakes.

"Mom, can _____ go right to the boa constrictor's cage?"

asked Nick. "_____ is my favorite reptile."

Nick and _____ parents peered through the glass at the large

snake. Kate, the zookeeper, was busy feeding the snake _____

dinner. _____ also fed the lizards, turtles, and other snakes in

_____ areas.

"Let's go see the turtles next!" said Nick.

"What do _____ like best about _____?" asked

_____ dad.

"Turtles hide in _____ shells!" exclaimed Nick.

After seeing the rest of the reptiles, Nick and _____ family

packed the van and headed home. _____ had been a wonderful

day.

In the Ark

In each  write a pronoun that could take the place of the underlined noun(s).

Example:

{ He }   <u>Bob</u> saw the movie twice.

1. The cat chased <u>the cat's</u> tail.

2. <u>Grandma and Grandpa</u> moved to Florida.

3. <u>My sister</u> was born in July.

4. We gave the puppy to <u>our neighbors</u>.

5. <u>Rick and I</u> played soccer on Monday.

6. Please give your coat to <u>Kim and me</u>.

7. <u>The ark</u> was overflowing with animals.

8. We played against <u>Justin's</u> team.

9. We went to see <u>Sue</u> in the hospital.

10. <u>Megan and Barb</u> played tennis.

Soar Like Eagles

⭐ **Verbs** are words that show action. Find and underline the verb in each sentence.

1. Eagles soar among the mountain's cliffs.

2. From tree to tree, a monkey swings.

3. A caterpillar wriggles out of its old skin.

4. Porpoises dive through the ocean spray.

5. Snakes slither on the hot desert sand.

6. Prairie dogs burrow in underground holes.

7. Deer leap through open fields.

8. Woodpeckers drill holes in hollow trees.

Jacob and Joseph

Joseph is speaking with his father, Jacob. Look at Joseph's sentences. Draw a smiley face beside the sentences that use correct verb tenses. Write the other sentences correctly on the lines below.

I will always trust God and follow him.

I love my new coat.

You has been a good father to me.

I come to see my brothers yesterday.

I seen my brothers do something bad.

Last night I had a dream about grain.

1. _____

_____

2. _____

_____

3. _____

_____

Spiders

★ To help explore God's world of spiders, Mrs. Cline's third grade class had an outdoor science lab. Afterwards, the class wrote about their experience and posted the results near the science table. The children used past tense verbs in each sentence. Find and underline each past tense verb. Then write the verbs in the puzzle boxes below.

1. We went on a nature walk.

2. We searched for spider webs.

3. We viewed the webs through magnifying glasses.

4. We looked for bugs in the webs.

5. The spiders caught many bugs.

6. We took photographs of the spider webs.

7. We shared information about spiders with each other.

8. We wrote about spiders and their webs.

9. Mrs. Cline mounted our photos and writing on the bulletin board.

10. We enjoyed our study of spider webs.

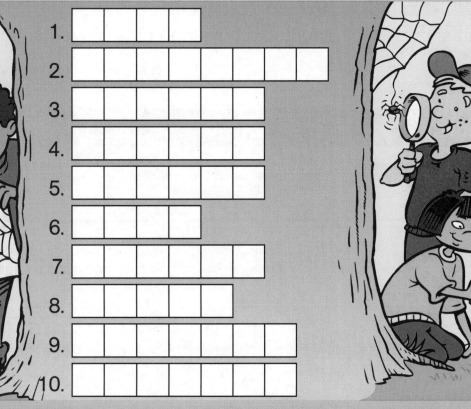

past tense verbs

Snow Everywhere

⭐ An **adverb** is a word that describes a verb. It tells **how, when,** or **where** an action takes place. Circle the adverbs in the story. Then write them under the correct category in the chart.

The snow began early in the day. Huge snowflakes floated gracefully to the ground. Soon the ground was covered with a blanket of white. Later the wind began to blow briskly. Outside the snow now drifted into huge mounds. Suddenly the snow stopped. The children went outdoors. Then they played in the snow there. They went sledding nearby. Others happily built snow forts. Joyfully the boys and girls played in the beautiful snow.

How	When	Where

Habits and Habitats

A sentence is a group of words that tells a complete thought. Write **yes** if the group of words make a sentence and write **no** if they do not. Punctuate the groups of words that are sentences.

_____ 1. The rain-drenched forest

_____ 2. Mountain goats can climb steep cliffs

_____ 3. Sharks never stop swimming

_____ 4. Migrate to lower areas

_____ 5. God created all types of animals

_____ 6. Leave in the winter

_____ 7. Insects reside all over the world

_____ 8. Favorite nighttime activity

_____ 9. Backyards attract many animals

_____ 10. Burrow in the ground

_____ 11. Spinning silken webs

_____ 12. Oceans are miles deep in some places

complete sentences

A Trip to the Circus

⭐ Some people use their special gifts by performing in the circus! Draw a line from the **subject** (peanut) to the **predicate** (elephant) that makes a complete sentence.

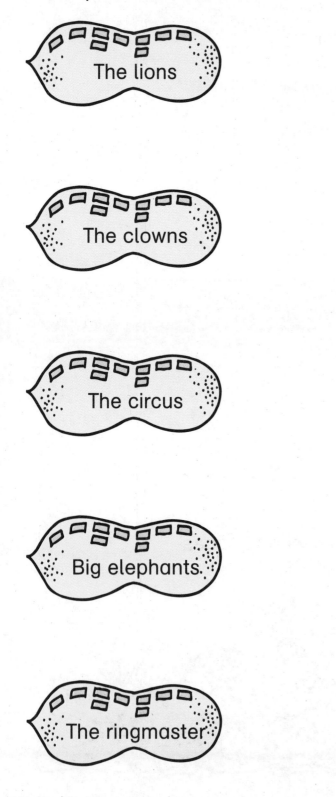

The lions

The clowns

The circus

Big elephants.

The ringmaster

began at 7 P.M.

wore brightly colored makeup.

announced the circus acts.

paraded in a line.

growled at the crowd.

⭐ Circle the 19 words in the story that need to begin with a capital letter.

> **Remember:**
>
> 1. All special names for people, places, and things begin with a capital letter. Don't forget that "I" is a special name, too.
>
> 2. The first word of a sentence always begins with a capital letter.

i took my dog, max, to a parade for pets. there we met lots of other pets and their owners. sammy's pet monkey, kong, held onto sammy's neck. rachel walked with her pet kitten named fluffy. freddie's frog, hopalong, jumped beside him. even sara came with her pet snake, slinky. each pet owner thought his or her pet was the best.

the other children asked me why max was wearing a watch. i told them that max is a "watch dog." they smiled as they looked at my little dog.

capital letters

Wow!

⭐ There are four different sentence types. They are explained below.

> **Statement**—tells something; ends with a period
>
> **Question**—asks something; ends with a question mark
>
> **Command**—tells someone to do something; ends with a period or an exclamation mark
>
> **Exclamation**—shows strong feeling such as fear, surprise, or excitement; ends with an exclamation mark

⭐ Read each sentence. Punctuate it, and write the sentence type on the line.

1. _____ Beware of rattlesnakes

2. _____ Will the sun rise in the Arctic tundra

3. _____ Where do zebras wander

4. _____ We should protect animal habitats

5. _____ Protect wildlife

6. _____ It's everyone's job to prevent forest fires

7. _____ Oceans are the earth's largest habitats

8. _____ I can't believe I just saw a whale

9. _____ Don't step on that plant

Calling All Commas

⭐ **Commas** are used to make the meaning of a sentence clearer. Use commas to separate a series of three or more words. Place the last comma just before the word *and*. Rewrite each sentence and add commas where they are needed.

1. In the stable, Mary saw hay cows and sheep.

   _____

2. In Sunday school, we studied Matthew Mark Luke and John.

   _____

   _____

3. Kindergartners used scissors magazines and glue to create collages.

   _____

   _____

4. The fourth grade made Christian symbol pins cards and magnets.

   _____

   _____

5. The second grade's mosaics featured fish doves and crosses.

   _____

   _____

6. The Praise Band sang played instruments and prayed.

   _____

   _____

7. The Bible tells us to love trust and obey.

   _____

Protect Our Oceans

Name _____

⭐ Read Jamie's letter to the editor. Help him by adding punctuation marks and capitals. (To capitalize a letter, draw three lines under it.) Then circle the six words that are misspelled and write them correctly on the numbered lines.

deer editor

    we have been studying oceans at school and I have learned a lot about animals and plants that live in the water i learned that humans do meny things to put ocean animals in danger we have not remembered to honor all god has given us

    some people use large nylon fishing nets that get loose and later trap ocean animals i wonder if they could use anuther kind of net or be more careful

    others, who use boats to ship oil, don't take very good care of there boats or they don't watch what they're doing and have crashes sometimes there are oil leaks this oil kills the ocean animals and plants that god created

    i want peeple to be more careful about our oceans this water can never be replaced it wuld be horrible if the ocean animals died and the water became so polluted we couldn't swim in it

    sincerely

    jamie johnson

1. _____ 4. _____

2. _____ 5. _____

3. _____ 6. _____

Dear Grandma

Letters require correct spelling, capitalization, and punctuation. Help Mark correct his letter by placing capital letters where they belong and adding any necessary punctuation. (To capitalize a letter, draw three lines under it.) Then circle the six words that are misspelled and write the words correctly on the lines below the letter.

June 8, 2003

dear grandma,

   I have been lerning about some of the wonderful animals god has made

   did you know that all animals are made to live right whare they are mountain goats have special hoofs so that climbing to the top of mountains is easy for them god also helps some peeple live high in the mountains

   i know you and grandpa have hikd up the mountains by your house have you seen any mountain goats

   pleese write bak and tell me what you've seen of god's creation on the mountain

                    Love

                    Mark

1. _____   4. _____

2. _____   5. _____

3. _____   6. _____

A Whale of a Tale

Name_____

Jonah had quite a story to tell his friends. If the pair of words on the whale rhyme, color the whale. If the words do not rhyme, put an **X** on the whale.

put   shut

those   chose

shall   fall

clean   mean

brown   crown

could   should

any   many

splash   flash

Name_____

If the two words on a shell make a compound word, write them together on a line. Put an **X** on the shell if they do not make a compound word.

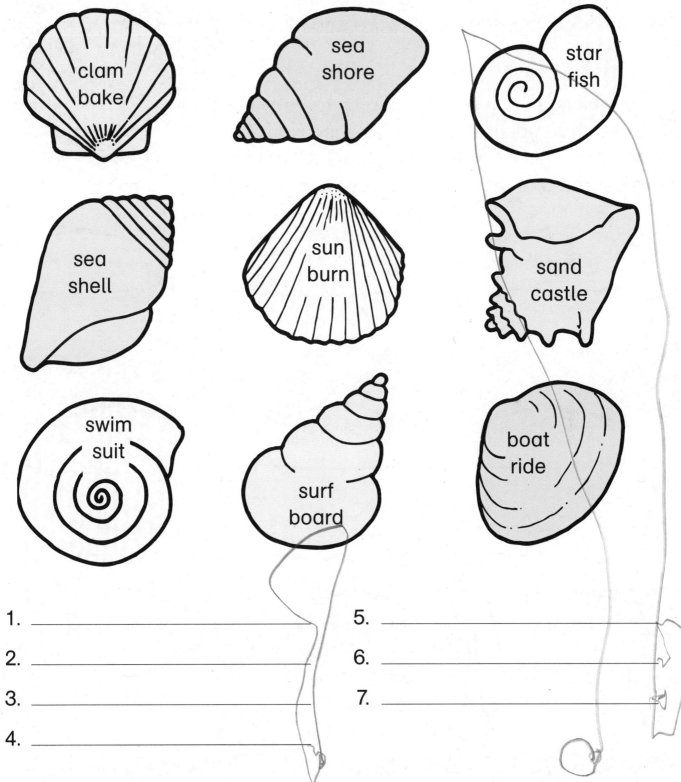

1. _____

2. _____

3. _____

4. _____

5. _____

6. _____

7. _____

On the Ark

Which is first, and which is last,
and which are in the middle?
All of these animals were on the ark.
Now can you solve each word riddle?

⭐ Rearrange each set of syllables to form
a word that makes sense. Write each word
in its ark. Then color the arks with 3-syllable
words—red and 4-syllable words—blue.

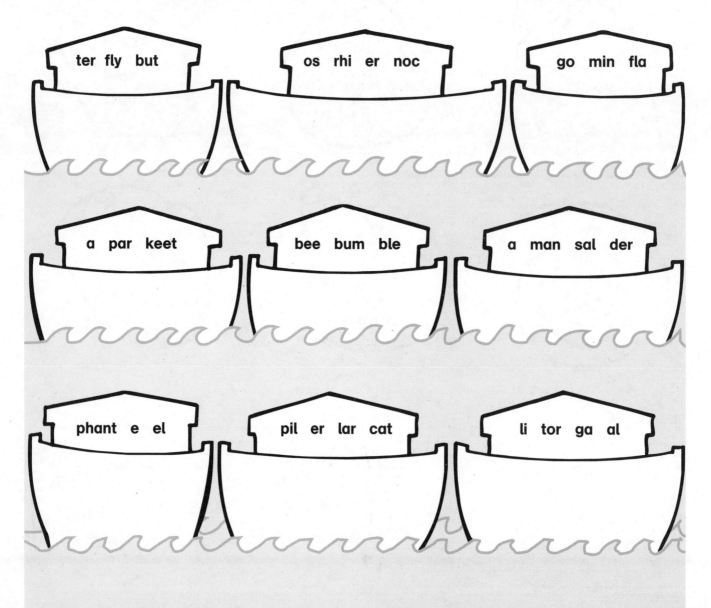

ter fly but

os rhi er noc

go min fla

a par keet

bee bum ble

a man sal der

phant e el

pil er lar cat

li tor ga al

Jesus, Our Redeemer

⭐ A word without any prefixes or suffixes is called a **base word** or **root word**. Prefixes and suffixes change a base word's meaning. A **prefix** is added to the beginning of a word. A **suffix** is added to the end of a word.

Look at each word. Does it have a prefix, suffix, or both? Write the prefixes and suffixes on the lines.

Prefix   **Suffix**

1. _____   redeemer   _____

2. _____   invaluable   _____

3. _____   righteous   _____

4. _____   lovely   _____

5. _____   uncovered   _____

6. _____   creation   _____

7. _____   smallest   _____

8. _____   unchanging   _____

9. _____   dislike   _____

prefix/suffix/base word

Jesus Loves Us!

⭐ Write the missing contraction in each sentence.

1. I _____ find my Bible for Sunday school.
   (aren't   couldn't)

2. Lisa shared her snack. _____ always showing love
   (She's   She'd)

   to others.

3. In the Bible, God gives us many promises. _____ why
   (That's   Let's)

   we _____ worried about God's love for us.
   (aren't   couldn't)

4. Jesus loves us very much! He tells us he _____ ever
   (isn't   won't)

   stop.

5. _____ going to invite our friends to church.
   (We're   We've)

6. Bob memorized many Bible verses. _____ very proud
   (He'd   He's)

   of his hard work.

Find the Twins

⭐ Even though twins may look identical, God made each twin unique. Words that have the same meaning are **synonyms**. Think of them as twins. Using the words in the Word Bank, find each pair of synonyms and write them on the box below the twin.

Word Bank

weary	watch	present	evening
gift	tired	night	observe
hurt	tale	injured	fable

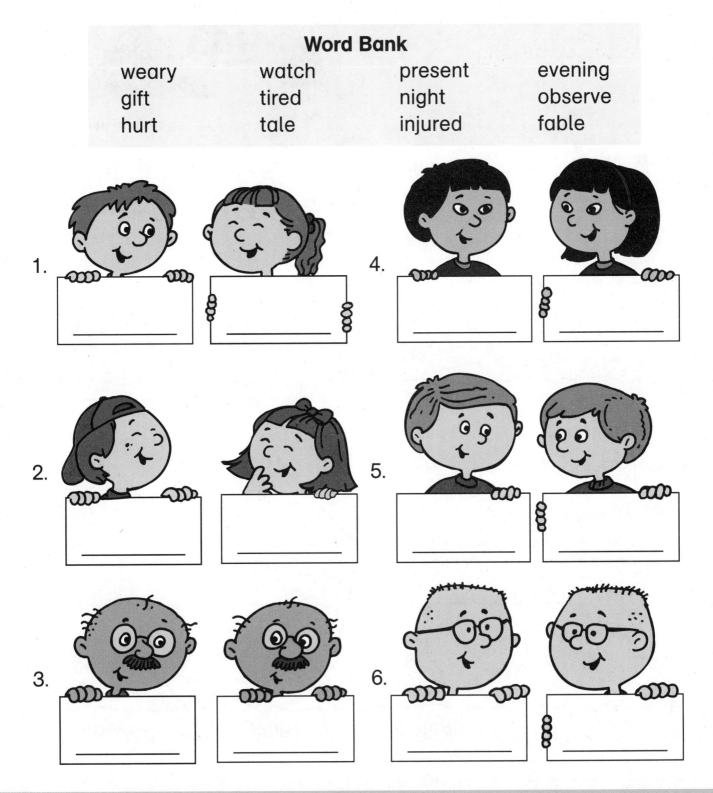

1.

2.

3.

4.

5.

6.

Go to the Ant!

Name_____

Words that have opposite meanings are **antonyms**. Find the matching antonym for each word listed under the anthills. Then draw the correct number of ants on each anthill to show the number of the matching antonym.

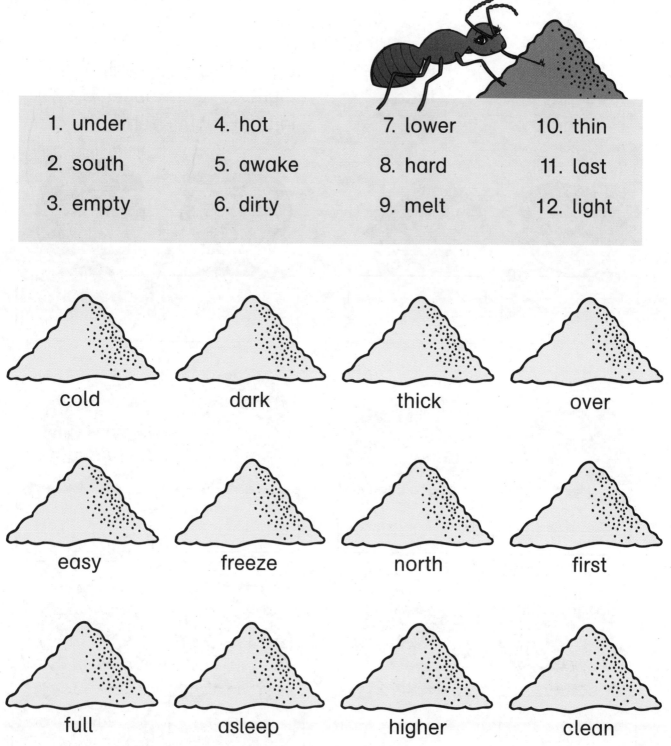

1. under	4. hot	7. lower	10. thin
2. south	5. awake	8. hard	11. last
3. empty	6. dirty	9. melt	12. light

cold   dark   thick   over

easy   freeze   north   first

full   asleep   higher   clean

Prickly Cactus

⭐ **Antonyms** are words with opposite meanings. Write each word from the Word Bank next to its antonym.

Word Bank

difficult	moist	day
chilly	dull	largest

1. dry _____

2. smallest _____

3. sharp _____

4. night _____

5. easy _____

6. warm _____

⭐ **Adjectives** are words that describe or tell about nouns. Circle the adjectives in each sentence. Be careful. Some sentences may have more than one adjective.

1. The scaly lizard crept across the desert.

2. In the daytime, scorching temperatures are common.

3. Animals come out to hunt during chilly nights.

4. A desert is home to poisonous snakes.

5. Birds build nests in prickly cactus plants.

antonyms/adjectives

Baby Talk

⭐ Did you know that God loved you before you were even born? Read the sentences describing some baby animals. Then write each baby animal's name under its picture.

1. An elephant has a baby **calf**.

2. The **tadpole** looks very different from its mother, a frog. Its tail helps it swim.

3. A **kid** eats lots of things, just as grown-up goats do.

4. A mother bear takes care of its **cub**.

5. A **piglet** says, "Oink."

6. This **colt** is white with black stripes.

_____

_____

_____

_____

_____

_____

Two for One

⭐ Some words have more than one meaning. Look at each pair of pictures. Unscramble the word that can be used for both pictures.

_____
(teabsk)

_____
(udck)

_____
(tab)

_____
(nteo)

_____
(bxo)

_____
(eterlts)

word meanings

Ask, Seek, Knock

⭐ Fill in the missing words from the Bible verse below. Use the words in the Word Bank to help you.

Word Bank			
seek	knock	ask	open

Jesus said,

"___ ___ ___ and it will be given to you;

___ ___ ___ ___ and you will find;

___ ___ ___ ___ ___

and the door will be

___ ___ ___ ___ to you."

Matthew 7:7 NIV

That's a Pizza!

Papa Luigi was having a bad day. He forgot to order some things that he used to make his very special pizza. Then he asked Jesus to help him have a good day anyway.

A man walked into the restaurant. "I'd like to order your 'Papa Luigi's Pizza Supremo,'" he stated.

"I'm sorry, but I do not have all of the toppings," explained Papa Luigi. "However, I can make you a large surprise pizza at a special price of $5.00."

"Okay, I'll try it," said the man.

Luigi had a great day. He sold lots of "surprise pizzas"!

Use the clues to find what toppings were on the pizza.

1. ____ ____ ____ ____ ____ ____
   (rhymes with sneeze)

2. ____ ____ ____ ato (Thomas's nickname)

3. saus____ ____ ____
   (the number of years one has lived)

4. pine____ ____ ____ ____ ____ (a red fruit)

5. o____ ____ ____ ____s (opposite of die)

Jesus Said . . .

Name_____

⭐ Jesus taught us many things about how we should live as his followers. Some of his teachings are listed here, but important words are missing. Fill in the blanks to complete the ideas using the words from the Word Bank. If you need a clue, you will find the answers in the verses listed at the bottom of the page.

Word Bank

always	forgiven	hearts	money	clothes
judge	neighbor	forgive	judged	others

1. "Love your _____ as yourself."

2. "You cannot serve both God and _____."

3. "Why do you worry about _____?"

4. "Do not let your _____ be troubled. Trust in God; trust also in me."

5. "Do not _____, or you too will be _____."

6. "_____, and you will be _____."

7. "Do to _____ as you would have them do to you."

8. "And surely I am with you _____, to the very end of the age."

Answers

1. Mark 12:31	3. Matthew 6:28	5. Matthew 7:1	7. Luke 6:31
2. Matthew 6:24	4. John 14:1	6. Luke 6:37	8. Matthew 28:20b

Danger!

⭐ Read the news release below. Then use the words from the Word Bank to fill in the blanks.

Word Bank		
fire	animals	rescue
safety	bedding	radio
resume	lows	frostbite
mountain	telephones	climbers

Mountain Press–Late Thursday, a group of _____ climbers

lost _____ contact with their home base causing concern

for their _____. Temperatures are expected to reach

record _____ this evening. Even though the climbers

are well-equipped with _____ and extra clothing, the

threat of _____ is great. These experienced

_____ are aware of predatory _____

and will likely light a _____ to keep them away. A

_____ party has been dispatched. Helicopters will search

until midnight and then _____ at daybreak. In the

meantime, families wait near their _____ as they pray

for news about loved ones.

Picture Gallery

⭐ Each Bible verse below is missing a word(s). Look at the pictures below each verse. Choose the picture that fits in the verse. Write the word represented by the picture on the line.

1. The prophet Jeremiah went to a potter's house. He saw the potter working at a _____. (Jeremiah 18:3)

2. Jesus told his disciples: "You are the _____ of the world." (Matthew 5:14)

3. In the Parable of the Lost Son, the older brother complained that his father had never given him even a _____ so he could celebrate with his friends. (Luke 15:28–29)

Seekers

⭐ Fill in the missing words from the Bible verse below. Use the words in the Word Bank to help you.

Word Bank

love   those   seek   find

I _____ those who love me.

And _____ who_____

me _____ me.

(Proverbs 8:17)

Marine Life

Name_____

⭐ In each blank, write a word from the paragraph below that matches the meaning given in parentheses.

The ocean contains a huge variety of marine life. Millions of tiny plantlike organisms and animals called plankton live near the ocean's surface because they need sunlight to make food. Plankton, which can be so small you need a microscope to see them, are eaten by large animals. Blue whales devour up to two tons a day. Another ocean plant, seaweed, is used as shelter for many animals and is eaten by animals and humans. Some ocean animals, such as the sponge, look like plants.

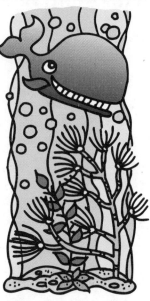

Near the _____ of the ocean live
　　　　　　　　(top)

_____ plantlike organisms and animals
　　(small)

called plankton. Blue whales _____
　　　　　　　　　　　　　　　　　　(gulp)

two tons of plankton a day. Seaweed is used by many

animals as _____.
　　　　　　　(proteted place)

⭐ Cross out the word in each line that does not fit with the others.

1. Atlantic　　　Pacific　　　Erie　　　Arctic

2. valleys　　　mud　　　volcanoes　　　mountains

3. shelter　　　enemy　　　hide　　　protection

Back to School

⭐ Write the missing words. Use words from the Word Bank.

Word Bank

summer	sit	work
new	happy	teacher
prayed	shoes	sleep

My dress is _____, and so are my tennis

_____. This year I get to _____ at a big

desk. I hope that the _____ is not too hard. I

_____ that my _____ at school is nice.

Last night I could hardly _____. I got bored during the

_____. So I am really _____ to be going

back to school today!

⭐ Read the questions. Underline the correct answers.

1. Who is talking?

the teacher   a girl   her mother

2. How does she feel?

glad   sad   lonely

3. When does she go back to school?

tomorrow   next week   today

African Animals

Name_____

⭐ Read the paragraph below. Then, using words from the Word Bank, write a word on each line that matches the meaning given in parentheses.

Word Bank

escape	disappearing	tropical	feed
herds	grazing	offer	quickly

In the grasslands of Africa, _____ of
                                                                (large groups)

_____ animals number more than one million. The
(grass-eating)

_____ climate is part of God's plan. It provides grass
(hot, muggy)

to _____ the animals. Animals that live in the grasslands
(provide food)

move _____ to _____ predators.
            (fast)   (get away from)

Grasslands are _____ as houses and farms take over
                              (vanishing)

the land. God wants us to _____ animals places to live,
                                              (give)

or they too will disappear.

⭐ Choose two of the words from the Word Bank above and use each one in a sentence.

1. _____

_____

2. _____

_____

Mountain Life

Name_____

⭐ Read the paragraph below. Then, using words from the Word Bank, write a word on each line that matches the meaning given in parentheses.

Word Bank			
survive	grip	hibernate	valuable
raise	farm	patches	

God helps animals and people _____ in the mountains.
                              (manage to live)

He created mountain goats with hoofs that _____ steep
                                          (take hold of)

cliffs. He made North American marmots _____ in
                                       (sleep all winter)

underground burrows. People who live in mountain villages

_____ animals and _____ on small
    (take care of)   (plant vegetables and grain)

_____ of land. Other people mine _____
    (areas)   (of great worth)

resources.

⭐ Alphabetize these mountain words.

1. eagles, sheep, marmots, goats   2. peaks, predators, prey, plants

_____   _____

_____   _____

_____   _____

_____   _____

Silly Sandwiches

⭐ Do you think Jesus ate silly sandwiches when he was little? Write the foods used in each sandwich in alphabetical order.

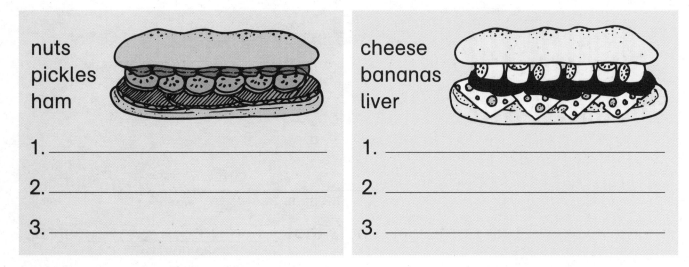

nuts
pickles
ham

1. _____

2. _____

3. _____

cheese
bananas
liver

1. _____

2. _____

3. _____

beans
popcorn
noodles

1. _____

2. _____

3. _____

peas
cookies
beef

1. _____

2. _____

3. _____

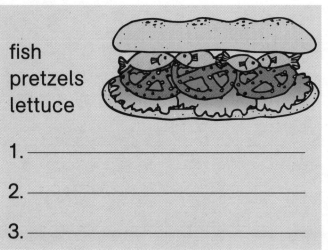

fish
pretzels
lettuce

1. _____

2. _____

3. _____

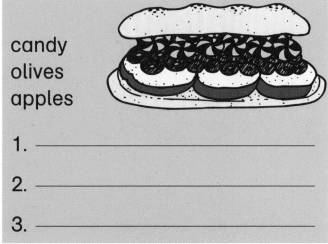

candy
olives
apples

1. _____

2. _____

3. _____

In Your Cupboard

Name_____

⭐ Many spices and flavorings come from the rainforest. Put their names, found in the Word Bank, in alphabetical order.

Word Bank

paprika	chili pepper	black pepper	cardamom
cocoa	cinnamon	cloves	ginger
vanilla	allspice	nutmeg	cayenne

1. _____   7. _____

2. _____   8. _____

3. _____   9. _____

4. _____   10. _____

5. _____   11. _____

6. _____   12. _____

⭐ Dictionary pronunciations help you learn how to say words correctly. Match the pronunciation to the appropriate word.

1. kī-ĕn´   cardamom

2. pĕp´ ər   cayenne

3. kar´də-məm   pepper

4. pă-prē´ kə   paprika

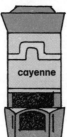

God's Awesome Plan

⭐ Dictionary **guide words** indicate the first and last words on a dictionary page. Show where to look for each word from the Word Bank by writing it on the line beside the correct guide words.

Word Bank			
desert	protection	survive	created
scaly	cactus	dunes	predators

1. save   scamp   _____

2. surprise   suspender   _____

3. crank   creative   _____

4. preach   prefix   _____

5. caboose   cake   _____

6. describe   desk   _____

7. dump   dwarf   _____

8. prose   proud   _____

⭐ Tell what a desert is in your own words. Then find the word **desert** in the dictionary and write its definition.

_____

_____

_____

_____

Galloping Gazelles

⭐ Dictionary **guide words** indicate the first and last words on a dictionary page. Show where to look for each word from the Word Bank by writing it on the line beside the correct guide words.

Word Bank

gazelle	giraffes
antelope	grasslands
pummel	release
rodents	rabbits

1. another   antic   _____

2. pulley   punch   _____

3. rocket   romp   _____

4. gill   give   _____

5. gather   general   _____

6. relate   relic   _____

7. grasp   gravy   _____

8. rabbi   radar   _____

Name_____

⭐ Match the people from the Bible with the correct picture.

1.

2.

3.

4.

The Path

⭐ Color the picture. Decode the rebus, then write the verse on the lines provided.

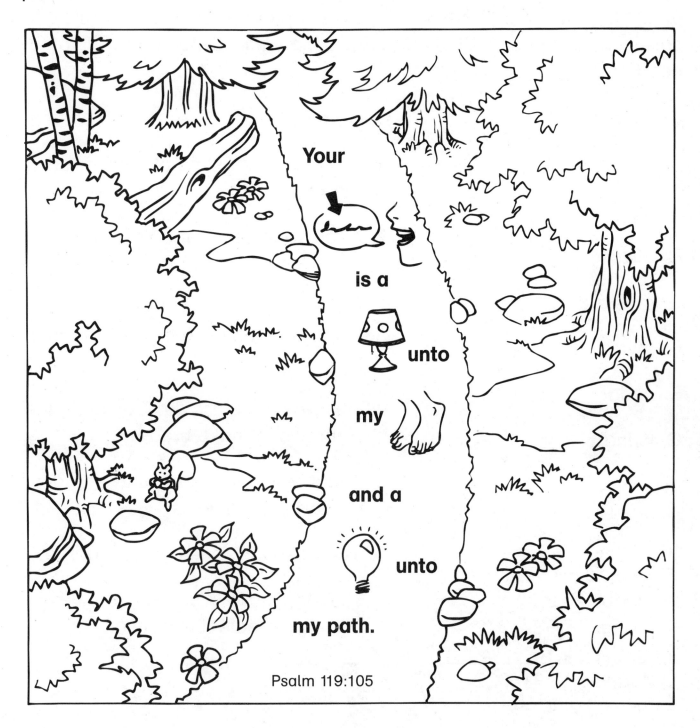

Your

is a

unto

my

and a

unto

my path.

Psalm 119:105

_____

_____

The Root of It All

People in biblical times lived off the land. Their crops and fields were very much a part of their everyday concerns. What were some of the plants mentioned in the bible? Match the plant in Column A with the correct description in Column B. Read the verses listed below if you need help.

Column A

A. sycamore-fig

B. fig

C. olive

D. mustard

E. myrrh

F. cedar

G. wheat

Column B

1. This was the first plant mentioned in the Bible.

2. After Noah sent out a dove from the ark, it returned with this leaf in its beak.

3. King Solomon used this tree to build his palace.

4. This was the basic grain used by the Hebrews to make bread.

5. Zacchaeus climbed this tree to get a good look at Jesus.

6. Jesus used this seed to tell a parable.

7. The Magi gave this as a gift to Jesus. It is an ingredient in holy oil.

Genesis 3:7
Genesis 8:11
Exodus 29:2
1 Kings 7:1–3
Matthew 2:11
Matthew 13:31–32
Luke 19:2–4

Up a Tree

⭐ A short man wanted to see Jesus, so he climbed a tree. Do you know his name? Read about him in Luke 19:1–10. Then fill in the puzzle.

Across

4. Who is this story about?
6. Jesus said that he had come to seek and to do what?
8. What kind of tree did the man climb?

Down

1. Where did this story take place?
2. Who asked the man to come down from the tree?
3. What was the man's job?
5. Jesus called him a son of whom?
7. What did the people call him?

recognizing details

⭐ Jesus performed many healing miracles. The Gospel of Luke tells us about some of them. Five stories of healing are listed in the verses below. Read the stories. In each case, discover the illness or condition that Jesus healed. Write it inside the shape. How did the person(s) healed respond to the miracle? Write it on the lines below.

Man in Jericho
(Luke 18:35–42)

Simon's mother-in-law
(Luke 4:38–39)

_____

_____

_____

Woman healed on the Sabbath
(Luke 13:10–13)

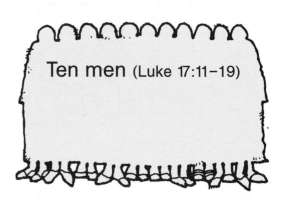

Ten men (Luke 17:11–19)

_____

_____

_____

True or False?

⭐ Read the statements below and decide if they are true or false. Color the **T** red if the statement is true. Color the **F** orange if the statement is false. The Bible verses will give you the answers.

Bethlehem was the town where Jesus was born.
(Matthew 2:1–2)

T   F

Eden was a place where God planted a garden.
(Genesis 2:8)

T   F

Timothy helped Paul and was like a son to him.
(Philippians 1:1; 2:22)

T   F

Revelation is the last book of the Bible.
(Check your Bible's table of contents.)

T   F

Uz is where Job lived.
(Job 1:1)

T   F

Twelve disciples were chosen by Jesus.
(Matthew 10:1)

T   F

Hosea is a book in the New Testament.
(Check your Bible's table of contents.)

T   F

Friendliness is a "fruit of the Spirit."
(Galatians 5:22)

T   F

Ur was Abram's home.
(Genesis 11:31)

T   F

Lot's wife turned into a pillar of salt.
(Genesis 19:26)

T   F

recognizing details

What Was That?

⭐ Read the story, then answer the questions below. Be sure to write your answers in complete sentences.

Kate and Nate walked by the old house. Windows were broken. The walls needed paint. Even the roof had a hole. No one had lived there for a long time. Suddenly Kate saw two big eyes at one window. Then they both heard a sound. It sounded like, "Boo!" The door swung open. Kate and Nate began to run. They looked back, and both children began to laugh. A cow stood in the doorway. It must have walked inside the open door in back.

1. By what did Kate and Nate walk? _____

_____

2. What was wrong with the windows? _____

_____

3. What was wrong with the roof? _____

_____

4. What did the children see in the window? _____

_____

5. Why did they laugh? _____

_____

6. How did the cow get inside the house? _____

_____

Do What?

⭐ Draw and color silly pictures for the sentences below.

1. Draw and color two orange zebras with yellow stripes climbing into the ark.

2. Add 10 green sheep to David's pen.

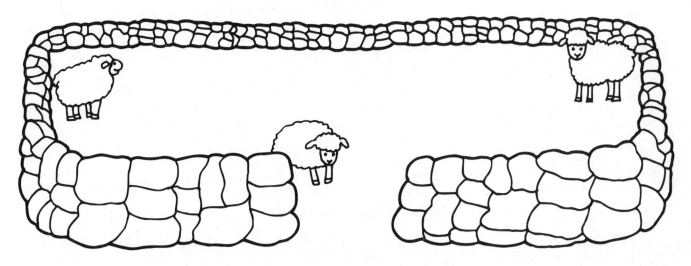

following directions

Love at First Croak

A little, green frog sat alone on a rock in the pond. "I wish I had a friend," he prayed quietly.

Soon a big butterfly flew down to the pond. She landed on a lily pad.

"She is very pretty and can fly," thought the frog.

"Will you be my friend?" asked the butterfly.

"Me?" answered the frog. "I am so ugly. Why do you want to be my friend?"

"You can hop and make croaking sounds. I think you are cute!" she said.

The frog smiled and croaked loudly. He and the butterfly became good friends. The frog thanked God for his new friend.

Read the sentences below and draw a cartoon strip.

Draw a happy frog holding a heart.	Draw a big, pretty butterfly sitting on a lily pad.	Draw a sad, little frog sitting on a rock in a pond.

Amazing Animals

⭐ Here are some of the wonderful animals God created. Draw and color silly pictures for the sentences below.

1. A pelican can hold up to 30 pounds of fish in its bill. Draw a fish inside the pelican's bill.

2. Snakes use their tongues to smell. Draw a silly nose on the end of the snake's tongue.

3. A crocodile carries its babies in its mouth. Draw a baby crocodile in the crocodile's mouth.

4. Horses sleep standing up. Draw a blanket on the horse's back and fuzzy slippers on its feet.

following directions

Good News!

Name_____

Choose the best answer to complete each sentence. Write the answer in the blank.

1. Shepherds were in their fields one night. Angels lit up the sky. "We have come with tidings of great joy," they said. It was

   _____.

   a. Easter   b. March   c. Jesus' birthday

2. One morning, Justin slept very late. He got dressed fast and ran downstairs. His family drove to a place where people worship God.

   It must have been _____.

   a. Sunday   b. Monday   c. summer

3. Adam and Eve were in the Garden of Eden. They saw an animal. It had no legs or arms and was very long. The animal told Eve to eat the fruit. It

   _____.

   a. was a hippo   b. was a snake   c. could see very well

4. Luis carried his Bible to the front pew. He sat with his mom and dad. They listened to the preacher teach about Jesus. He was at

   _____.

   a. the store   b. the library   c. church

Read for Clues

⭐ Read each passage. Then underline the sentence that correctly answers each question.

1. Joe tried to read the book. He pulled it closer to his face and squinted. What is wrong?

   a. The book isn't very interesting.

   b. Joe needs glasses.

   c. Joe has the book closed.

2. "My shoes are too tight," said Eddie, "and my pants are too short!" What has happened?

   a. Eddie has put on his older brother's clothes.

   b. Eddie has become shorter.

   c. Eddie has grown.

3. Patsy went to the beach. She stayed outside for six hours. When she came home, she looked into the mirror. Her face was very red. Why did she look different?

   a. Patsy had gotten a bad sunburn.

   b. Patsy got red paint all over herself.

   c. Patsy was very cold.

drawing conclusions

And the Answer Is . . . Name_____

⭐ Read each passage. Then circle the picture that correctly finishes each sentence.

1. I am on a field trip with my class. I see cows eating grass. The horses are in the barn. The hens are sitting on their eggs. I am visiting a . . .

2. Timmy wore his best suit. He walked into the room and sat in a tall chair. His mom combed his hair. The man told Timmy to say, "Cheese!" The man is a . . .

3. Mark spilled his milk on the floor. He knew to do the right thing by cleaning up the mess. He went into the closet and got a . . .

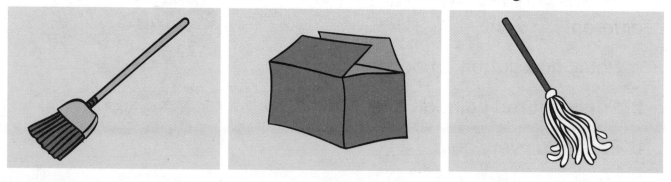

drawing conclusions

Mountain Climbing

Name_____

⭐ Read each sentence below. Write whether it is fact (**F**) or opinion (**O**).

1. _____ Mountains are great places to live.

2. _____ Goats have gripping hoofs to help them climb mountains.

3. _____ It is harder to breathe at the top of a mountain than at its base.

4. _____ Mountain climbers are foolish.

5. _____ Valuable rocks and minerals are found in mountains.

⭐ Circle the word that does not belong in each list.

1. rain, snow, slippery, sleet

2. hibernate, fly, climb, run

3. copper, iron ore, lumber, emeralds

4. grass, bushes, insects, trees

⭐ Use complete sentences to write a paragraph telling why you would or would not want to be part of a mountain-climbing team.

_____

_____

_____

_____

_____

_____

Time to Eat!

⭐ Are you hungry? If you want to try something different, go to an Arab wedding in the desert. Here is a recipe for a special wedding meal.

1. Cook some eggs.

2. Stuff the eggs into fish.

3. Put the fish inside cooked chickens.

4. Place the chickens into a roasted sheep.

5. Set the sheep inside a whole camel and roast.

6. Enjoy!

Show the recipe order by numbering the ingredients from 1 to 5.

_____   _____   _____

_____   _____

R-r-r-r-ring!

⭐ Read the passage, then number the pictures 1, 2, 3, 4, and 5 in order.

The alarm clock rang loudly. Cathy jumped out of bed. She pulled on her clothes and then ran down the steps. She thanked God for her food and ate breakfast. Then she brushed her teeth. When Mom told Cathy that school was cancelled, she moaned. Then she thought of all the fun things she could do.

sequence

Emily's Zoo Trip

Name_____

The order of events in a story is called its **sequence**. Read the passage below. Then number the events listed at the bottom of the page. Look back at the story as you number the events in order.

Emily woke up early and thanked Jesus that it was a beautiful, sunny day. Until now, Emily had only seen zoo animals in books. Today she would visit the zoo with her family.

Emily burst through the zoo gates at 10 A.M., just as the zoo opened. She was eager to visit every display. First she saw the Siberian tigers and the leopards. Emily loved the size of those cats. Next she watched the zookeeper feed three elephants. Then, just before stopping at the Snack Shack for lunch, Emily and her family went to the petting zoo where they fed and touched a variety of barnyard animals.

In the afternoon, Emily saw monkeys, zebras, and giraffes. It was one of the best days Emily could ever remember! That night she thanked God for all the animals she had seen.

_____ Emily visited the tigers and leopards.

_____ She visited the petting zoo.

_____ Emily's family arrived at the zoo at 10 A.M.

_____ The zookeeper fed the elephants.

_____ They had lunch at the Snack Shack.

_____ Emily was excited. She would visit the zoo today.

_____ She visited the monkeys, zebras, and giraffes.

Rainforest Trivia

Paraphrasing is stating the same information in new words. Writers use this skill all the time. Read the numbered sentences below and check (✔) the line for the best paraphrase of each statement.

1. Plants thrive in the rainforest.

    _____ In the rainforest, plants grow fast and well.

    _____ Plants grow slowly in the rainforest.

2. Rainforest plants and trees provide many spices, fruits, and vegetables.

    _____ Grocery stores get supplies from the rainforest.

    _____ Rainforests are a source of good foods.

3. About a third of South America is covered by tropical rainforests.

    _____ A lot of rainforests are located in South America.

    _____ South America has many pine forests.

4. The temperature in the rainforest is near 75° Fahrenheit year round.

    _____ It is warm all year in the rainforest.

    _____ Rainforests are hot or cold depending on the rain.

paraphrasing

Polar Life

⭐ **Paraphrasing** is stating the same information in new words. Read the numbered sentences below and then check (✔) the line for the best paraphrase of each statement.

1. Insects are the only permanent residents of Antarctica.

   _____ Insects are not found in Antarctica.

   _____ Insects live in Antarctica year round.

2. The tundra regions burst with plant life as snow and ice melts.

   _____ Plants begin to grow in the tundra in the springtime.

   _____ Plants explode like fireworks in the tundra.

3. God gave Arctic wolves white fur and keen eyesight to help them live in the Arctic.

   _____ Arctic wolves like to hunt for food.

   _____ Arctic wolves are well-adapted to life in the Arctic.

⭐ Paraphrase this sentence.

In the summer, birds migrate to the South Pole to feast on insects.

_____

_____

_____

Nathan's Backyard

⭐ Read about Nathan and his backyard. Then complete the story map.

The sky was overcast and gloomy outside Nathan's window. He watched a pair of robins who lived in the maple tree beside his window. He thought of how God cared for them.

For days, the pair of birds had been carrying twigs, string, and grasses to build a nest. Nathan was very thankful he could watch as he kept a close eye on the birds to see what they would do next.

As Nathan watched, the cloudy weather quickly changed to a storm. The old maple tree swayed in the forceful wind. Soon Nathan heard thunder and saw a bolt of lightning dart across the sky and strike the maple tree. All Nathan could think about was the pair of robins and their nest. He prayed that God would protect them and keep them safe.

The storm lasted nearly an hour before Nathan could rush outside to the shattered maple tree. Among the fallen branches, he found the nest. With his father's help, Nathan placed the nest in another tree. He hoped the robins would continue to call the nest home.

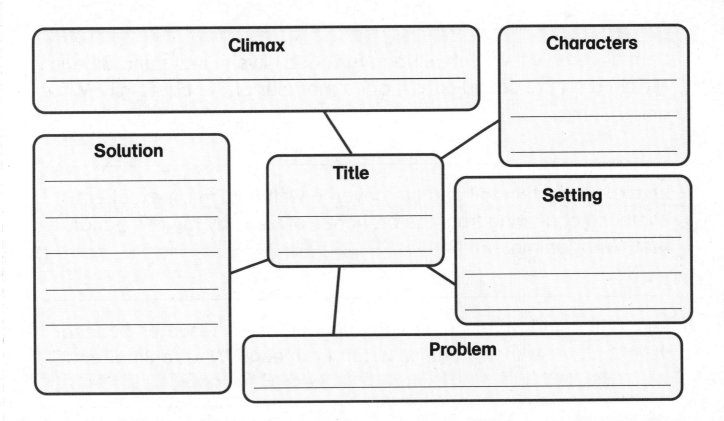

Climax

Characters

Solution

Title

Setting

Problem

story map

Animal Riddles

Imagine all the animals that rode on the ark. Use the animal names in the Word Bank to help you answer the animal riddles below.

Word Bank

tiger   penguin   snake   monkey   cheetah   elephant

1. I am large and have no fur. My skin is gray and wrinkled. I eat plants and spray myself with my trunk. What animal am I?

_____

2. I'm a mammal whose furry coat is covered with spots. I'm known for how fast I can run. I'm a member of the cat family. What animal am I?

_____

3. I am a reptile. My skin is cool and scaly. I am long and slender. I slither on the ground and in trees. What animal am I?

_____

4. I am covered with a soft, striped fur coat. I live in India and Siberia. My children are called cubs. I am a member of the cat family. What animal am I?

_____

5. I have a long, thin tail and am covered with fur. I'm an excellent climber. I can swing from the branches of trees by my tail, hands, or feet. What animal am I?

_____

6. I am black and white. I am happy on land or in the water. I cannot fly, but I can swim. My babies hatch from eggs. What animal am I?

_____

inference   82

Animal Homes

Name_____

⭐ Look at the Table of Contents below and decide which chapter would contain each sentence listed below.

Table of Contents

1. _____ Wasps collect pellets of wet mud that they mold into a ribbon of mud to create nests.

2. _____ Beavers make lodges of sticks and twigs piled on top of one another. These lodges have two or more underwater entrances.

3. _____ Animals build homes from surrounding materials.

4. _____ The harvest mouse builds the strongest grass nest of all.

5. _____ Rabbits build a system of linked burrows that have many different entrances.

table of contents

It's in the Book

⭐ Use the table of contents below to help answer the questions.

Table of Contents

1. _____ You have been asked to write a report on vegetation in the rainforest. Which chapter will likely have this information?

2. _____ To learn where cashew nuts are found, where should you look?

3. _____ From floor to sky, you must explain the growth of plants and trees in the rainforest. Which chapter, do you think, has this information?

4. _____ With a partner, you must compare animals of the rainforest with those of the desert. Where can you find which animals live in the rainforest?

⭐ **Read the passage below, then complete the sentences that follow.**

I have a pen pal named Anne. She lives in England. We write letters to each other. We share our favorite Bible verses. Sometimes her words make me giggle. She watches the "telly" after school. Her father drives a "lorry." On Saturdays, her family likes to see a "flick."

Sometimes my words make Anne laugh, too. The funny thing is that we both speak English! I'm so glad God made Anne.

1. Anne lives in _____.

2. Anne and her pen pal _____ to each other.

3. Anne and her pen pal share favorite _____.

4. What does Anne call these things?

_____

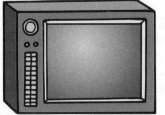

_____

_____

Love One Another

⭐ The bible shows us how we should treat one another. What do the three ideas below mean to you: Write your answers in the boxes.

Serve one another. (Galatians 5:13)

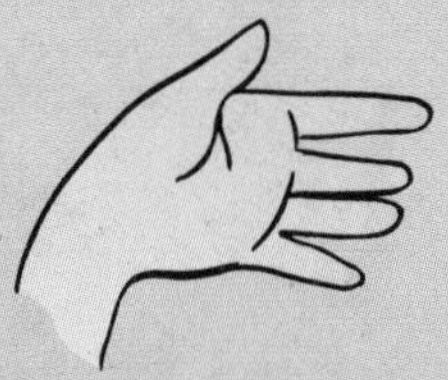

_____

_____

_____

_____

Honor one another. (Romans 12:10)

_____

_____

_____

_____

Instruct one another (Romans 15:14)

_____

_____

_____

_____

Look Who's Talking

⭐ Read what each child is saying. Then write in the correct name to complete each sentence below.

"Let me bat first!" yelled Butch.

"A new doll!" said Missy. "Wow! It's just what I wanted!"

"I stayed up too late," yawned Yvonne. "I am going to bed."

I have two different colored socks," cried Tom. "Everyone is looking at me!"

"Oh, no! We can't go to the zoo today," said Ben sadly. "It's closed."

⭐ Write the name.

1. _____ feels silly.   4. _____ is upset.

2. _____ is sleepy.   5. _____ is surprised.

3. _____ acts bossy.

⭐ Remember, Jesus is with you no matter what you are feeling. Draw the correct mouth on each face above.

upset   silly   sleepy   surprised   bossy

character analysis

Who Said It?

God made each animal special. Draw a line from the animal to what it might say.

"I live in the forest. Some day I may grow antlers."

"I live in the ocean and have sharp teeth."

"I hop on lily pads in a pond with my webbed feet."

"I save lots of bones and bury them in the yard."

"I slither on the ground because I have no arms or legs."

Design It!

⭐ Most people like to be outdoors enjoying nature. Design a T-shirt that expresses your feelings about the world that God has created for us.

"In the beginning God created the heavens and the earth"

(Genesis 1:1).

creative writing

What's the Question?   Name_____

⭐ In this activity, the answers are provided for you. You need to think of a question for each answer. Look up the chapter and verse listed for each answer and write the question on the line. All the questions are about Noah and his ark.

Here are the answers!
What are the questions?

1. A righteous man (Genesis 6:9)

_____

2. Ham, Shem, and Japheth (Genesis 6:10)

_____

3. Cypress wood (Genesis 6:14)

_____

4. 600 years (Genesis 7:6)

_____

5. Forty days (Genesis 7:12)

_____

6. A dove (Genesis 8:8)

_____

7. A rainbow (Genesis 9:12–13)

_____

_____

God's World

⭐ Draw a picture in the globe that illustrates the verse at the bottom of the page.

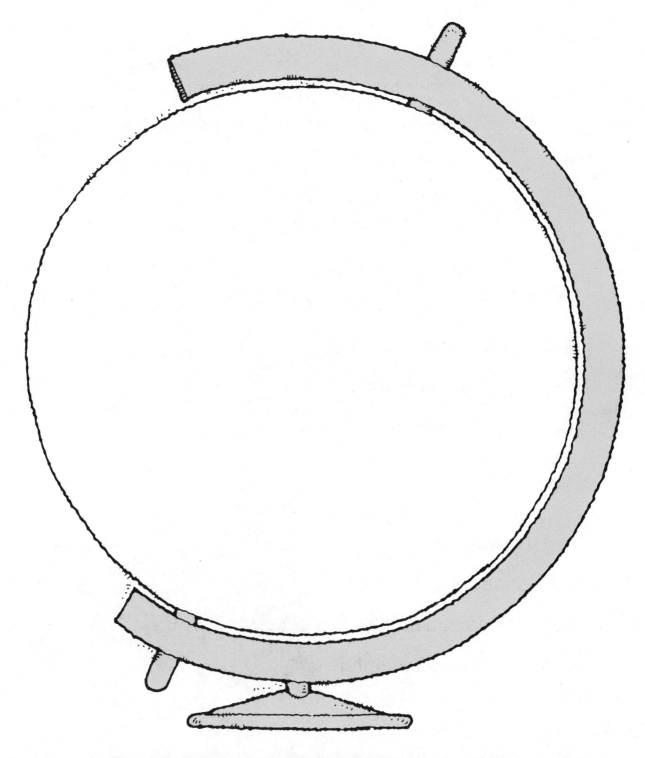

"The earth is the Lord's and everything in it, the world, and all who live in it." (Psalm 24:1).

You're a Puma

God made you a special child, but what if you had been a puma?! Pretend you're a puma. Use the Fact Box below to help you answer the interview questions from a puma's point of view.

Fact Box

- Pumas may be up to 5 feet long, not counting the tail.

- The largest puma on record weighed 227 pounds.

- Pumas are also known as cougars or mountain lions.

- A puma's cry sounds similar to a person screaming in pain. The puma also has a soft whistle call.

- Pumas eat deer, elk, and other animals.

- Adult pumas have a gray or tawny coat which makes them hard to see when they hide in the grass and sneak up on their prey.

Answer these questions on the next page. Use complete sentences.

1. What animal are you?

2. Describe what you look like and how big you can grow.

3. What do you eat?

4. What sounds do you make?

5. How is your plain coat helpful to you?

6. What do they call you besides puma?

You're a Puma

⭐ Answer the questions from the bottom of page 92. Make sure to use complete sentences.

1. _____

_____

2. _____

_____

3. _____

_____

4. _____

_____

5. _____

_____

6. _____

_____

creative writing using facts

Creative Writing

⭐ Choose a title from the list below. Then write and illustrate a story.

Titles

My Day with Jesus   What Would Jesus Do If . . .

I Was on the Ark   In the Desert

_____

_____

_____

_____

_____

_____

_____

_____

Dear Noah

⭐ The ark is crowded, smelly, and damp. The animals got together to talk about how to improve it. Pretend you are one of the animals. Write your letter to Noah below.

_____

Dear _____ ,

_____

_____

_____

_____

_____

_____

_____

_____

_____

_____ ,

_____

writing a letter

Lydia's Ads

Lydia was a merchant who sold purple cloth. People who sell products need to advertise. Help Lydia sell her cloth by creating two ads for her. Design a sign in the frame below that she could have used outside a shop. Then create an ad for a flyer she could give to people as they passed. Use your imagination. Read about her in Acts 16:13–15.

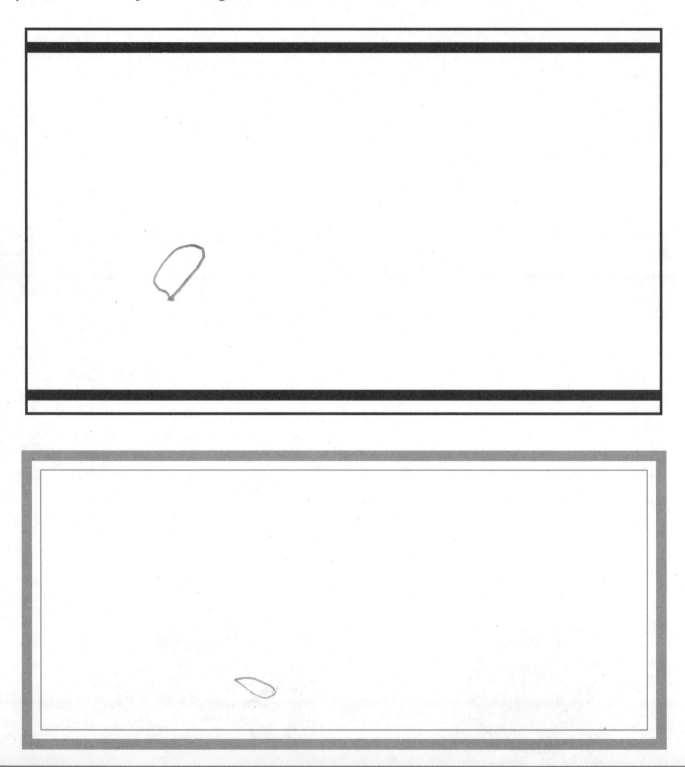

The Big Story

Name_____

⭐ Imagine that you were living during the time of Jesus and were a reporter for the local paper, *The Jerusalem Times*. Your job is to report on the miracle that occurred at Siloam. Read the story in John 9:1–12. Then write your "eye-witness" account of what happened in the space below.

The Jerusalem Times

Miracle at the Pool of Siloam

_____

_____

_____

_____

_____

_____

_____

_____

_____

_____

Cyber Mail

Today, we send e-mail messages to people all over the world using our computers and the Internet. Imagine that you could e-mail people who lived in biblical times. Read about Mary Magdalene and John the Baptist in the verses below. Then write them a note on the lines under their imaginary e-mail addresses. What would you like to say to them or ask them about their experiences?

marymagdalene@newtestament.com (John 20:1–18)

_____

_____

_____

_____

_____

johnthebaptist@newtestament.com (Matthew 3:1–17)

_____

_____

_____

_____

Hello,

In Your Mind's Eye

⭐ Choose one of your favorite Bible verses. Think about how you could illustrate it. How you illustrate it is all in your mind's eye. Draw your illustration in the light bulb below.

The verse says: _____

_____

_____

_____

Mathematics

Table of Contents

God's Promise

⭐ God gave us a promise that He will never flood the earth again. Connect the dots and discover the beautiful image of God's promise.

In the Beginning

Name_____

⭐ God created the world in six days. Each day's creation is pictured. What did God create on each of the days? Read Genesis 1, and then label each picture with the correct day.

fish and birds

Day_____

day and night

Day_____

sun, moon, and stars

Day_____

trees and plants

Day_____

water and sky

Day_____

animals and people

Day_____

Countdown

⭐ The box below contains seven questions labeled from A to G. Each question has a number for an answer. Put the correct letter from the box under the number that answers that question.

A. How many books are in the Bible?
(Check your Bible's table of contents.)

B. How many smooth stones did David pick up for his slingshot when he went to meet the Philistine, Goliath?
(1 Samuel 17:38–40)

C. How many days did Joshua march around Jericho?
(Joshua 6:2–5)

D. How many men did Jesus feed with five loaves of bread and two fish? (Mark 6:39–44)

E. How many coins did the widow put in the offering?
(Mark 12:41–44)

F. How many disciples did Jesus choose?
(Luke 6:13)

G. How many times did Daniel pray each day?
(Daniel 6:13)

_____   _____   _____   _____

_____   _____   _____

counting

Words to Count On

⭐ Draw a line from each numeral to the matching number word.

19	nineteen	72	eighty-three
26	fifty-five	18	sixteen
12	twelve	68	sixty-eight
55	twenty-six	16	eighteen
13	thirteen	83	seventy-two

one hundred twenty-five	915
seven hundred thirty-one	125
four hundred eighty-nine	397
nine hundred fifteen	731
three hundred ninety-seven	489

How Many Candles?

⭐ What is the age of each person listed on this cake? Read the Bible verses if you need help.

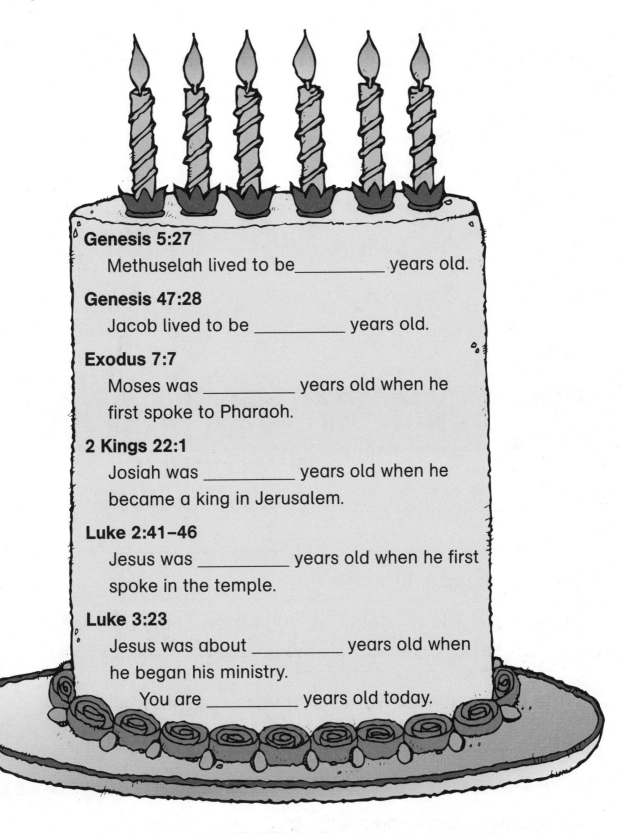

Genesis 5:27

   Methuselah lived to be_____ years old.

Genesis 47:28

   Jacob lived to be _____ years old.

Exodus 7:7

   Moses was _____ years old when he first spoke to Pharaoh.

2 Kings 22:1

   Josiah was _____ years old when he became a king in Jerusalem.

Luke 2:41–46

   Jesus was _____ years old when he first spoke in the temple.

Luke 3:23

   Jesus was about _____ years old when he began his ministry.

   You are _____ years old today.

Going Fishing

The disciples were going fishing. They needed worms, so they began to dig in the dirt.

Use the pictograph to complete each sentence below.
Each ⌇ = 2 worms

Peter	⌇ ⌇ ⌇ ⌇
James	⌇ ⌇ ⌇ ⌇ ⌇
John	⌇ ⌇ ⌇ ⌇
Andrew	⌇ ⌇
Philip	⌇ ⌇ ⌇ ⌇ ⌇ ⌇
Thomas	⌇ ⌇ ⌇

1. _____ got the fewest worms.

2. _____ dug up the most worms.

3. _____ and _____ found

the same number of worms.

4. Andrew and Thomas together dug up the same number of worms

as _____.

5. Write the number of worms that each disciple found.

Peter _____   John _____   Philip _____

James _____   Andrew _____   Thomas _____

6. Altogether, the disciples dug up _____ worms.

Fundraiser

Name_____

One way to take care of God's world is to recycle. The third-grade classrooms at Valleywood School collected 2-liter soda bottles to help fund a field trip. Each bottle could be returned to the store for a 10-cent refund. This pictograph shows the number of bottles collected by each class. Each 🍶 = 5.

Teacher	Bottles Collected	Total
Townsend	🍶🍶🍶🍶🍶🍶🍶🍶🍶🍶	
Parks	🍶🍶🍶🍶🍶🍶	
Beach	🍶🍶🍶🍶🍶🍶🍶🍶	
Williams	🍶🍶🍶🍶🍶🍶🍶	
DeGroot	🍶🍶🍶🍶🍶	
Blue	🍶🍶🍶🍶🍶🍶🍶	

⭐ Count by fives to find out how many bottles each class collected. Fill in the totals on the chart.

1. How many bottles did the third grade collect altogether?_____

2. Whose class was able to contribute the most money toward the

   field trip?_____ How much?_____

3. Whose class contributed the least?_____ How much?_____

4. The third-grade classes needed a total of $20 in order to take their

   field trip. Did they earn enough money? _____

reading a pictograph

Chew on This!

God made your jaw bones strong. Color the gumballs with **even** numbers **purple**. Color the gumballs with **odd** numbers **green**.

Remember: Even numbers end with 0, 2, 4, 6, and 8.
Odd numbers end with 1, 3, 5, 7, and 9.

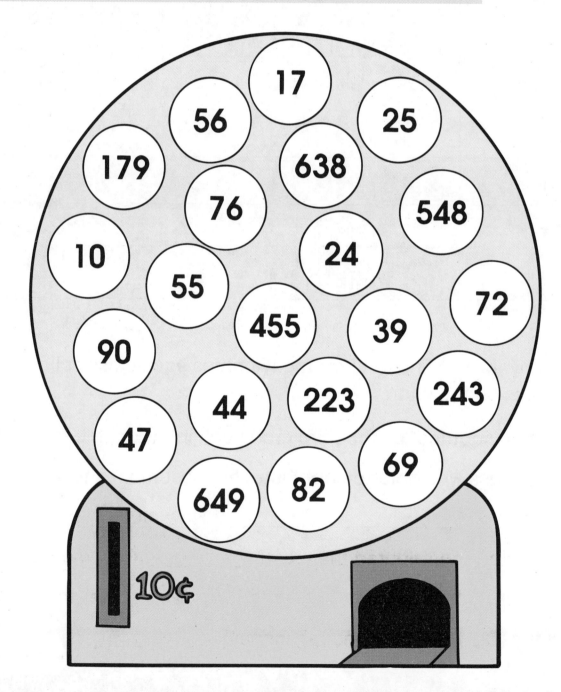

Exercise in Addition

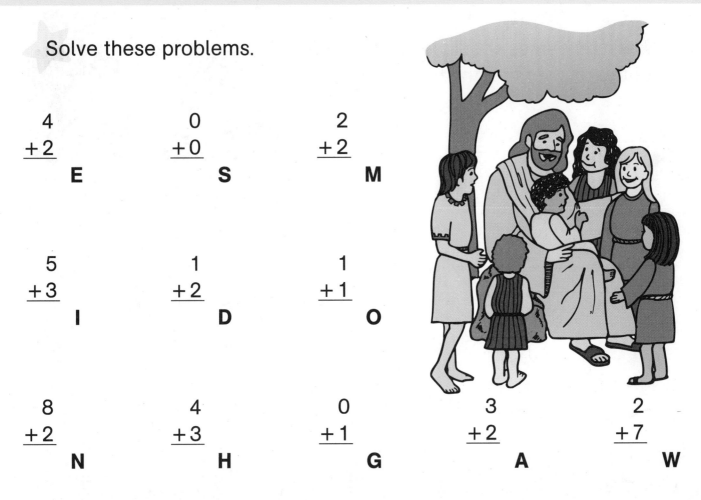

Solve these problems.

```
  4        0        2
 +2       +0       +2
 ___      ___      ___
  E        S        M


  5        1        1
 +3       +2       +1
 ___      ___      ___
  I        D        O


  8        4        0        3        2
 +2       +3       +1       +2       +7
 ___      ___      ___      ___      ___
  N        H        G        A        W
```

Solve the Bible verse using the letters from the problems above. We know Jesus was without sin because of what Paul tells us.

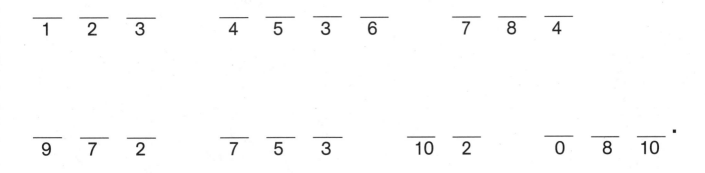

```
___  ___  ___     ___  ___  ___  ___     ___  ___  ___
 1    2    3       4    5    3    6        7    8    4


___  ___  ___     ___  ___  ___     ___  ___     ___  ___  ___ .
 9    7    2       7    5    3      10    2        0    8   10
```

(2 Corinthians 5:21)

addition facts 1-10

Forgive Each Other

Name_____

How many times should we forgive others?
Write the answers on the hearts.

7 +6	9 +3	8 +7	4 +7	8 +8
5 +6	3 +8	6 +8	9 +6	8 +5
5 +7	9 +8	4 +9	9 +9	6 +6

Run the Race

⭐ How far can the runner go in one minute? Write the answers. After one minute, circle where you are. Then finish the page.

2	7	8	9	6	1
+8	+9	+1	+4	+6	+2

8	4	6	7	5	7
+5	+4	+3	+3	+6	+8

7	7	3	8	2	5
+6	+7	+4	+6	+2	+7

0	6	8	3	5	4
+0	+8	+8	+4	+9	+2

9	6	3	8	5	2
+9	+4	+3	+9	+5	+3

Paul told us to "run in such a way as to get the prize" (1 Corinthians 9:24)

addition facts 0-18, timed

Angels

Add the numbers in each problem. Then decode the verse using the letters from the problems.

A 3 + 2 = _____   **H** 5 + 2 = _____   **R** 4 + 2 = _____

C 2 + 1 = _____   **I** 8 + 7 = _____   **S** 9 + 7 = _____

D 7 + 3 = _____   **L** 5 + 4 = _____   **T** 7 + 7 = _____

E 6 + 5 = _____   **M** 6 + 6 = _____   **U** 1 + 1 = _____

F 9 + 9 = _____   **N** 8 + 5 = _____   **W** 8 + 9 = _____

G 4 + 4 = _____   **O** 2 + 2 = _____   **Y** 1 + 0 = _____

Verse

___ ___ ___   ___ ___   ___ ___ ___ ___
18   4   6   7   11   17   15   9   9

___ ___ ___ ___ ___ ___ ___   ___ ___ ___
3   4   12   12   5   13   10   7   15   16

___ ___ ___ ___ ___ ___
5   13   8   11   9   16

___ ___ ___ ___ ___ ___ ___ ___ ___ ___
3   4   13   3   11   6   13   15   13   8

___ ___ ___   ___ ___   ___ ___ ___ ___ ___
1   4   2   14   4   8   2   5   6   10

___ ___ ___   ___ ___   ___ ___ ___
1   4   2   15   13   5   9   9

___ ___ ___ ___   ___ ___ ___ ___ . . .
1   4   2   6   17   5   1   16

(Psalm 91:11 NIV)

The Missing Sheep

⭐ An addend in each problem is missing. Write it in the lamb.

```
  ___
+  7
  ___
   8
```

```
  ___
+  2
  ___
  10
```

6
```
  ___
+
  ___
   9
```

```
  ___
+  5
  ___
  10
```

6
```
  ___
+
  ___
  11
```

```
  ___
+  9
  ___
  15
```

8
```
  ___
+
  ___
  16
```

9
```
  ___
+
  ___
  18
```

8
```
  ___
+
  ___
  17
```

```
  ___
+  8
  ___
  14
```

9
```
  ___
+
  ___
  12
```

```
  ___
+  6
  ___
  13
```

missing addends

How Many Bees?

⭐ Solve each problem to find the number of bees in each hive.

26
+13

82
+15

12
+32

34
+45

13
+35

46
+31

61
+22

92
+ 6

56
+12

70
+15

addition - no regrouping

Salvation

Add 10 to each number. Write your answers on the lines. Then decode the verse using the letters next to your answers.

23	47	38	51	29	77	34	41
A ___	B ___	D ___	E ___	H ___	I ___	L ___	N ___

82	15	25	64	58	86	12	30
O ___	P ___	R ___	S ___	T ___	V ___	W ___	Z ___

Verse

"

—— —— —— —— —— —— ——
22 39 92 61 96 61 35

—— —— —— —— —— —— —— ——   —— —— ——
57 61 44 87 61 96 61 74   33 51 48

—— ——   —— —— —— —— —— —— —— ——
87 74   57 33 25 68 87 40 61 48

—— —— —— ——   —— ——
22 87 44 44   57 61

—— —— —— —— —— ...."
74 33 96 61 48   (Psalm 91:11 NIV)

"Eggs"tra Work

Tommy felt bad because he was always dropping eggs. His mom forgave him and told him she still loved him.

⭐ How many unbroken eggs were left in each carton? Finish each number sentence.

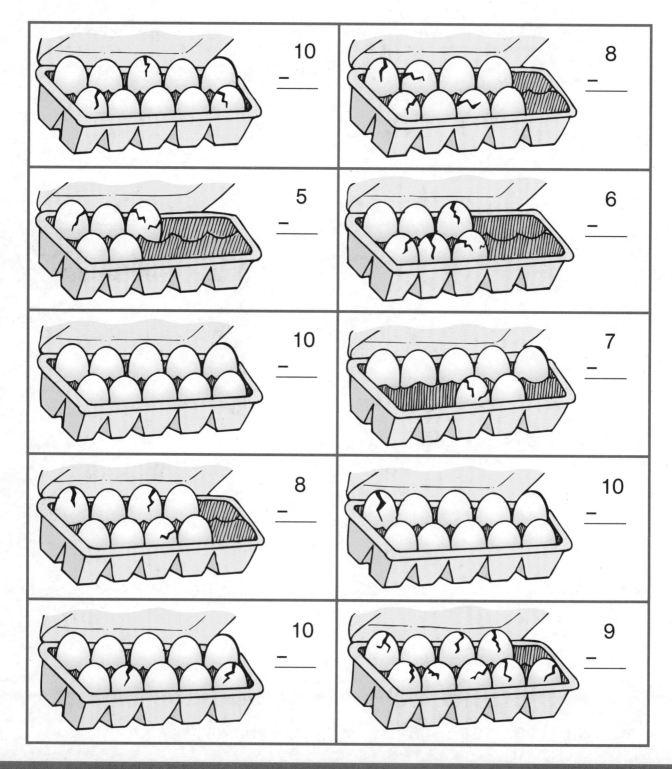

Like Pulling Teeth

⭐ Draw the total number of teeth in each alligator's mouth. (This is the top number.) Then, color the number of lost teeth black. (This is the bottom number.) Last, write the number of teeth left. (This is the answer.)

Example:

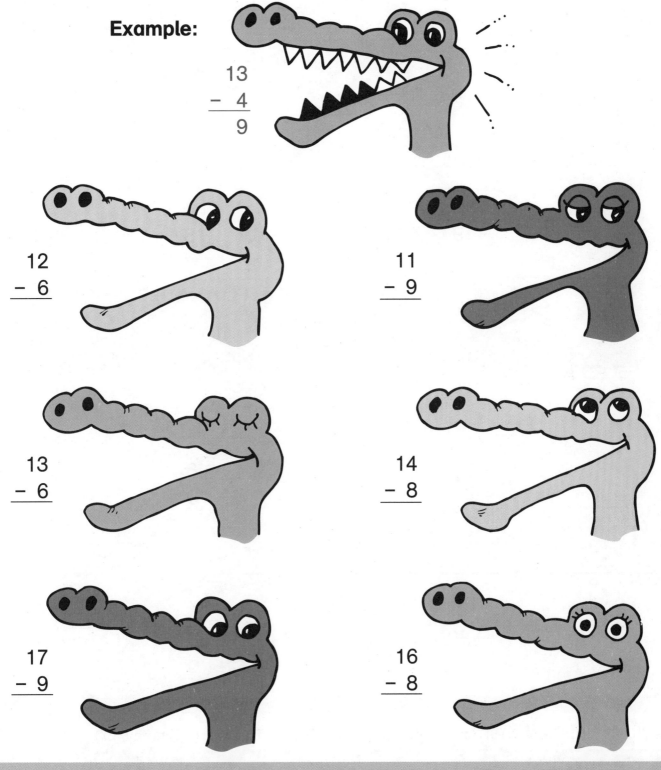

$$\begin{array}{r} 13 \\ -\ 4 \\ \hline 9 \end{array}$$

$$\begin{array}{r} 12 \\ -\ 6 \\ \hline \end{array}$$

$$\begin{array}{r} 11 \\ -\ 9 \\ \hline \end{array}$$

$$\begin{array}{r} 13 \\ -\ 6 \\ \hline \end{array}$$

$$\begin{array}{r} 14 \\ -\ 8 \\ \hline \end{array}$$

$$\begin{array}{r} 17 \\ -\ 9 \\ \hline \end{array}$$

$$\begin{array}{r} 16 \\ -\ 8 \\ \hline \end{array}$$

subtraction facts 1-17

The Race is On!

How far can the jogger run in one minute? Write the answers. After one minute, circle where you are. Then finish the page.

$$
\begin{array}{r} 17 \\ -\ 9 \\ \hline \end{array}
\qquad
\begin{array}{r} 11 \\ -\ 6 \\ \hline \end{array}
\qquad
\begin{array}{r} 12 \\ -\ 7 \\ \hline \end{array}
\qquad
\begin{array}{r} 9 \\ -\ 5 \\ \hline \end{array}
\qquad
\begin{array}{r} 13 \\ -\ 8 \\ \hline \end{array}
$$

$$
\begin{array}{r} 6 \\ -3 \\ \hline \end{array}
\qquad
\begin{array}{r} 16 \\ -\ 9 \\ \hline \end{array}
\qquad
\begin{array}{r} 0 \\ -0 \\ \hline \end{array}
\qquad
\begin{array}{r} 14 \\ -\ 8 \\ \hline \end{array}
\qquad
\begin{array}{r} 16 \\ -\ 8 \\ \hline \end{array}
$$

$$
\begin{array}{r} 4 \\ -3 \\ \hline \end{array}
\qquad
\begin{array}{r} 15 \\ -\ 7 \\ \hline \end{array}
\qquad
\begin{array}{r} 10 \\ -\ 4 \\ \hline \end{array}
\qquad
\begin{array}{r} 3 \\ -2 \\ \hline \end{array}
\qquad
\begin{array}{r} 9 \\ -9 \\ \hline \end{array}
$$

$$
\begin{array}{r} 8 \\ -6 \\ \hline \end{array}
\qquad
\begin{array}{r} 7 \\ -4 \\ \hline \end{array}
\qquad
\begin{array}{r} 2 \\ -1 \\ \hline \end{array}
\qquad
\begin{array}{r} 18 \\ -\ 9 \\ \hline \end{array}
\qquad
\begin{array}{r} 8 \\ -4 \\ \hline \end{array}
$$

$$
\begin{array}{r} 14 \\ -\ 5 \\ \hline \end{array}
\qquad
\begin{array}{r} 10 \\ -\ 3 \\ \hline \end{array}
\qquad
\begin{array}{r} 4 \\ -2 \\ \hline \end{array}
\qquad
\begin{array}{r} 12 \\ -\ 6 \\ \hline \end{array}
\qquad
\begin{array}{r} 14 \\ -\ 7 \\ \hline \end{array}
$$

"I have finished the race, I have kept the faith." (2 Timothy 4:7)

Open Arms

⭐ Cross out each heart that has the wrong answer.

26
−15
11

34
−21
13

53
−10
43

46
−12
54

75
−32
43

38
−18
20

96
−74
23

82
−71
11

66
−35
31

84
−11
73

57
−24
73

70
−60
10

subtraction - no regrouping

Creation

⭐ Subtract the numbers in each problem. Then decode the verse using the letters from the problems.

77 -25 **A**	73 -23 **D**	96 -15 **H**	79 -43 **O**	57 -34 **T**
98 -24 **B**	67 -32 **E**	39 -27 **I**	48 -32 **R**	99 -35 **V**
46 -25 **C**	56 -24 **G**	45 -23 **N**	86 -25 **S**	

Verse

$\overline{12}$ $\overline{22}$ $\overline{23}$ $\overline{81}$ $\overline{35}$

$\overline{74}$ $\overline{35}$ $\overline{32}$ $\overline{12}$ $\overline{22}$ $\overline{22}$ $\overline{12}$ $\overline{22}$ $\overline{32}$ $\overline{32}$ $\overline{36}$ $\overline{50}$

$\overline{21}$ $\overline{16}$ $\overline{35}$ $\overline{52}$ $\overline{23}$ $\overline{35}$ $\overline{50}$ $\overline{23}$ $\overline{81}$ $\overline{35}$

$\overline{81}$ $\overline{35}$ $\overline{52}$ $\overline{64}$ $\overline{35}$ $\overline{22}$ $\overline{61}$ $\overline{52}$ $\overline{22}$ $\overline{50}$

$\overline{23}$ $\overline{81}$ $\overline{35}$ $\overline{35}$ $\overline{52}$ $\overline{16}$ $\overline{23}$ $\overline{81}$.   (Genesis 1:1 NIV)

King of Kings

Who is the King of kings and Lord of lords? Add or subtract. Find out his name by coloring the spaces with answers greater than **12** red. Color the rest of the spaces blue.

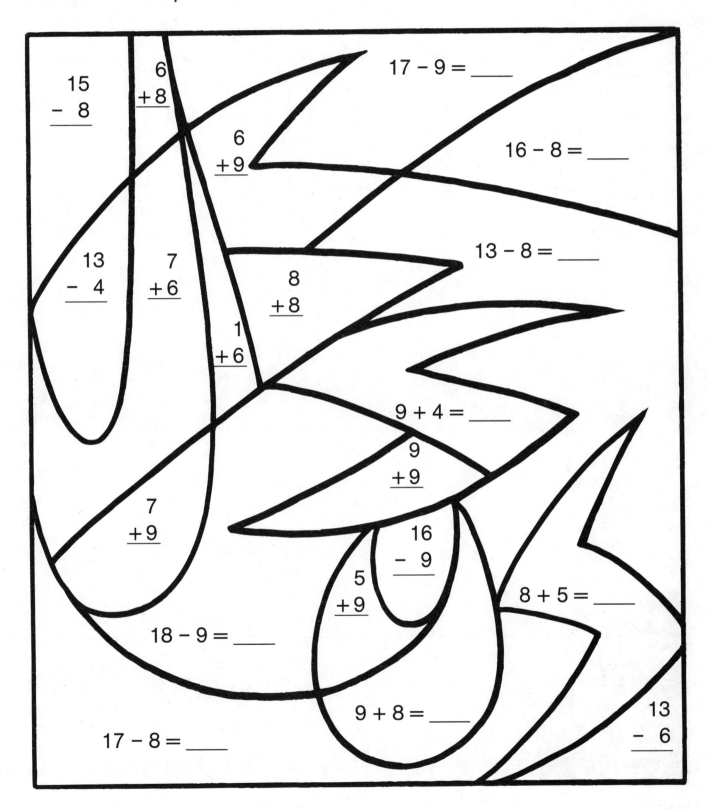

$$15 - 8$$

$$6 + 8$$

$$6 + 9$$

$$17 - 9 = \underline{\quad}$$

$$16 - 8 = \underline{\quad}$$

$$13 - 4$$

$$7 + 6$$

$$8 + 8$$

$$13 - 8 = \underline{\quad}$$

$$1 + 6$$

$$9 + 4 = \underline{\quad}$$

$$9 + 9$$

$$7 + 9$$

$$16 - 9$$

$$5 + 9$$

$$8 + 5 = \underline{\quad}$$

$$18 - 9 = \underline{\quad}$$

$$9 + 8 = \underline{\quad}$$

$$13 - 6$$

$$17 - 8 = \underline{\quad}$$

addition and subtraction

The Trumpet Blast

⭐ Solve the problems on the wall. In the Book of Joshua, the priests blew the trumpets, and Joshua's army shouted. The walls of Jericho fell down.

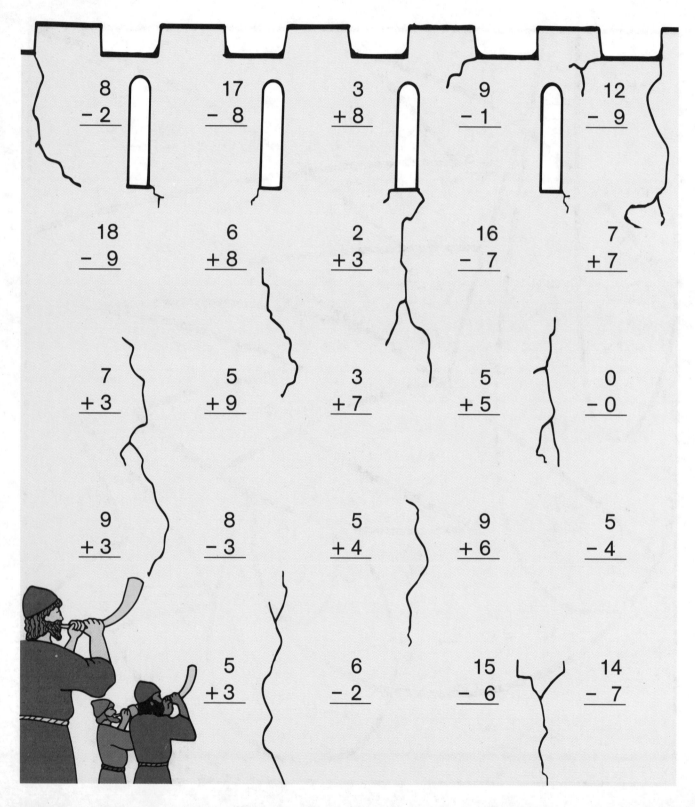

$$\begin{array}{r} 8 \\ -2 \\ \hline \end{array} \qquad \begin{array}{r} 17 \\ -8 \\ \hline \end{array} \qquad \begin{array}{r} 3 \\ +8 \\ \hline \end{array} \qquad \begin{array}{r} 9 \\ -1 \\ \hline \end{array} \qquad \begin{array}{r} 12 \\ -9 \\ \hline \end{array}$$

$$\begin{array}{r} 18 \\ -9 \\ \hline \end{array} \qquad \begin{array}{r} 6 \\ +8 \\ \hline \end{array} \qquad \begin{array}{r} 2 \\ +3 \\ \hline \end{array} \qquad \begin{array}{r} 16 \\ -7 \\ \hline \end{array} \qquad \begin{array}{r} 7 \\ +7 \\ \hline \end{array}$$

$$\begin{array}{r} 7 \\ +3 \\ \hline \end{array} \qquad \begin{array}{r} 5 \\ +9 \\ \hline \end{array} \qquad \begin{array}{r} 3 \\ +7 \\ \hline \end{array} \qquad \begin{array}{r} 5 \\ +5 \\ \hline \end{array} \qquad \begin{array}{r} 0 \\ -0 \\ \hline \end{array}$$

$$\begin{array}{r} 9 \\ +3 \\ \hline \end{array} \qquad \begin{array}{r} 8 \\ -3 \\ \hline \end{array} \qquad \begin{array}{r} 5 \\ +4 \\ \hline \end{array} \qquad \begin{array}{r} 9 \\ +6 \\ \hline \end{array} \qquad \begin{array}{r} 5 \\ -4 \\ \hline \end{array}$$

$$\begin{array}{r} 5 \\ +3 \\ \hline \end{array} \qquad \begin{array}{r} 6 \\ -2 \\ \hline \end{array} \qquad \begin{array}{r} 15 \\ -6 \\ \hline \end{array} \qquad \begin{array}{r} 14 \\ -7 \\ \hline \end{array}$$

In the Desert

⭐ How far will you get in one minute? Solve the problems in the desert. After one minute, circle where you are. Then finish the page.

2 + 8	3 + 3	3 + 5	8 + 9	10 − 1
6 − 4	7 + 7	2 + 7	8 − 4	5 + 4
12 − 4	15 − 6	9 − 6	7 − 5	3 + 2
0 + 0	10 − 5	17 − 9	6 + 8	
8 + 1	4 − 3	14 − 5	9 + 3	

Weather Wise

Meg kept her class's weather chart for two months. Write a number sentence to solve each problem.

1. Meg counted 11 rainy days and 3 foggy days. How many fewer foggy days than rainy days were there?

_____   _____ days

2. There were 6 rainy days in one week and 3 in the next. How many rainy days were there in 2 weeks?

_____   _____ days

3. In one week, 5 of the days were snowy. How many days were not snowy?

_____   _____ days

4. Meg needed 12 stickers to put on the chart for sunny days. She only had 8. How many more stickers did she need?

_____   _____ days

5. There were 9 days when the temperature was 60° and 5 days when it was 50°. How many more days was the temperature 60°?

_____   _____ days

Bugs, Bugs, Bugs

Name_____

⭐ God made every creature, even bugs! Solve these problems.

1. Justin saw 15 butterflies.

    He saw 14 more.

    How many butterflies did Justin see in all?

    _____ butterflies

2. At first, 40 ants came to Clara's picnic.

    Then 22 more ants came.

    How many ants visited altogether?

    _____ ants

3. Barney found 26 beetles.

    Then he found 32 more.

    How many beetles did Barney find altogether?

    _____ beetles

4. Nick heard 25 bees buzzing.

    15 bees flew away.

    How many bees were left?

    _____ bees

5. Travis found 29 ladybugs.

    14 flew away.

    How many were left?

    _____ ladybugs

story problems - no regrouping

The Pet Shop

Name_____

⭐ God wants us to take care of our pets with love and kindness. Solve these problems.

1. The pet shop owner had 56 white rabbits and 23 gray rabbits.

   He had _____ more white rabbits than gray rabbits.

2. There were 26 hamsters.

   They had 32 babies.

   There are now _____ hamsters.

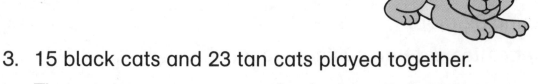

3. 15 black cats and 23 tan cats played together.

   There were _____ cats playing altogether.

4. 12 out of 24 puppies were sold.

   _____ puppies were left.

5. 39 lizards lived in the pet shop.

   15 lizards ran away.

   There were _____ lizards left.

How Many?

Name_____

Solve these story problems.

1. Jack brought 7 quarters for the church offering.

   Jill brought 8 quarters for the church offering.

   How many quarters did they have for the offering altogether?

   _____ quarters

2. The Sunday school class has 6 girls and 9 boys.

   How many children are in the class?

   _____ children

3. The shepherd had 14 sheep.

   He lost 6 of them.

   How many sheep were still in the pen?

   _____ sheep

4. Nancy first grew 9 roses and 2 lilies.

   Then she grew 5 daisies.

   How many flowers does she have altogether?

   _____ flowers

5. Mary lit 7 candles.

   Two candles burned out.

   How many candles were still lit?

   _____ candles

story problems

How Old?

⭐ Solve these story problems.

HAPPY BIRTHDAY JESUS LOVES YOU!

1. Beth is 10 years old.

   Bobby is 6 years old.

   Beth is _____ years older than Bobby.

2. Mike, who is 12, has a sister who is 3.

   Mike's sister is _____ years younger than Mike.

3. Sally and her twin brother are 8 years old today.

   They will need _____ candles altogether for two cakes.

4. It is Ben and Barb's birthday.

   Mom puts up balloons to show their ages.

   If Ben is 6 years old and Barb is 7 years old, Mom

   will need _____ balloons in all.

5. Kathy is 11 years old.

   Carla is 9 years old.

   Kathy is _____ years older than Carla.

How Many Hearts?

⭐ Complete each number sentence by writing the number or symbol that is missing. Use small objects or draw pictures to help you solve the problems.

Example: 7 − _4_ = 3	♡̸ ♡̸ ♡̸ ♡̸ ♡ ♡ ♡

_____ + 6 = 11	
7 + _____ = 13	
4 + _____ + 1 = 9	
5 _____ 4 = 9	
_____ + 5 = 14	
4 + _____ + 3 = 13	
2 + _____ + 2 = 9	
7 − _____ = 2	
9 _____ 3 = 6	
7 _____ 6 = 1	

"Love the Lord your God with all your heart."   (Mark 12:30a)

operation sense

The Shepherd's Staff

Name_____

Don't be led astray. Follow the numbers from left to right on each staff by adding and subtracting to reach the final answer.

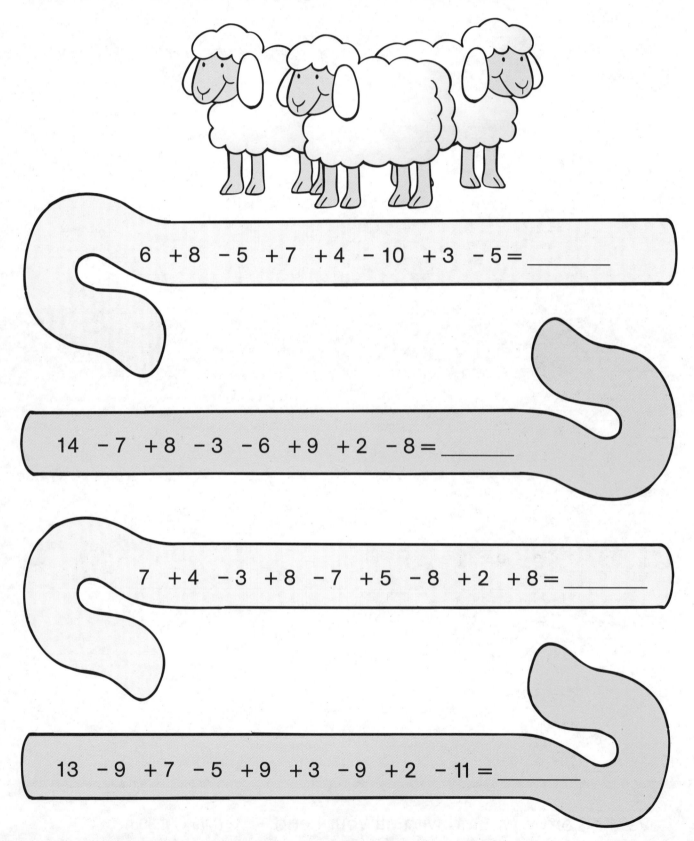

$6 \ +8 \ -5 \ +7 \ +4 \ -10 \ +3 \ -5 =$ _____

$14 \ -7 \ +8 \ -3 \ -6 \ +9 \ +2 \ -8 =$ _____

$7 \ +4 \ -3 \ +8 \ -7 \ +5 \ -8 \ +2 \ +8 =$ _____

$13 \ -9 \ +7 \ -5 \ +9 \ +3 \ -9 \ +2 \ -11 =$ _____

Jesus Loves Kids

Draw a red ♡ around the problem if you must add.

Draw a yellow ✝ around the problem if you must subtract.

Solve each problem.

26 +72	78 − 45	66 − 14	32 +35
82 − 41	75 − 34	22 +66	82 − 51
21 +38	81 +18	46 − 14	59 − 35
71 +15	26 +63	42 +46	68 − 36

Hop Along Quickly

Name_____

⭐ How far can the frog hop in one minute? Solve the problems. After one minute, circle where you are. Then finish the page.

15 +20	96 −83	52 +43	44 +24	67 −34
62 −41	56 −20	45 +32	70 +29	39 −18
78 −45	83 +12	50 +19	47 +51	82 −61
27 −15	81 +17	35 −23	64 +25	66 −45

A Whale of a Problem

Find the sums of these three-digit addition problems.

```
   9        7        4        2
   7        3        3        9
 + 4      + 8      + 9      + 3
```

```
   9        5        4        4
   2        6        7        5
 + 1      + 8      + 6      + 2
```

```
   2        2        6        7
   6        7        3        1
 + 1      + 6      + 4      + 2
```

addition with three addends

It all Adds Up!

⭐ Solve the problems.

2	6	7	3
7	5	0	6
+ 9	+ 4	+ 9	+ 2

5	4	5	4
5	7	2	3
+ 2	+ 2	+ 1	+ 7

6	3	4	3
8	4	5	5
+ 3	+ 2	+ 1	+ 9

Good Deeds

Name_____

⭐ Add the numbers in each problem. Then decode the verse using the letters by the problems.

A 8 + 8 + 3 = _____	**B** 3 + 9 + 4 = _____	**C** 7 + 7 + 7 = _____
D 7 + 4 + 2 = _____	**E** 5 + 9 + 9 = _____	**F** 8 + 9 + 8 = _____
G 6 + 2 + 2 = _____	**H** 9 + 9 + 9 = _____	**I** 7 + 3 + 5 = _____
L 4 + 4 + 4 = _____	**N** 6 + 5 + 3 = _____	**O** 9 + 7 + 8 = _____
R 6 + 5 + 9 = _____	**S** 7 + 6 + 4 = _____	**T** 9 + 9 + 8 = _____
W 3 + 3 + 5 = _____	**Y** 3 + 3 + 3 = _____	

Verse

9 23	19 20 23	26 27 23

12 15 10 27 26	24 25	26 27 23

11 24 20 12 13.	19	21 15 26 9

26 27 19 26	15 17	17 23 26

24 14	19	27 15 12 12

21 19 14 14 24 26	16 23	27 15 13.

(Matthew 5:16 NIV)

addition

Count On It

The king is counting the coins in each pile of gold. He doesn't know that Jesus wants us to store up treasures in heaven, not on Earth. Help the king by writing the missing numbers in the blanks below.

156, _____, _____, 159, _____

241, 242, _____, _____, _____

_____, 330, 331, _____, _____

478, _____, _____, _____, 482

501, 502, _____, _____, _____

627, _____, _____, 630, _____

_____, _____, _____, 720, 721

838, _____, _____, 841, _____

_____, _____, _____, 998, 999

Chariot Chase

How far can the Egyptian chariot travel in one minute? Solve the problems. After one minute, circle where you are. Then finish the page.

83 +12	96 +58	75 +46	33 +23	99 +42
56 +27	30 +14	64 +18	26 +15	88 +39
47 +29	53 +32	28 +16	71 +25	69 +48
87 +34	65 +38	34 +47	42 +22	70 +36

addition - some regrouping, timed

Seaside Aquarium

Name_____

The town of Seaside attracts thousands of visitors each year. Its aquarium is a wonderful place to see some of the many fish God created. Attendance records are kept for both morning and afternoon visitors. Solve these problems.

Day 1	Day 2	Day 3	Day 4	Day 5
247	502	101	517	436
+ 358	+ 469	+ 603	+ 244	+ 304

Day 6	Day 7	Day 8	Day 9	Day 10
185	327	299	316	402
+ 464	+ 428	+ 501	+ 317	+ 529

Now answer these questions.

1. Which day had the most visitors?_____

2. Which day had the least visitors?_____

3. What is the difference between

   these two totals?_____

Palm Sunday

Find each sum. Connect the sums of **83** to make a path for Jesus to follow.

17 +66	58 +25	42 +19	38 +25
48 +26	17 +75	57 +26	28 +38	65 +29
58 +37	64 +24	48 +35	65 +16	37 +39
39 +59	59 +27	55 +28	39 +44

two-digit addition, regrouping

Bird Watching

In Matthew 10:29–31, Jesus tells us he watches over the sparrows and, better yet, watches over us!

 Joy has a bird feeder in her yard. Help her solve the following problems.

Example: On Monday, she saw 27 robins and 35 chickadees. How many birds did she see?

$$\begin{array}{r} 1 \\ 27 \\ +35 \\ \hline 62 \end{array}$$

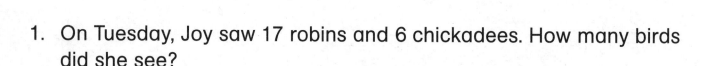

1. On Tuesday, Joy saw 17 robins and 6 chickadees. How many birds did she see?

2. On Wednesday, she saw 32 robins and 19 chickadees. How many birds did she see?

3. On Thursday, she saw 59 robins and 26 chickadees. How many birds did she see?

4. On Friday, she saw 73 robins and 19 chickadees. How many birds did she see?

Number Crunch

Name_____

Your answers on this page will be numbers. Put the answer to question number 1 in the box marked 1. Put the answer to question number 2 in the box marked 2, and so on. Add up each row across. Read the Bible verses if you need help.

1. How many "great lights" did God create? (Genesis 1:16)
2. How old was Jotham when he became king in Jerusalem?
   (2 Chronicles 27:1)
3. How many days was Jonah in the huge fish? (Matthew 12:40)
4. How many years did it take Solomon to build his palace?
   (1 Kings 7:1)
5. How many years did Jacob agree to serve Laban before he could marry Rachel? (Genesis 29:20)
6. How many talents did the first servant receive in the Parable of the Talents? (Matthew 25:15)
7. How old was Joseph when his father gave him a beautiful robe?
   (Genesis 37:2–3)
8. How many anchors did the sailors put in the water to save Paul's ship from hitting the rocks? (Acts 27:29)
9. After Jesus healed ten lepers, how many did not thank him?
   (Luke 17:11–19)

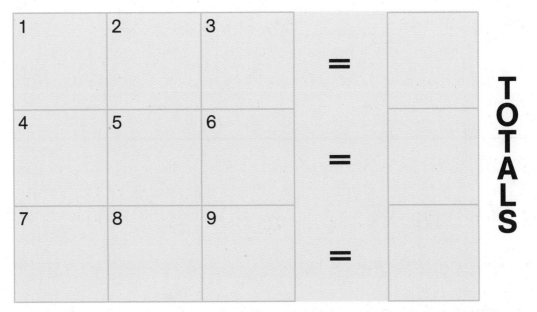

1	2	3	=		T O T A L S
4	5	6	=		
7	8	9	=		

addition with regrouping

Unlock This Riddle

Add the numbers vertically to find the sum. Then write the letters from the problems in the answer blanks below to solve the riddle.

Riddle:
What did Samson use less of after
his encounter with Delilah?

- $24 + 16 + 32 =$ _____ **R**   • $15 + 21 + 9 =$ _____ **N**

- $17 + 26 + 11 =$ _____ **S**   • $36 + 26 + 12 =$ _____ **S**

- $7 + 24 + 19 =$ _____ **H**   • $21 + 24 + 33 =$ _____ **O**

- $17 + 9 + 27 =$ _____ **Y**   • $11 + 31 + 26 =$ _____ **P**

- $30 + 17 + 29 =$ _____ **E**   • $16 + 15 + 32 =$ _____ **A**

- $22 + 39 + 14 =$ _____ **M**   • $9 + 34 + 23 =$ _____ **O**

Answer:

___ ___ ___ ___ ___ ___ ___
74   50   63   75   68   78   66

Bound for Bethlehem

Name _____

Work the problems to help Mary and Joseph reach Bethlehem.

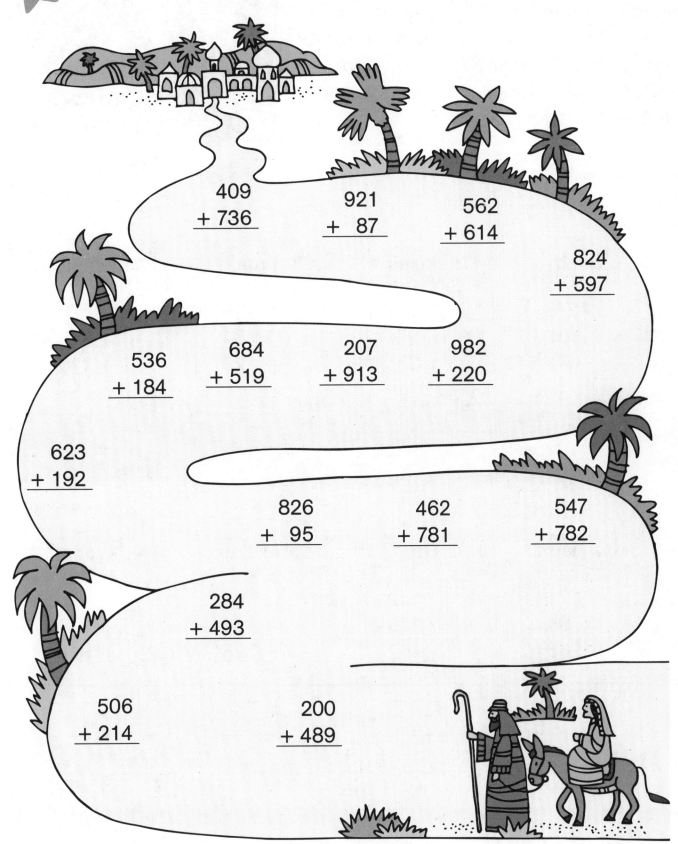

$$409 + 736$$

$$921 + 87$$

$$562 + 614$$

$$824 + 597$$

$$536 + 184$$

$$684 + 519$$

$$207 + 913$$

$$982 + 220$$

$$623 + 192$$

$$826 + 95$$

$$462 + 781$$

$$547 + 782$$

$$284 + 493$$

$$506 + 214$$

$$200 + 489$$

addition - regrouping hundreds

Baseball Stats

⭐ The men below have special talents given to them by God. These figures show the total number of hits per player for the last three seasons. Write an estimate of the total. Then add to find the true answer.

1. Smith

```
  278
  162
+ 641
```

Est. _____

_____

2. Jones

```
  371
  274
+ 321
```

Est. _____

_____

3. Frank

```
  410
   84
+ 129
```

Est. _____

_____

4. Manning

```
  173
   52
+ 310
```

Est. _____

_____

5. Johnson

```
  121
   94
+ 268
```

Est. _____

_____

6. Gray

```
   72
  139
+ 402
```

Est. _____

_____

7. Nettles

```
   83
  174
+ 326
```

Est. _____

_____

8. Evans

```
   62
  408
+ 101
```

Est. _____

_____

Take a Giant Step

How far will the Philistines run? Solve the problems. After one minute, circle where you are. Then finish the page.

98	57	82	35	46
−17	−34	−69	−13	−28

72	67	26	47	50
−56	−35	−19	−28	−37

54	42	66	83	75
−37	−31	−47	−62	−38

74	23	54	92	57
−33	−15	−21	−85	−28

subtraction - some regrouping, timed

Joseph's Robe

⭐ Subtract. Regroup as needed. Color the spaces with differences of:

10–19 red	20–29 blue	30–39 green
40–49 yellow	50–59 purple	60–69 orange

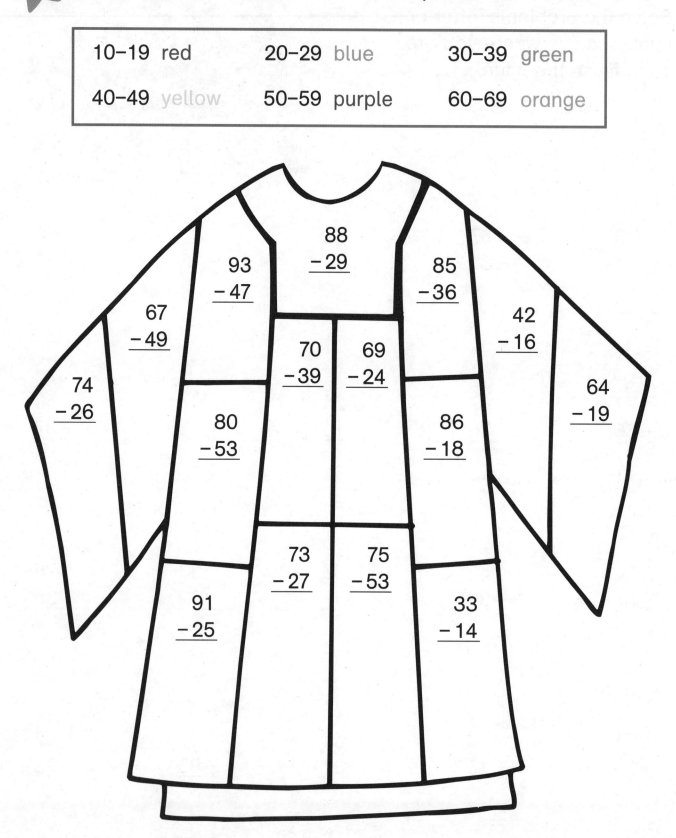

88
− 29

93
− 47

85
− 36

67
− 49

42
− 16

70
− 39

69
− 24

74
− 26

80
− 53

86
− 18

64
− 19

73
− 27

75
− 53

91
− 25

33
− 14

Bon Appetit!

⭐ Jerry and his friends were very hungry! Solve the problems to find out how many leaves were left on each tree after Jerry and his friends ate dinner.

56 − 47	32 − 18	44 − 29	26 − 18	67 − 38

| 80
− 15 | 73
− 58 | 51
− 28 | 65
− 47 | 92
− 83 |

"Give thanks to the Lord of lords . . . who gives food to every creature." (Psalm 136:3, 25)

subtraction - regrouping

Sports Bonanza

Name_____

Do you think Jesus played games with his friends? Subtract. Regroup as needed.

```
  33        62
- 18      - 47
```

```
  81        75
- 19      - 46
```

```
  52        44        70
- 33      - 26      - 22
```

```
  76
- 58
```

```
  87        61
- 69      - 55
```

High-Scoring Scoreboards Name_____

⭐ Give the difference in points between the team scores on each scoreboard. Show your work.

Praise Singers	112
Prayer Warriors	96

Sandals	112
Chariots	88

Staffs	117
Halos	98

Donkeys	92
Camels	85

Shepherds	91
Carpenters	74

Psalms	108
Proverbs	89

Israelites	92
Egyptians	76

Tablets	113
Scrolls	97

subtraction with regrouping

Let's Weigh In!

Name_____

⭐ According to God's plan, all baby animals are different. Use the chart below to solve the problems.

Weight Chart	
baby elephant	92 pounds
baby hippo	83 pounds
baby alligator	47 pounds
baby shark	26 pounds
baby snake	5 pounds

1. The baby shark weighs _____ pounds more than the baby snake.

2. The baby elephant and the baby shark together weigh _____ pounds.

3. If the baby hippo and the baby shark were weighed together, the scale would show_____ pounds.

4. The difference between the lightest animal and the heaviest animal is _____ pounds.

5. The baby snake weighs _____ pounds less than the baby hippo.

6. The baby alligator and the baby snake together weigh _____ pounds.

Shoot for the Stars

You are a super math star! How many stars can you catch in one minute? After one minute, stop and circle where you are. Then finish the page.

74
+15

52
−10

76
−28

83
+38

54
−28

65
+24

93
+27

39
−12

47
+45

32
−24

87
−23

56
+11

71
−19

52
−32

40
+42

65
+99

Fantastic Freckles

⭐ Fred knows that God made him like no one else. During some months, Fred has more freckles. During other months, Fred has fewer freckles. Solve each problem to see how many freckles Fred has each month.

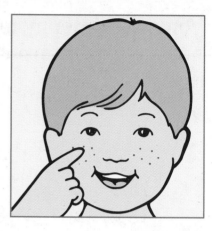

January	**February**	**March**	**April**
52 − 9	43 − 6	37 − 9	28 − 6

May	**June**	**July**	**August**
34 + 9	43 + 9	52 + 9	61 −15

September	**October**	**November**	**December**
46 − 9	37 − 9	28 +44	72 −29

Playing with blocks

⭐ How many blocks? Write the numbers.

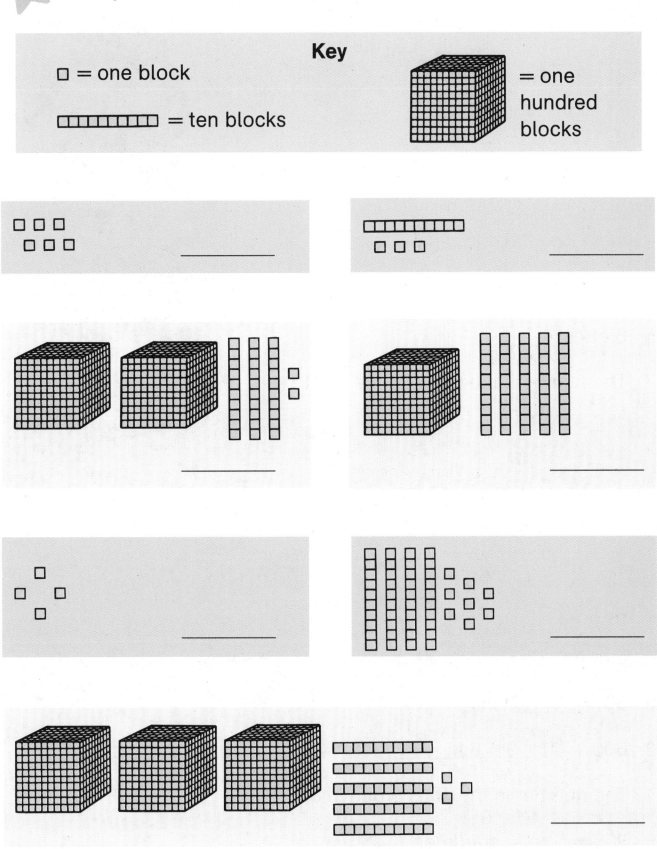

Key

☐ = one block

▭▭▭▭▭▭ = ten blocks

= one hundred blocks

Numbered

Use the Word Bank to complete the crossword puzzle.

Word Bank

one	three	five	seven	nine
two	four	six	eight	

Across:

1. The number in the hundreds place in 425

2. 600 + 30 + 7 = 63_____

5. 8 ones = _____

7. The number in the tens place in 913

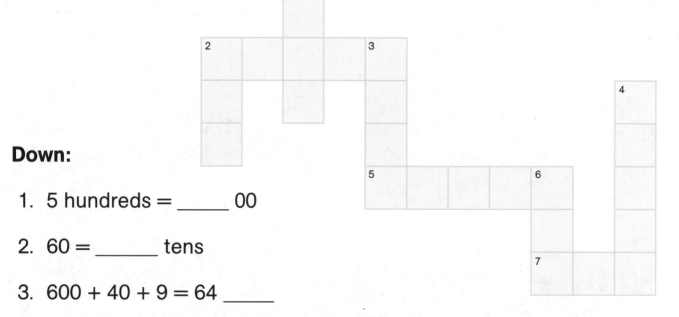

Down:

1. 5 hundreds = _____ 00

2. 60 = _____ tens

3. 600 + 40 + 9 = 64 _____

4. The number in the ones place in 853

6. 200 = _____ hundreds

Asking

⭐ Write the numbers described. Then decode the verse using the letters next to your answers.

Three ones	Seven tens	One ten	Three tens
A ___	F ___	N ___	U ___
Five ones	Two tens	Seven ones	Six tens
B ___	H ___	O ___	V ___
Six ones	Eight ones	Nine ones	Zero ones
C ___	I ___	P ___	W ___
Five tens	Eight tens	Two ones	Four tens
D ___	L ___	R ___	Y ___
Nine tens	Four ones	One one	
E ___	M ___	T ___	

Verse

"... ___ ___ ___ ___   ___ ___ ___ ___   ___ ___
    6   3 80 80   30 9 7 10   4 90

___ ___   ___ ___ ___   ___ ___ ___
8 10   1 20 90   50 3 40

___ ___   ___ ___ ___ ___ ___ ___ ___;   ___
7 70   1 2 7 30 5 80 90   8

___ ___ ___ ___   ___ ___ ___ ___ ___ ___ ___
0 8 80 80   50 90 80 8 60 90 2

___ ___ ___,   ___ ___ ___   ___ ___ ___
40 7 30   3 10 50   40 7 30

___ ___ ___ ___   ___ ___ ___ ___ ___   ___ ___."
0 8 80 80   20 7 10 7 2   4 90

(Psalm 50:15)

place value

Communion

For each number pair, draw a goblet 🏆 around the smaller number and make an arrow (< or >) pointing to the goblet. If the numbers in the pair are the same draw a loaf of bread 🍞 around both numbers and draw an equal sign (=) between them.

Examples:

56 > ⟨24⟩   ⟨134⟩ < 200   🍞263 = 🍞263

1.	35	27	8.	237	237
2.	47	82	9.	265	344
3.	165	156	10.	52	52
4.	384	391	11.	41	33
5.	972	972	12.	80	76
6.	83	38	13.	362	501
7.	15	24	14.	492	284

comparing numbers

Match the Plagues

Pharaoh would not let God's people go, so God sent plagues to Pharaoh's land. Draw a line from each Pharaoh to the plague with the addition that checks the subtraction on Pharaoh.

$$46 - 27$$

$$34 + 28$$

$$62 - 28$$

$$19 + 27$$

$$85 - 37$$

$$48 + 37$$

checking subtraction with addition

Across the U.S.A.

Name_____

⭐ Compare the temperatures in the following cities using <, >, or =.

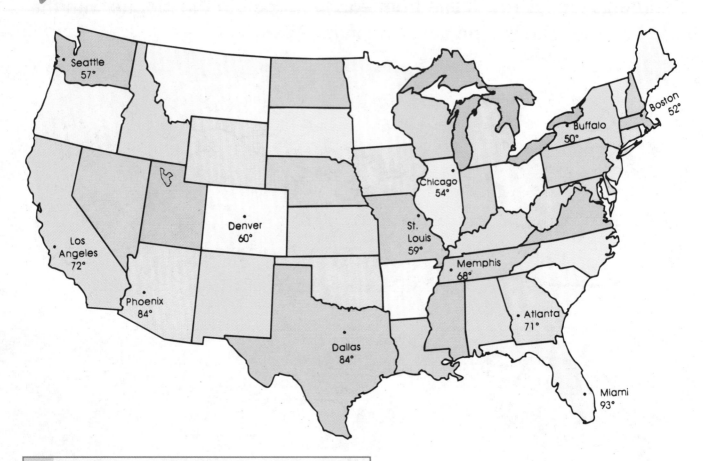

1. Los Angeles		Miami
2. Boston		Chicago
3. Dallas		Atlanta
4. Phoenix		Dallas
5. Chicago		St. Louis
6. Memphis		Denver

Ski the Number Line

⭐ How do you enjoy nature during the winter? Go skiing across the number line by doing the following problems.

Give the number that is one greater than . . .

1. 256 _____   2. 294 _____   3. 248 _____

4. 299 _____   5. 311 _____   6. 272 _____

Give the number that is one less than . . .

1. 263 _____   2. 313 _____   3. 291 _____

4. 250 _____   5. 285 _____   6. 310 _____

Write the numbers that are between . . .

1. 253 and 262 _____

2. 287 and 295 _____

3. 241 and 250 _____

4. 296 and 305 _____

ordering numbers

Beach Trip

The Harris family took a trip to the beach. The trip created the following problems. Use your math skills to solve them, showing your work beneath each.

1. How many miles would the Harris family travel to the beach if the odometer read 1,278 when they left their house and showed 1,314 when they got to the beach?

    _____

3. The odometer read 1,314 when the Harris family left the beach. They drove 47 miles to the grocery store. What was the new reading?

    _____

2. If the family arrived at the beach at 1:15 P.M. and stayed three and one half hours, at what time would they leave?

    _____

4. It takes 1 hour and 10 minutes to drive home from the beach. If the family left the beach at 4:45 and went directly home, when would they have arrived?

    _____

Name_____

★ God created many different fruits and vegetables. Clarissa is excited to plant a variety of seeds in her garden and to watch how God helps them grow. Read each problem carefully and solve it. Show your work.

1. Clarissa planted 210 bean seeds, and 183 bean plants grew. How many seeds did not grow?

   _____

3. After picking 348 carrots on Wednesday, Clarissa gave 175 to a friend. How many did she have left?

   _____

2. On Monday, she picked 74 strawberries, and on Tuesday she picked 109 more. How many strawberries did she pick altogether?

   _____

4. On Saturday, Clarissa's friends helped her to pick 27 pumpkins, 35 tomatoes, and 108 beans. How many items were picked?

   _____

What's Missing?

⭐ What fraction is shaded? Show this by writing the missing numeral in each fraction.

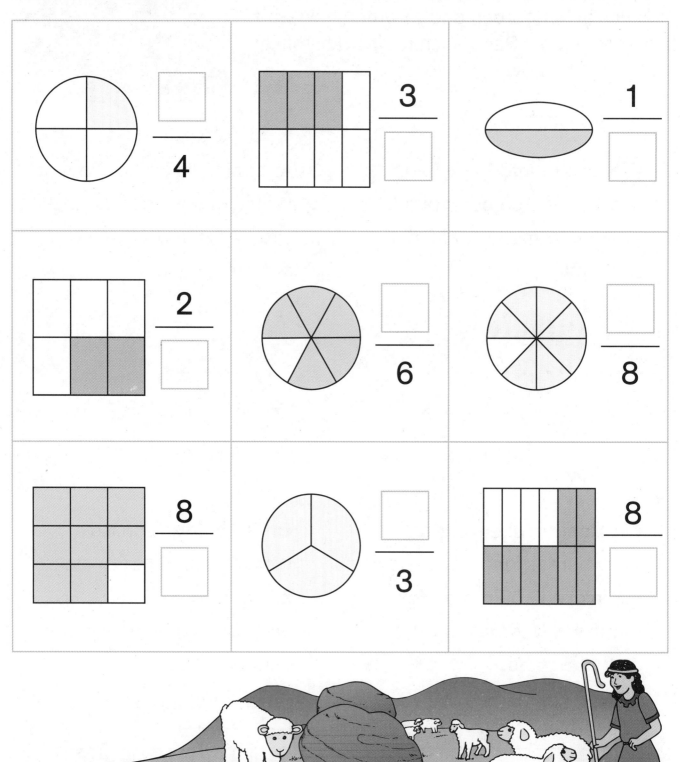

Focus on Fractions

Name_____

⭐ Color the correct amount of pictures to show the fraction listed for each problem.

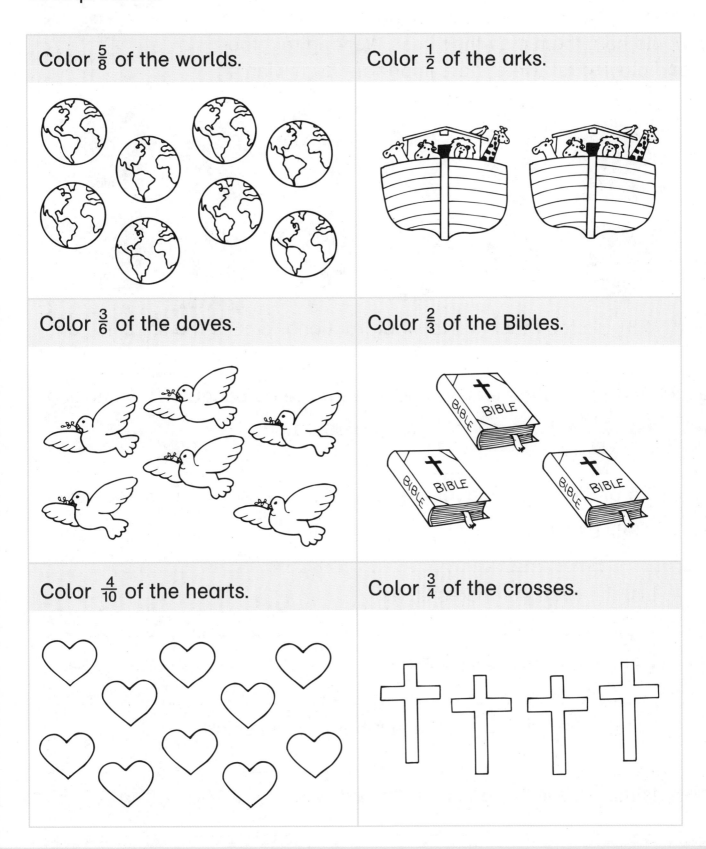

Color $\frac{5}{8}$ of the worlds.

Color $\frac{1}{2}$ of the arks.

Color $\frac{3}{6}$ of the doves.

Color $\frac{2}{3}$ of the Bibles.

Color $\frac{4}{10}$ of the hearts.

Color $\frac{3}{4}$ of the crosses.

fractions

Soccer Team Jerseys

Name_____

There are 12 girls on the church soccer team. Coach Bryant unwrapped their new team shirts and spread them on the gym floor. He reminded them that God would help them play their best. Working together and playing fair were more important than winning.

1. If 3 girls took their shirts, what fractional part of the shirts is gone?

   _____

2. One-sixth of the jerseys had to be returned because the stitching was weak. How many shirts were returned?

   _____

3. If $\frac{1}{2}$ of the team paid for their shirts by the end of the week, how many girls paid?

   _____

4. List the even-numbered shirts.

   _____

   List the odd-numbered shirts.

   _____

5. What is the total of all the numbers on the shirts?

   _____

   Is this an even or an odd number?

   _____

Fruity Fractions

Name_____

⭐ To help keep our bodies healthy, God has given us fruits and vegetables. Color each fractional part.

Color $\frac{3}{4}$ orange	Color $\frac{3}{6}$ green
Color $\frac{1}{2}$ brown	Color $\frac{1}{3}$ green
Color $\frac{2}{4}$ yellow	Color $\frac{1}{3}$ pink

fractional parts

The Praise Band celebrated the release of their CD and expressed their thanks to God by giving a concert each night for six days. They also served a chocolate cake each day. The shading shows the portion eaten of each cake. Write a fraction for each shaded portion.

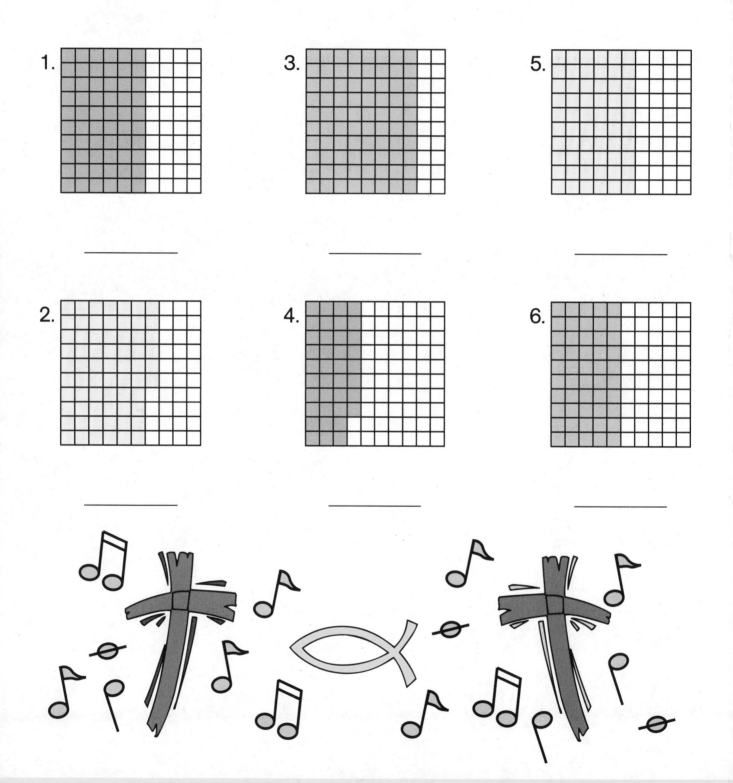

1. _____

3. _____

5. _____

2. _____

4. _____

6. _____

Creepy Crawlies

⭐ Look at a ruler to compare inches and centimeters. Circle the correct answer.

1. The world's shortest snake, the thread snake, is about 4 inches long. This is about _____ long.

   6 centimeters   10 centimeters   13 centimeters

2. The smallest frog, the Cuban frog, is less than 1/2 inch long. This is about _____ long.

   1 centimeter   3 centimeters   5 centimeters

3. The largest spider, the goliath bird-eating spider, has legs about 28 centimeters long. This is about _____ long.

   10 inches   11 inches   12 inches

4. The biggest scorpion, the emperor scorpion, can be over 7 inches long. This is about _____ long.

   16 centimeters   17 centimeters   18 centimeters

5. One shark, the spined pygmy shark, grows to be about 15 centimeters long. This is about _____ long.

   5 inches   6 inches   7 inches

Fishers of Men

Peter and Andrew agreed only to keep fish that measured greater than 6 centimeters. One day the brothers caught the fish below. Estimate how many Peter and Andrew will keep. _____
Then measure to find out the length of each.

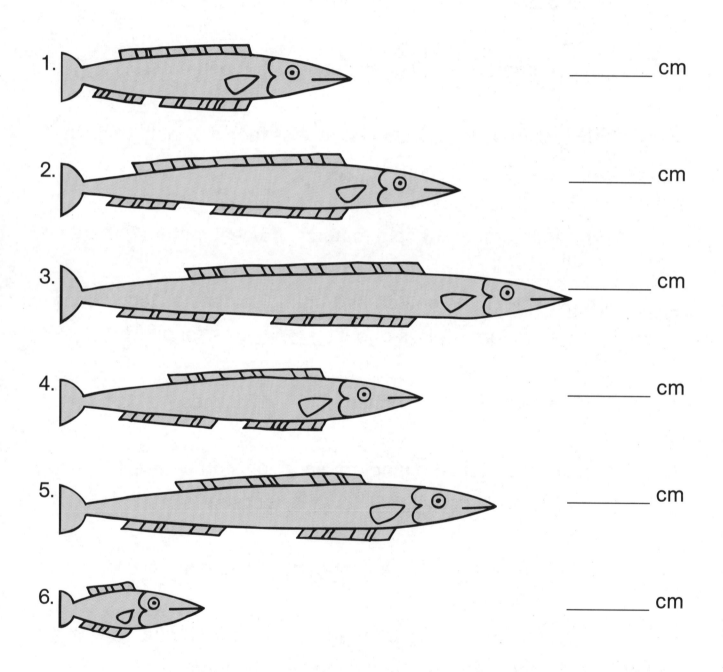

1. _____ cm

2. _____ cm

3. _____ cm

4. _____ cm

5. _____ cm

6. _____ cm

If the fish were laid end to end, what would they measure altogether?

_____

It's Time!

⭐ Answer each question below.

1. Andrew's music lesson begins in 1 hour. It is now 8:00. What time does the music lesson begin? _____

2. Melanie reads her Bible from 7:00 to 8:00 every day. How many minutes does she read? _____

3. Mrs. Hall tells her children that lunch is in half an hour. It is now 11:30. What time is lunch? _____

4. Quiet time lasts for 15 minutes. If it begins at 12:15, when will quiet time be over? _____

5. In the afternoon, Mrs. Hall reads to her children from 1:00 to 1:20. For how long does she read? _____

6. Alex and Rachel began to put a puzzle together at 1:20 and were finished at 1:50. How many minutes did it take to do the puzzle? _____

time

What Time Is It?

⭐ Write the time. Then draw the hands on each clock.

1. Lilly ate breakfast at 7:00 A.M.
   She took 15 minutes to finish eating.
   What time did she finish? _____

2. Daniel began praying at 11:30 A.M.
   He finished praying in 30 minutes.
   What time did he finish? _____

3. Paul ran in the gym for 30 minutes.
   If he began at 2:00 P.M., when did he
   finish running? _____

4. The last school bell rang 25 minutes after
   Sarah's gym class ended. Her gym class
   ended at 2:30 P.M. What time did the last
   bell ring? _____

Bible Times

Read each sentence from a Bible story that has a made-up time in it. Write the number of the matching clock by each sentence.

_____ Moses saw the burning bush at 10:33.

_____ Eve took a bite of the fruit at 1:04.

_____ The wise men arrived in Bethlehem at 5:16.

_____ The lamb has been missing since 6:30!

_____ The wedding banquet began at 9:47.

_____ David's suppertime is 5:52.

_____ Jesus rode into Jerusalem at 4:39.

_____ The disciples threw their nets to the other side of the boat at 8:21.

time

Prayer Time

Jesus hears our prayers any time we pray. Draw the hands on the clock to show the time when you could pray.

10:15

7:27

2:04

5:47

11:58

1:11

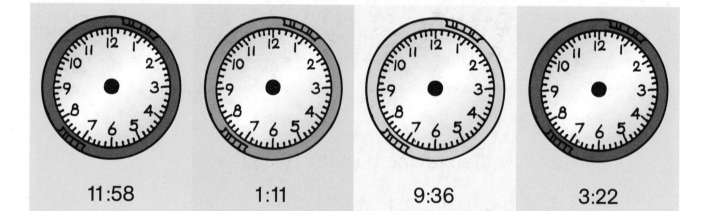
9:36

3:22

12:13

8:09

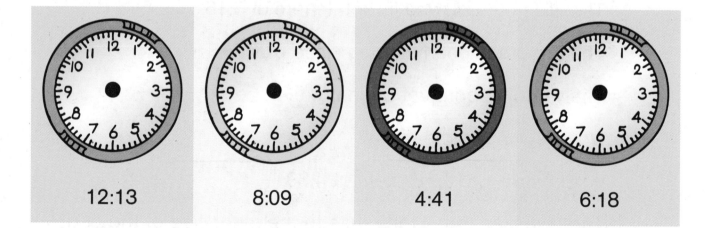
4:41

6:18

Mark's Busy Schedule

Name_____

★ Mark had a busy day. Use a clock to help you answer these questions about his schedule.

1. School starts at 8:45. Mark gets up at 7:30. How much time does Mark have before school? _____

2. Mark eats breakfast ½ hour after he gets out of bed. What time does he eat breakfast? _____

3. After breakfast, Mark and his brother work on their homework for 15 minutes. When are they done with this task? _____

4. Music class starts at 10:20 and ends at 10:50. How long is this class? _____

5. The afternoon runs from 12:45–3:25. How long is the afternoon session? _____

6. After school, Mark has soccer practice. It starts at 4:00 but it takes him 25 minutes to get there. What time must he leave home? _____

7. Mark eats supper at 5:45. It takes him 15 minutes to eat. After supper, he spends 30 minutes doing his homework, two hours playing with his friends, and 30 minutes watching his favorite TV show until bedtime. What time does Mark go to bed? _____

figuring elapsed time

Tithes and Offering

Name_____

⭐ Everyone in Mrs. Johnson's Sunday school class put money in the offering plate each Sunday. Write the total amount in each offering plate.

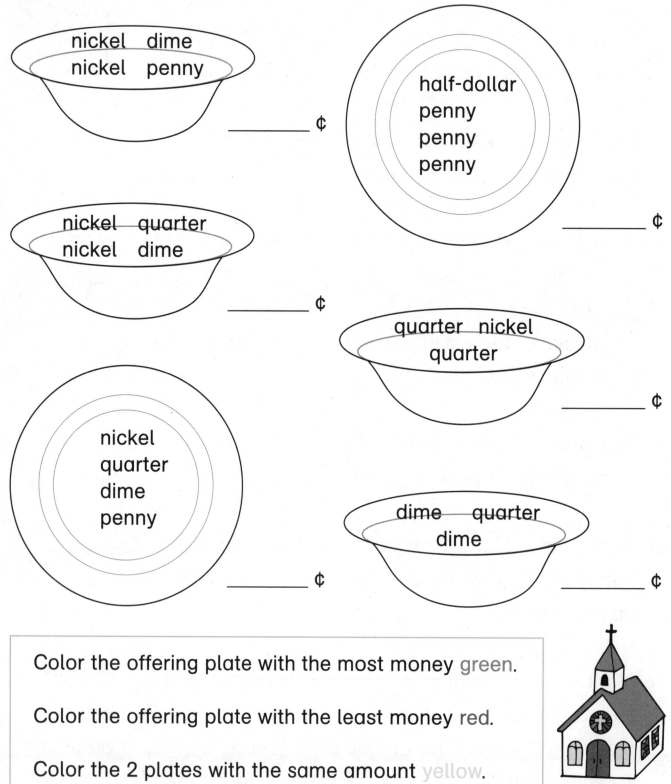

nickel   dime
nickel   penny

_____ ¢

half-dollar
penny
penny
penny

_____ ¢

nickel   quarter
nickel   dime

_____ ¢

quarter   nickel
quarter

_____ ¢

nickel
quarter
dime
penny

_____ ¢

dime   quarter
dime

_____ ¢

Color the offering plate with the most money green.

Color the offering plate with the least money red.

Color the 2 plates with the same amount yellow.

Money Matters

Name_____

Use the work spaces to solve the problems. Write the answers in the blanks.

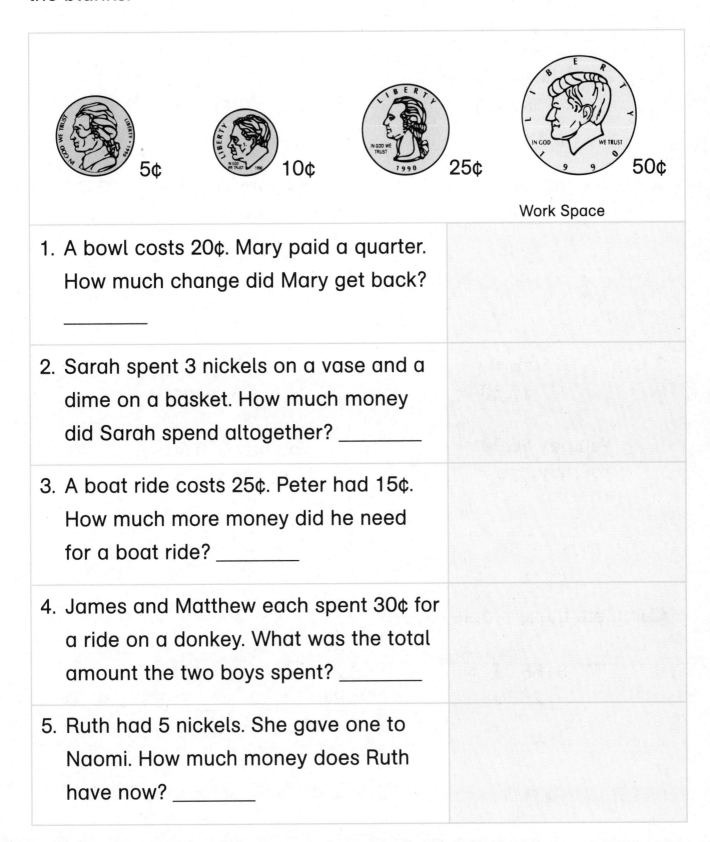

5¢   10¢   25¢   50¢

Work Space

1. A bowl costs 20¢. Mary paid a quarter. How much change did Mary get back?

   _____

2. Sarah spent 3 nickels on a vase and a dime on a basket. How much money did Sarah spend altogether? _____

3. A boat ride costs 25¢. Peter had 15¢. How much more money did he need for a boat ride? _____

4. James and Matthew each spent 30¢ for a ride on a donkey. What was the total amount the two boys spent? _____

5. Ruth had 5 nickels. She gave one to Naomi. How much money does Ruth have now? _____

money

Change Back

God wants us to use our money wisely and to not make it the most important thing in our lives. Complete these problems.

1.
cheeseburger and cola
$2.54

You pay $3.00
Your change = _____

2.
3 pairs of jeans 2 shirts
$78.41

You pay $80.50
Your change = _____

3.
movie
$5.60

You pay $6.00
Your change = _____

4.
2 large pizzas
$16.36

You pay $16.50
Your change = _____

Complete these problems.

$155.75
− 25.75
———

$98.20
− 74.87
———

$328.74
− 71.93
———

The Amusement Park

The King's Youth Group spent a day at an amusement park. While there, Tyrone made many purchases. Fill in the blanks for each purchase.

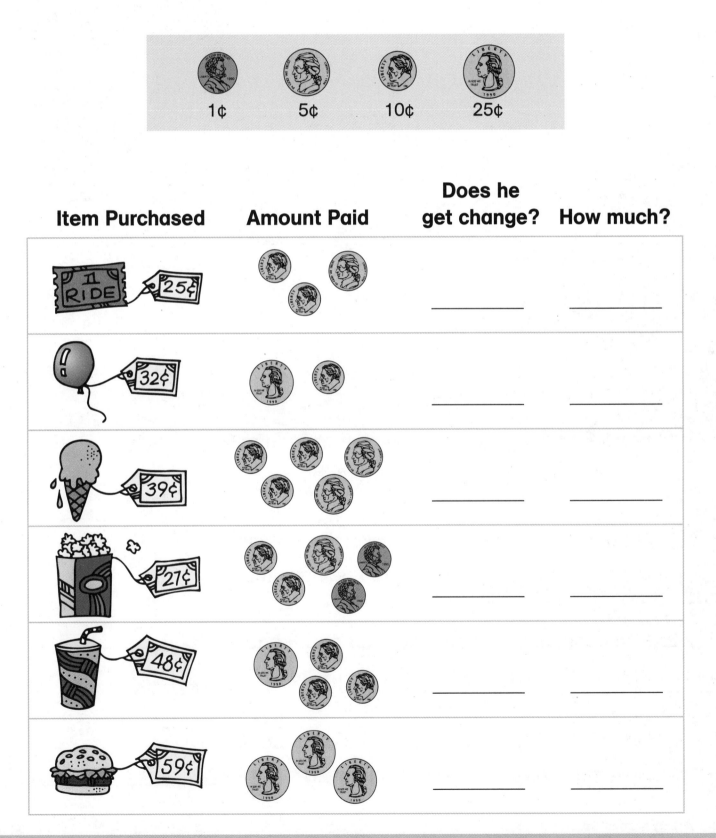

Item Purchased	Amount Paid	Does he get change?	How much?
		_____	_____
		_____	_____
		_____	_____
		_____	_____
		_____	_____
		_____	_____

179

Eating Out

Name_____

The youth group went out on Wednesday night. Use the menu to solve the problems.

Menu

Hot Dog . . . . 52¢

Hamburger . . . . .69¢

Milk . . . . 40¢

Cupcake . . . . 47¢

French Fries . . . . .63¢

1. Frank bought a hot dog, French fries, and milk. How much did Frank spend altogether? _____

2. Greg had five dimes and a nickel. He bought a cupcake. How much money did he have left? _____

3. Ron decided to get a hamburger and French fries. How much money in all did he need? _____

4. Doris had 39¢. She really wanted a cupcake. How much more money did she need? _____

Sweet Treats

⭐ Mr. Morgan owns a candy shop. To share God's love, he gives children a free piece of candy if they can tell him a Bible verse from memory. He has the sweetest treats in town. Use a calculator to work the problems below.

peppermints 12¢

candy hearts 26¢

jellybeans 8¢

lemon drops 28¢

caramels 23¢

licorice 44¢

gum 38¢

cinnamon drops 6¢

gumdrops 35¢

fudge 56¢

sourballs 22¢

Aaron has $1.00 to spend. Show three different ways he can spend that amount. List each treat and its price.

- 2 items: _____   _____

- 3 items: _____   _____

  _____

- 4 items: _____   _____

  _____

Tally It Up

⭐ A trip to the grocery store can cost a lot of money. Use a calculator to find the totals for each set of grocery items. Then add the totals to learn the grand total of the grocery bill.

1. English muffin bread $1.79
   pretzel snacks   2.49
   baby carrots   1.99
   flower bouquet   + 5.99
   _____

4. milk $2.09
   orange juice   1.49
   noodle soup   1.13
   spaghetti sauce   + 2.89
   _____

2. roast beef $3.44
   sandwich bags   2.19
   cheese slices   1.79
   bleach   + 1.19
   _____

5. wheat crackers $2.81
   bread   .79
   rice cereal   2.19
   marshmallows   + .89
   _____

3. bananas $1.39
   magazine   1.99
   grape jelly   1.59
   dish soap   + 1.79
   _____

6. salad dressing $1.79
   mustard   .83
   broom   6.99
   soy sauce   + 1.29
   _____

Grand Total: _____

Ned's Grill

Name_____

Sue has been hired at Ned's Grill to wait tables. On her first night, two families order from the children's menu. Help her total these orders and figure the change owed. You may use a calculator.

Kids' Menu

Hot Dog . . . . $1.50   Chicken Fingers $2.95

Grilled Cheese . . $1.95   Cheese Nachos $1.50

Hamburger. . . . . $2.25   Cheeseburger. $2.50

Cheese Pizza. . . .$1.95   PBJ Sandwich $1.35

Item	# of Items	Amount Per Item	Total
1. Chicken Fingers	2	_____	_____
Cheese Nachos	1	_____	_____
PBJ Sandwich	1	_____	_____

Total Cost: _____

Amount Paid: $10.00

Change: _____

Item	# of Items	Amount Per Item	Total
2. Cheese Pizza	3	_____	_____
Chicken Fingers	1	_____	_____
Grilled Cheese	2	_____	_____

Total Cost: _____

Amount Paid: $15.00

Change: _____

Two by Two

Finish numbering the animals 1–20. Color the second animal in each pair red. Then, read the numbers on the red animals aloud.

Solve the problems.

7 x 2 = _____   1 x 2 = _____

4 x 2 = _____   5 x 2 = _____

3 x 2 = _____   9 x 2 = _____

8 x 2 = _____   2 x 2 = _____

10 x 2 = _____   6 x 2 = _____

Helping Hands

⭐ Finish numbering the fingers 1–50. Color the fifth finger on each hand brown. Then, read the numbers on the brown fingers aloud.

Solve the problems.

4 x 5 = _____   5 x 5 = _____

1 x 5 = _____   9 x 5 = _____

6 x 5 = _____   8 x 5 = _____

10 x 5 = _____   7 x 5 = _____

2 x 5 = _____   3 x 5 = _____

multiplication - table of 5s

Time to Multiply

Remember to thank God for your talents. Complete the mulitplication grid by writing the products in the boxes.

X	4	9	0	3	8	5	1	7	2	6
2										
8				24						
1										
6								42		
7										
4					32					
0										
9										
5										
3										

"For nothing is impossible with God."
Luke 1:37

Help Moses Up Mt. Sinai

Name_____

⭐ Help Moses up Mt. Sinai. Start at the bottom of the boulder and work the problems up to the top!

$$8 \times 9 \qquad 7 \times 8 \qquad 0 \times 4$$

$$9 \times 9 = \underline{} \qquad 3 \times 3 = \underline{}$$

$$4 \times 8 = \underline{} \qquad \begin{array}{r} 4 \\ \times 6 \end{array} \qquad 3 \times 5 = \underline{}$$

$$7 \times 7 = \underline{} \qquad \begin{array}{r} 6 \\ \times 6 \end{array} \qquad 2 \times 8 = \underline{} \qquad \begin{array}{r} 9 \\ \times 1 \end{array}$$

$$6 \times 1 = \underline{} \qquad \begin{array}{r} 6 \\ \times 7 \end{array} \qquad 6 \times 6 = \underline{} \qquad \begin{array}{r} 2 \\ \times 2 \end{array}$$

$$8 \times 6 = \underline{} \qquad \begin{array}{r} 8 \\ \times 7 \end{array} \qquad 7 \times 9 = \underline{} \qquad \begin{array}{r} 5 \\ \times 5 \end{array}$$

$$3 \times 6 = \underline{} \qquad \begin{array}{r} 2 \\ \times 3 \end{array} \qquad 6 \times 7 = \underline{} \qquad \begin{array}{r} 3 \\ \times 9 \end{array}$$

multiplication

How Many Times?

⭐ Write each product in the grid as shown.

X 3	Product
4	12
0	
8	
5	
6	
2	
9	

X 8	Product
7	
4	
3	
1	
9	
6	
5	

X 5	Product
2	
9	
4	
7	
8	
6	
0	

X 6	Product
4	
1	
5	
9	
6	
3	
7	

X 9	Product
7	
4	
6	
8	
2	
9	
5	

X 4	Product
9	
4	
7	
5	
6	
3	
2	

X 7	Product
3	
7	
4	
9	
5	
6	
8	

X 2	Product
8	
5	
0	
4	
7	
3	
6	

Tic-Tac-Times

Name_____

God has given you a good mind. Use it to check each problem. Circle the three problems in each game that are correct.

3 x 2 = 6	4 x 5 = 20	1 x 4 = 4
1 x 7 = 8	7 x 5 = 2	6 x 5 = 11
3 x 3 = 6	2 x 2 = 0	9 x 5 = 4

8 x 2 = 10	5 x 2 = 7	5 x 5 = 25
6 x 3 = 6	3 x 3 = 9	9 x 3 = 6
7 x 2 = 14	2 x 8 = 10	9 x 1 = 8

3 x 5 = 8	6 x 2 = 12	8 x 3 = 11
2 x 7 = 9	3 x 5 = 15	4 x 4 = 0
3 x 4 = 7	1 x 2 = 2	5 x 6 = 11

multiplication - tables 1-10

Picture Day

Name_____

⭐ Photographs help us remember special days and people God places in our lives. It's picture day at your school. Help the photographers with some problem solving.

1. If 292 students came to have pictures taken in the a.m. and 373 students in the p.m., how many students came in all? _____

2. All of the students in the three first-grade classes had pictures taken. There were 26 students per room. How many first-grade students had pictures taken?

_____

3. The 20 kindergarten students each bought a $10 picture packet. How much did they spend in all?

_____

4. Extra wallet pictures are available for $.50 apiece. How much would 8 extra wallet pictures cost?

_____

5. One student's mother wants three 8" x 10" photos for relatives. They cost $1.85 each. How much money does she need for these pictures? _____

Moses and Manna

⭐ Read the problems. Then circle the picture that answers each question.

1. The boy ate 2 fish for lunch. He ate 3 times as many fish for dinner. How many did he eat at dinner?

2. Noah loves bananas. He eats them for snacks. Each snack consists of 4 bananas. If Noah has 3 snacks each day, how many bananas does he eat altogether?

3. Moses loves manna. He eats 5 manna cakes each day. Aaron eats twice as many. How many does Aaron eat?

4. Mrs. Smith has twins. Her best friend, Mrs. Jones, has 6 times as many children. How many children does Mrs. Jones have?

story problems - multiplication

Everyday Math

There are many ways to use math every day. Solve these story problems. Show your work.

1. If a family of 6 people ate a Chinese meal with chopsticks, how many chopsticks would they need altogether?

   _____

2. Joe and his dad refinished 8 dining room chairs. How many chair legs altogether did they sand and stain?

   _____

3. John loves to play tennis and always keeps spare balls on hand. He has 6 cans with 3 balls in each. How many tennis balls does John have?

   _____

4. Gina needed cans of soda for a Sunday school party. She bought 7 six-packs. Will she have enough for 32 children to each have one can?

   _____

5. Jill used $2\frac{1}{2}$ dozen eggs to make bake sale goodies. How many eggs did she use?

   _____

Walls of Jericho

Name_____

⭐ Help build this colorful wall of Jericho before Joshua knocks it down! Write each quotient. Then color the bricks according to the code.

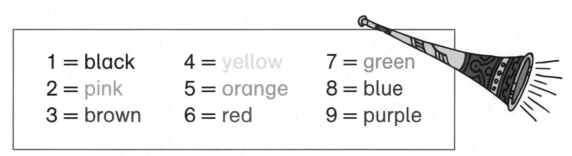

1 = black	4 = yellow	7 = green
2 = pink	5 = orange	8 = blue
3 = brown	6 = red	9 = purple

16 ÷ 4 = _____

12 ÷ 2 = _____

30 ÷ 6 = _____

4 ÷ 2 = _____

36 ÷ 9 = _____

7 ÷ 7 = _____

21 ÷ 3 = _____

72 ÷ 8 = _____

32 ÷ 4 = _____

56 ÷ 7 = _____

6 ÷ 1 = _____

48 ÷ 6 = _____

9 ÷ 3 = _____

8 ÷ 4 = _____

35 ÷ 7 = _____

18 ÷ 9 = _____

36 ÷ 6 = _____

40 ÷ 5 = _____

20 ÷ 4 = _____

28 ÷ 4 = _____

54 ÷ 6 = _____

12 ÷ 3 = _____

64 ÷ 8 = _____

42 ÷ 6 = _____

division facts

Packaging Plants

Name_____

⭐ All of the beautiful flowers you see are gifts from God! When packaging plants at a greenhouse, workers put equal amounts of plants in each box. Help the workers divide the plants for packaging. Draw pictures in the boxes to help you solve the problems.

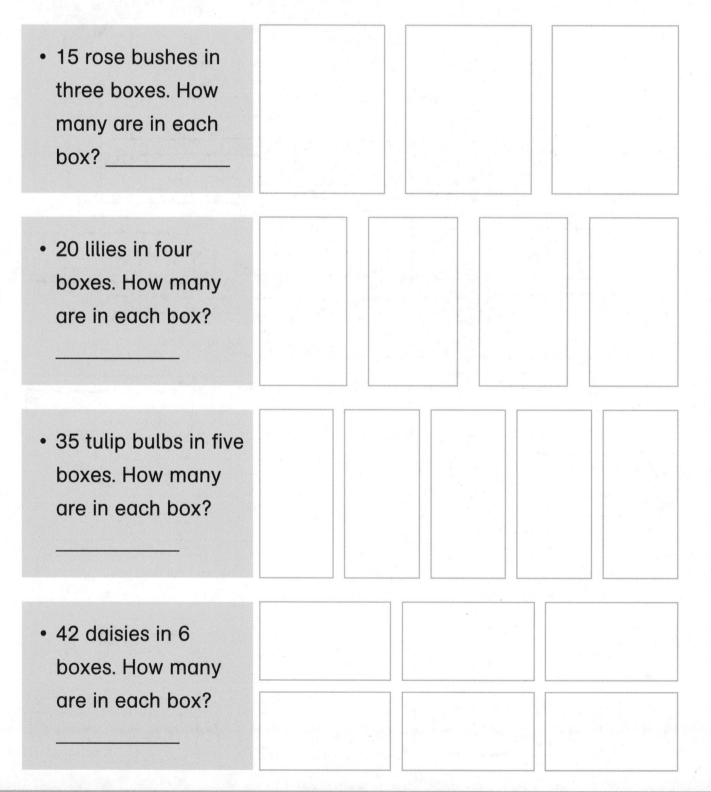

- 15 rose bushes in three boxes. How many are in each box? _____

- 20 lilies in four boxes. How many are in each box? _____

- 35 tulip bulbs in five boxes. How many are in each box? _____

- 42 daisies in 6 boxes. How many are in each box? _____

You're Great!

Name_____

These two animals were busy on the ark! What did they do that you also can do to become good at division? To find out, work the problems in the key. Then write the letters in the blanks above the matching quotients.

Key:

$$D = 2\overline{)64} \qquad V = 4\overline{)48} \qquad N = 2\overline{)86}$$

$$P = 2\overline{)88} \qquad R = 3\overline{)69} \qquad I = 2\overline{)84}$$

$$A = 3\overline{)93} \qquad C = 4\overline{)44} \qquad G = 4\overline{)84}$$

$$T = 2\overline{)68} \qquad E = 3\overline{)66} \qquad Y = 2\overline{)48}$$

$$! = 2\overline{)66}$$

44	23	31	11	34	42	11	22

32	42	12	42	32	42	43	21

22	12	22	23	24		32	31	24	33

The Great Divide

⭐ Watch out for remainders as you divide these problems.

Example:

```
      6  R3
  4⟌27
    24
     3
```

6⟌40   3⟌13   7⟌50

8⟌44   9⟌17   5⟌19   6⟌21

4⟌35   2⟌9   3⟌29   9⟌57

6⟌52   7⟌24   8⟌35   4⟌17

3⟌17   2⟌11   6⟌56   7⟌60

Pizza and Licorice

Jenny loves to share things equally with her friends and family. It's one way she shows God's love to others. To share equally, she must divide. Answer the questions below.

1. Jenny shared a 24-piece bag of licorice with two other girls. How many pieces did each girl receive?

   _____

2. Mark and Jenny split a box of 8 markers. How many markers will each of them have?

   _____

3. Jenny and her younger sister divided a box of 64 crayons. How many crayons will each girl put in her school box?

   _____

4. Mandy and Lisa joined Jenny for a sleepover. They ate a 16-piece pizza. If they each ate the same number of pieces, how many were left over?

   _____

story problems - division

Sticky Stamps

Name_____

A stamp got stuck on each of these problems. What number does each stamp cover? Write the missing number below each stamp.

• 6 + [W.W.J.D?] = 14

_____

• 2 x 4 =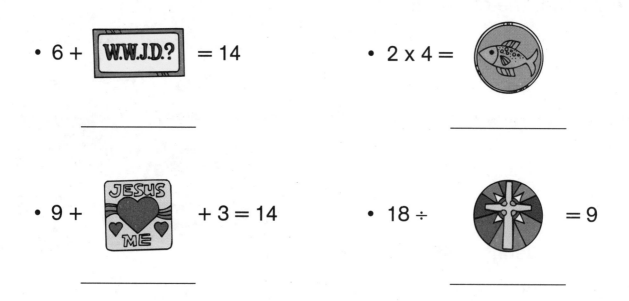

_____

• 9 + [JESUS ♥ ME] + 3 = 14

_____

• 18 ÷ = 9

_____

Write the correct symbol (<, >, or =) in the circle. (Hint: Solve the problems before filling in the symbols.)

• 12 – 7   ◯   2 x 4

• 45 ÷ 9   ◯   30 ÷ 6

• 2 x 9   ◯   4 x 4

• 81 ÷ 9   ◯   31 – 24

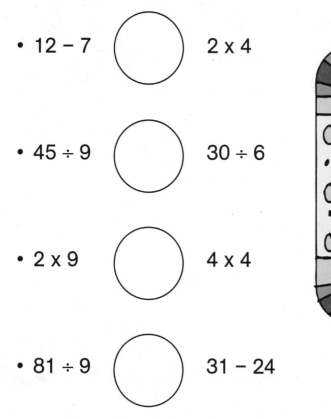

The Sticker Club

Name_____

⭐ A group of friends formed a sticker club. They bought, sold, traded, and shared stickers. Solve these problems. Show your work.

1. For her birthday, Erin got a set of 8 animal stickers from three different people. How many animal stickers did she recieve?

   _____

2. Erin placed equal amounts of the new animal stickers on 2 pages of her album. How many stickers were on each page? _____

3. Jeff made a bookmark for each of 7 friends. He put 3 stickers on each bookmark. How many stickers did he use? _____

4. Each time Jeff bought 5 stickers, he recieved 2 free stickers. If he bought 20 stickers, how many total would he recieve?

   _____

story problems - mixed operations

Church Street

⭐ Jesus knows right where you live. He shines his love on you every day. Fill in the number line to show the addresses on Church Street. Notice that the top numbers are even and the bottom numbers are odd.

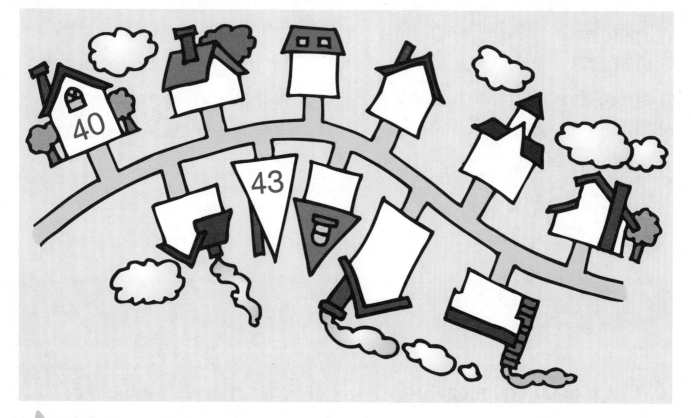

⭐ Complete these problems. Then write whether the answer is even or odd. Use the number line to check your answers.

• 20 + 20 = _____ _____   • 5 x 8   = _____ _____

• 54 – 7   = _____ _____   • 10 x 5   = _____ _____

• 6 x 7   = _____ _____   • 57 – 9   = _____ _____

• 50 – 6   = _____ _____   • 7 x 7   = _____ _____

• 48 – 5   = _____ _____   • 52 – 7   = _____ _____

Goose and Gander

Name_____

Work each problem on your calculator. Then, turn the calculator upside down and write the word which should match each clue.

Example: 256 + 362 = __618__   antonym of small ____Big____

	Answer	Clue	Word
• 139 + 524	= _____	a nest occupant	_____
• 11,862 − 4,757	= _____	a synonym for dirt	_____
• 29,331 + 5,675	= _____	a gander's wife	_____
• 609 x 5	= _____	a foot warmer	_____
• 12,955 − 9,251	= _____	a gopher's home	_____
• 323 x 25	= _____	a messy, unkempt person	_____
• 9,867 + 25,140	= _____	an antonym of tight	_____
• 2,428 ÷ 4	= _____	fireplace fuel	_____
• 918 x 6	= _____	an employer	_____
• 3,412 + 4,304	= _____	a fish uses this to breathe	_____

calculator

In My Estimation

Sarah's teacher just gave her the following math problems. Help her estimate the answers. To do that, round any numbers greater than 10, and then multiply the numbers in your head. Use that estimate to help you choose the exact answer. Check your work with a calculator.

$9 \times 105 = 945$

1. 107 x 6   **a.** 762   **b.** 536   **c.** 642

2. 4 x 311   **a.** 1,178   **b.** 1,244   **c.** 1,202

3. 8 x 295   **a.** 2,741   **b.** 2,360   **c.** 2,064

4. 512 x 7   **a.** 3,584   **b.** 2,486   **c.** 3,106

5. 5 x 406   **a.** 2,030   **b.** 1,870   **c.** 2,242

6. 215 x 8   **a.** 1,468   **b.** 1,524   **c.** 1,720

7. 9 x 105   **a.** 945   **b.** 961   **c.** 1,010

8. 2 x 621   **a.** 1,242   **b.** 1,308   **c.** 1,181

Pleasantville Events

⭐ The town of Pleasantville hosted many events last year. Help the town newspaper reporter round the attendance figures so that they can be used in headlines to report the events.

Event	Attendance	Round to Nearest 10	Round to Nearest 100	Round to Nearest 1,000
Vacation Bible School	1,246			
Family Fun Day	9,367			
Prayer Power	4,822			
Jesus' Kids Carnival	5,111			
Youth Rally	6,781			
Bible Bike Ride	3,759			
Harvest Festival	2,674			
Easter Musical	8,888			

rounding

Going Buggy

Each bug has a special shape inside. Draw a line from the shape to its name.

pyramid

cube

octagon

cone

circle

triangle

rectangle

square

"Go to the ant,... consider his ways and be wise!" (Proverbs 6:6)

Fun with Shapes

Name_____

⭐ Create each object using the geometric shapes indicated.

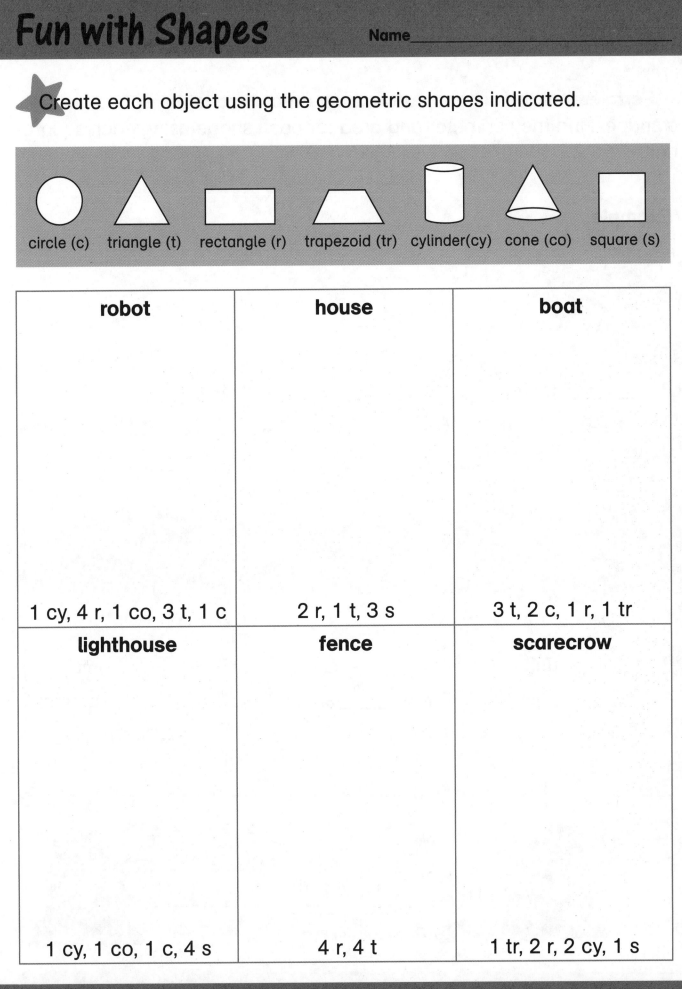

| circle (c) | triangle (t) | rectangle (r) | trapezoid (tr) | cylinder(cy) | cone (co) | square (s) |

robot	**house**	**boat**
1 cy, 4 r, 1 co, 3 t, 1 c	2 r, 1 t, 3 s	3 t, 2 c, 1 r, 1 tr
lighthouse	**fence**	**scarecrow**
1 cy, 1 co, 1 c, 4 s	4 r, 4 t	1 tr, 2 r, 2 cy, 1 s

geometric shapes

⭐ **Perimeter** is the distance around an area. **Area** is the space inside a shape. Find the perimeter and area for each shape using each square unit.

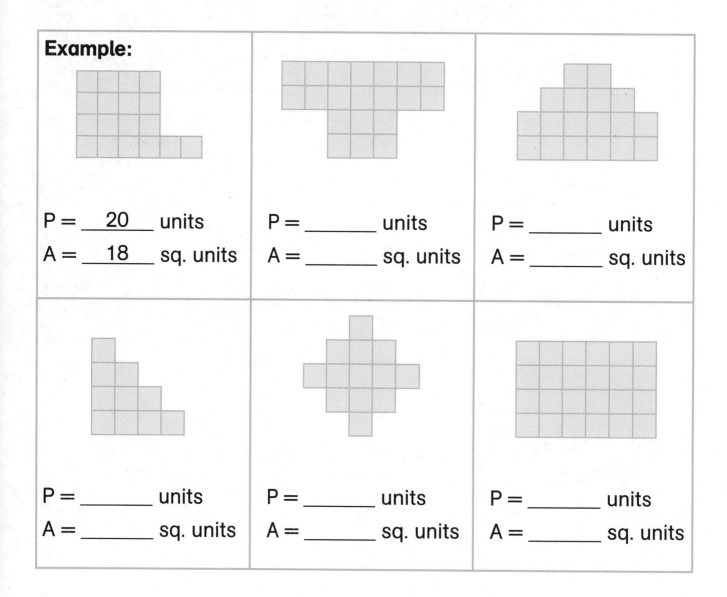

Example:

P = ___20___ units

A = ___18___ sq. units

P = _____ units

A = _____ sq. units

P = _____ units

A = _____ sq. units

P = _____ units

A = _____ sq. units

P = _____ units

A = _____ sq. units

P = _____ units

A = _____ sq. units

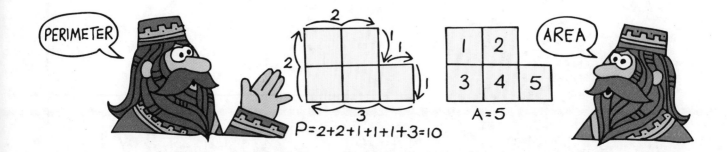

PERIMETER

2

2

1

1

1

3

P=2+2+1+1+1+3=10

AREA

1	2
3	4	5

A=5

Animal Creations

⭐ What is your favorite animal that God created? Draw that animal on this grid, using complete squares. When you have finished drawing, write the area of your animal.

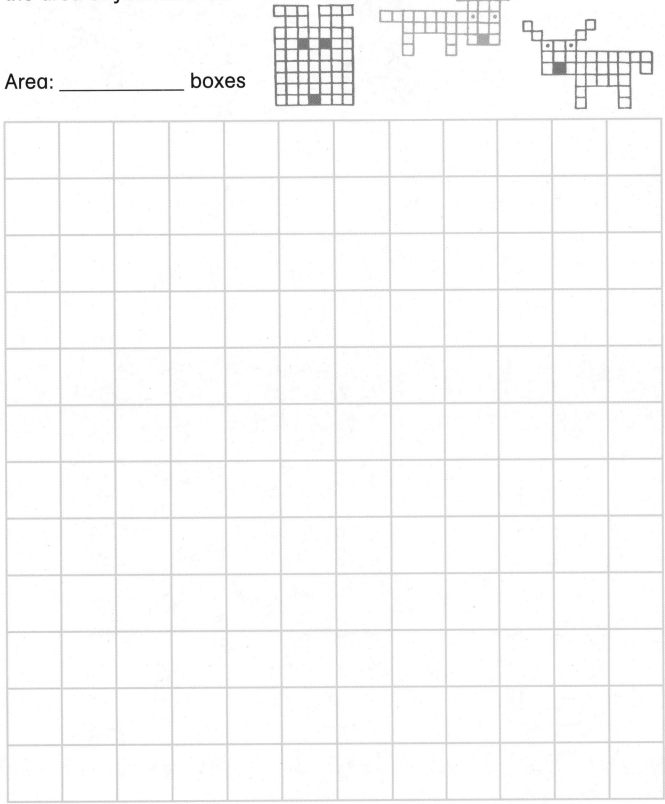

Area: _____ boxes

Looking Good

You have 3 T-shirts
and 3 pairs of shorts.

 Using the different colors of the clothes above, color these 9 outfits
so that each one is different.

Full Hearts

⭐ Matthew 22:37 tells us to "Love the Lord your God with all your heart." The Bible contains dozens of other verses that talk about the heart. The hearts on this page may look alike, but they are not. One is slightly different. Can you find which one it is? Look carefully.

Symbol Survey

The youth group asked 60 church members which Christian symbol they liked best. Show the results of the survey on the graph using a different color for each type of symbol.

Favorite Symbol							
heart							
dove							
fish							
praying hands							
cross							

0   5   10   15   20   25   30   35

Survey Results

15 chose a fish.

10 chose a cross.

5 chose a dove.

20 chose a heart.

10 chose praying hands.

Read the questions. Then using the graph above, fill in the correct answers.

1. What was the most favorite symbol? _____

2. What was the least favorite symbol? _____

3. Which was more popular—a fish or praying hands?

   _____

4. How many more people chose a heart than chose a cross?

   _____

5. How many more people chose a heart than chose praying hands?

   _____

bar graph   210

Faraway Friends

⭐ Sharing Jesus' love with friends who live far away is fun. Refer to the chart to determine the cost of mailing each package.

If it weighs this amount or less...	5 oz.	10 oz.	15 oz.	1 lb. 4 oz.	1 lb. 9 oz.	1 lb. 14 oz.	2 lb. 3 oz.	2 lb. 8 oz.
It costs	50¢	$1.00	$1.25	$1.50	$1.75	$2.00	$2.25	$2.50

1.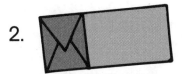

weight: 3 oz.

cost:_____

3.

weight: 2 lbs.

cost:_____

5.

weight: 2 lbs. 5 oz.

cost:_____

2.

weight: 1 lb. 12 oz.

cost:_____

4.

weight: 9 oz.

cost:_____

6.

weight: 16 oz.

cost:_____

reading a table

Summer Earnings

The Bethlehem Boys Choir held fundraisers during the summer to raise money for a mission trip to Mexico. The church kept accounts for each boy. The table below shows the money each boy earned. Add the rows to fill in the total column.

Choir Members	June	July	August	Total
Tim	$12.50	$14.00	$10.00	
Jeff	$19.00	$17.60	$14.75	
Nick	$16.50	$13.85	$21.00	
Dan	$11.75	$14.25	$16.50	
Blake	$9.90	$11.20	$17.80	
Kyle	$15.00	$15.00	$15.00	

1. How much altogether did Dan earn? _____

2. How much more did Blake earn in August than in June?

   _____

3. Which two boys earned the same total amount?

   _____

4. Boys who were able to raise $45 or more received a prayer journal for the trip. Which boys raised enough funds to receive a prayer journal?_____

Cool Collections

Name_____

People love to collect things! Refer to the chart to answer each of the story problems. Show your work.

Sue	Mike	Ryan	Lisa	Mary	Austin
342 shells	425 baseball cards	1,098 coins	1,387 stamps	139 teddy bears	216 rocks

1. If Sue and Mary combined their collections, how many items would they have? _____

2. If Lisa gave 248 stamps to a friend, how many stamps would remain in her collection? _____

3. Do the girls or the boys own more items in their collections? How many more? _____

4. _____ has collected 83 more items than Sue.

5. How many more items are in Mike's collection than in Austin's collection? _____

6. If Ryan sold 312 of his coins at a collectors' show, how many coins would remain in his collection? _____

7. _____ has 77 less items than Austin.

8. Ryan needs _____ more coins to equal the number of items in Lisa's collection.

reading a table/story problems

Bible Verse Activities

Table of Contents

Star Bright

⭐ God promised Abraham that his descendants would be as plentiful as the stars in the sky. You can read this promise in Genesis 15:5. How many stars can you count in the picture below? Write the number in the blank. Color the stars using bright colors.

I see _____ stars in the box.

Moses

⭐ Moses brought the commandments down from Mount Sinai. Can you decode the first two commandments using the letter key below?

A	B	D	E	F	G	H	I	L	M	N	O	R	S	T	U	V	Y
4	16	13	3	17	6	10	1	12	11	18	5	7	14	9	2	15	8

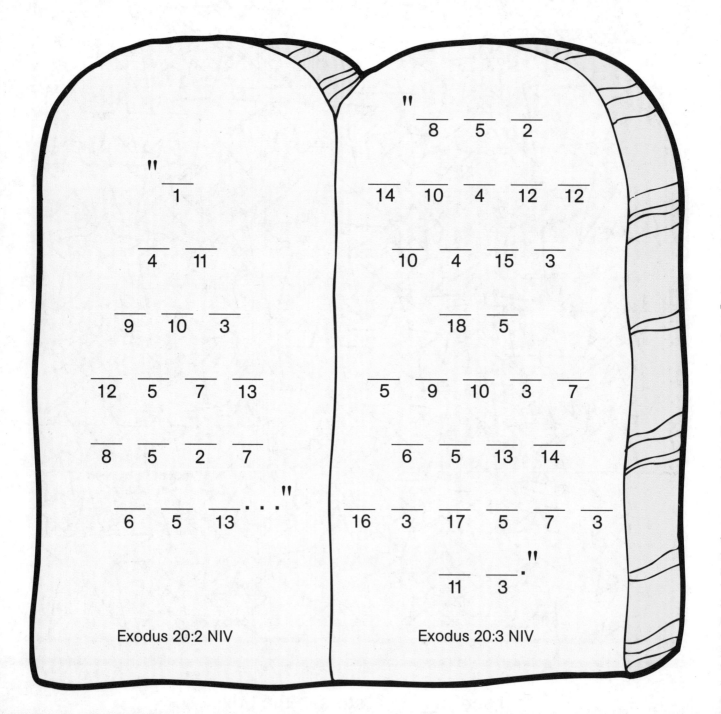

"___
 1

___ ___
 4   11

___ ___ ___
 9   10   3

___ ___ ___ ___
12   5   7   13

___ ___ ___ ___
 8   5   2   7

___ ___ ___..."
 6   5   13

"___ ___ ___
 8   5   2

___ ___ ___ ___ ___
14 10   4   12   12

___ ___ ___ ___
10   4   15   3

___ ___
18   5

___ ___ ___ ___ ___
 5   9   10   3   7

___ ___ ___ ___
 6   5   13   14

___ ___ ___ ___ ___ ___
16   3   17   5   7   3

___ ___."
11   3

Exodus 20:2 NIV   Exodus 20:3 NIV

218

Which Disciple?

⭐ There are many stories about the disciples in the Bible. Read the questions below and look up the Bible verses to find the answers. Then, instead of writing a disciple's name, draw the symbol from the bottom of the page that represents that disciple. Names and symbols can be used more than once.

The Disciples	Their Symbols
1. Who were the first two disciples chosen? (Matthew 4:18–19)	
2. Who walked on water? (Matthew 14:29)	
3. Who was at the transfiguration? (Mark 9:2)	
4. Who betrayed Jesus? (Luke 22:3–6)	
5. Who doubted that Jesus had risen from the dead? (John 20:24–31)	
6. Who preached in Samaria after Jesus died? (Acts 8:4–6)	

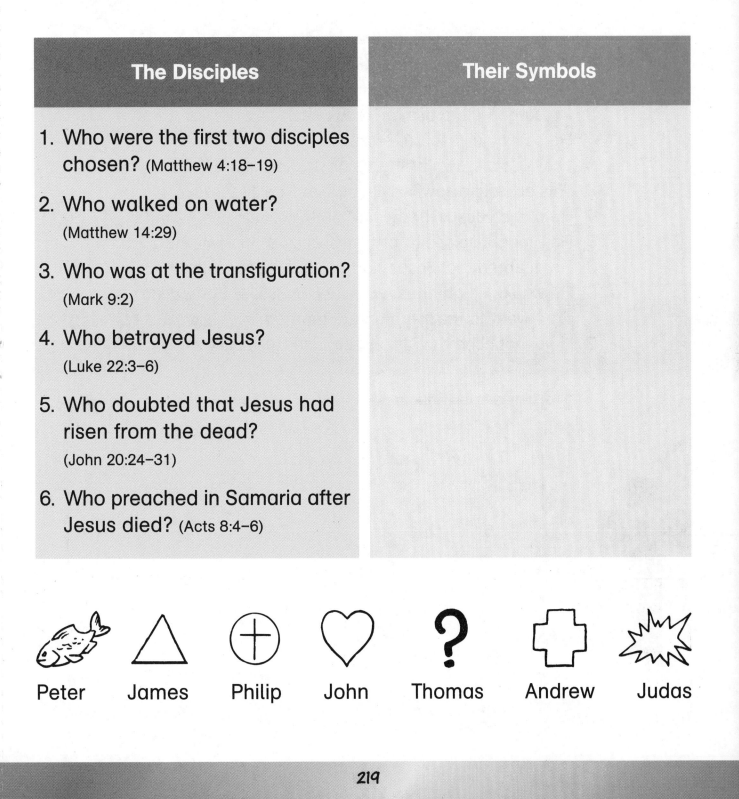

Peter   James   Philip   John   Thomas   Andrew   Judas

Roll Call

★ The crucifixion and the resurrection of Jesus are two of the most important events in Christian history. Many people were part of those stories. Who were they? Some of them are mentioned in the Bible verses below. Fit their names around the word resurrection.

Clues

1. He was set free instead of Jesus. (Mark 15:6–15)
2. He was the Roman governor. (Matthew 27:12–14)
3. He carried the cross for Jesus. (Mark 15:21)
4. He betrayed Jesus. (Luke 22:3–4)
5. They put a crown of thorns on Jesus. (Matthew 27:27–29)
6. This disciple disowned Jesus. (Matthew 26:69–75)
7. He placed Jesus' body in a tomb. (Matthew 27:57–60)
8. He brought spices to bury Jesus. (John 19:39–40)
9. He doubted that Jesus had risen. (John 20:24–25)
10. He was the high priest who tried Jesus. (Matthew 26:57)
11. They went to the tomb on Easter morning. (Luke 24:1)
12. He announced that Jesus had risen. (Matthew 28:5–6)

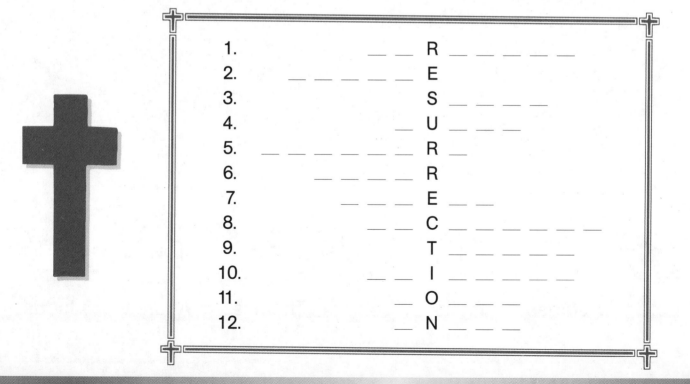

1. __ __ R __ __ __ __ __
2. __ __ __ __ __ E
3. S __ __ __ __
4. __ U __ __ __
5. __ __ __ __ __ R __
6. __ __ __ __ R
7. __ __ __ E __ __
8. __ __ C __ __ __ __ __
9. T __ __ __ __ __
10. __ __ I __ __ __ __ __
11. __ O __ __ __
12. __ N __ __ __ __

Name_____

⭐ Decode the Bible verse using the key below.

Key

A ●	D †	E ⁄	G ○
H □	I ✳	L ⊙	M ◇
N ▽	O ✕	P ∨	R ＞
S —	T ■	U ◇	V ÷
W ·⫶·	Y △		

Matthew 4:10 NIV

Fishing for Men

⭐ Jesus taught his disciples about the importance of believing in God. What did Jesus say when he asked them to be disciples? Catch the fish in order and write the words in the spaces.

" _ _ _ _ , _ _ _ _ _ _ _ _ _ , . . .

_ _ _ _ _ _ _ _

_ _ _ _ _ _ _ _ _ _ . "

Let Others See Jesus in You Name_____

Jesus wants us to tell others about Him. Decode the Bible verse using the key below.

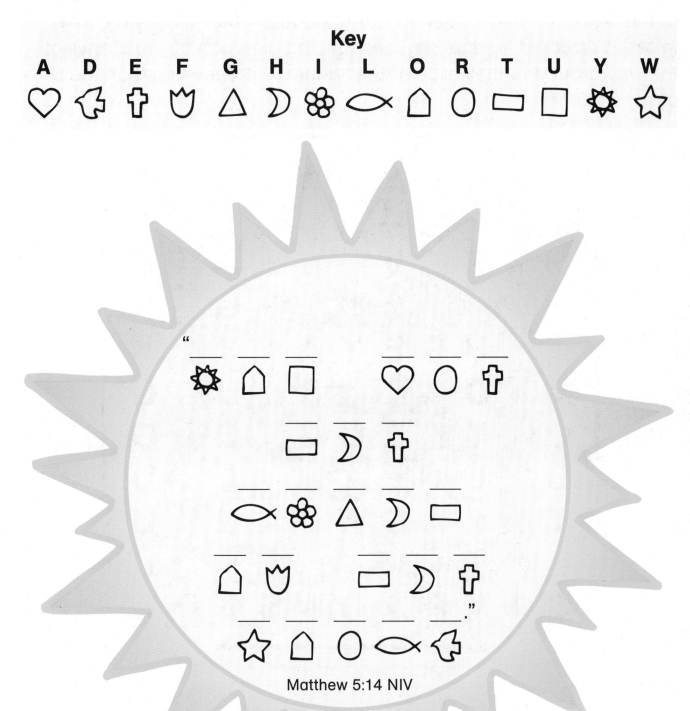

Matthew 5:14 NIV

223

Squared Off

⭐ This puzzle reveals a promise that Jesus gave to his disciples before he ascended into heaven. Start with the letter **I** in the upper left corner of the grid. This is the first letter of the quote. Then skip every other letter to discover the message. Follow the direction of the arrows all the way around to the inside of the square. Write the verse on the lines at the bottom.

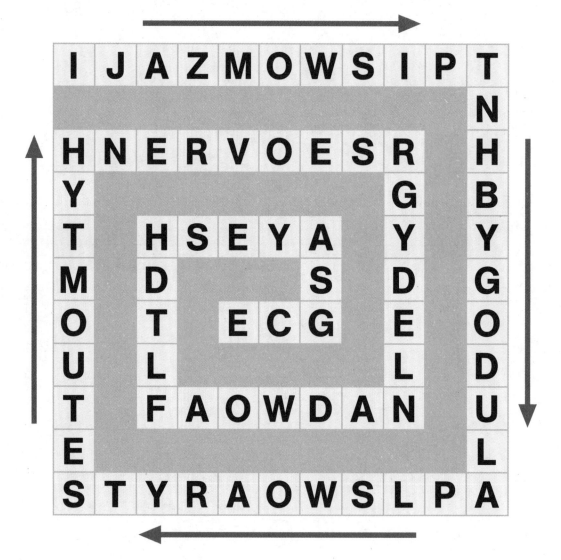

Matthew 28:20

_____

_____

_____

Name_____

⭐ Jesus told a parable of a man who owned 100 sheep. One sheep was lost, so the man left the other 99 and went searching for it. When he found his sheep, he was so happy he told his friends all about it.

Jesus also told the parable of a woman who lost a coin. After searching everywhere and then finding it, she was so happy that she called her neighbors to rejoice with her.

Jesus told these stories to teach us about God. God searches for sinners to come to him, and when they do, he rejoices.

Search for the lost sheep in the first puzzle. Clue: This sheep is different from the others. Then find the word **coin** hidden in the second puzzle.

Luke
15:3–7

Luke
15:8–10

```
B  P  I  O  C  N  C  O  I  F  C  V
M  G  T  R  O  W  W  O  H  S  O  I
C  O  I  Z  I  N  C  M  U  A  K  T
O  N  K  J  V  K  S  O  C  Y  J  C
A  T  O  C  A  P  F  C  O  I  D  O
M  I  I  D  T  N  C  O  I  L  A  I
S  Y  N  B  I  R  O  H  B  C  N  F
O  C  T  O  S  O  I  K  U  S  J  A
S  T  C  D  C  M  X  C  O  I  R  I
N  A  V  T  B  C  O  I  E  D  G  O
L  K  R  Y  C  O  I  P  R  I  O  C
C  O  I  S  D  P  T  G  A  T  R  O
```

I Am

Name_____

⭐ Jesus often used the phrase "I am" in describing himself. For example, he said, "I am the way and the truth and the life." Many of these sayings come from the Book of John. Three "I am" phrases are illustrated for you below. Look up the verse to discover what Jesus said about himself and write it on the line by the picture. The last verse is for you to look up and illustrate in the box.

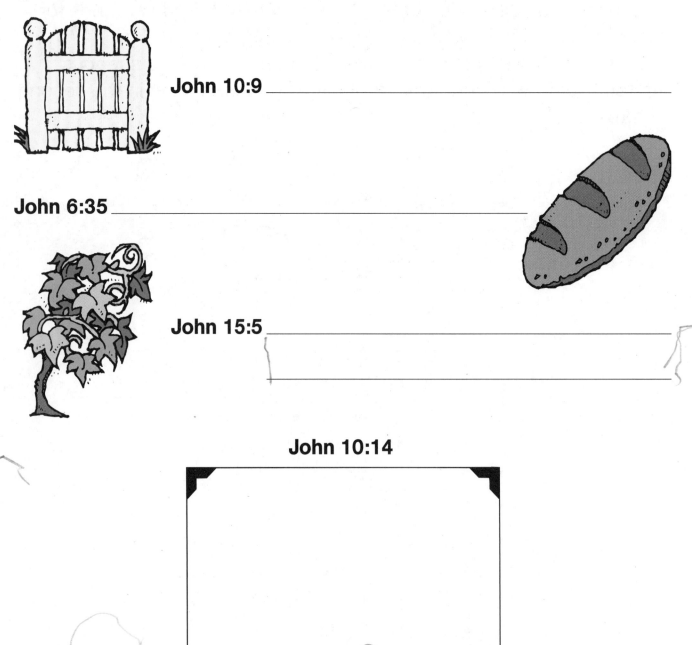

John 10:9 _____

John 6:35 _____

John 15:5 _____

_____

John 10:14

Love

⭐ Jesus teaches us many things. He gave us a command to live by. Use the key below to find out what Jesus wants us to do.

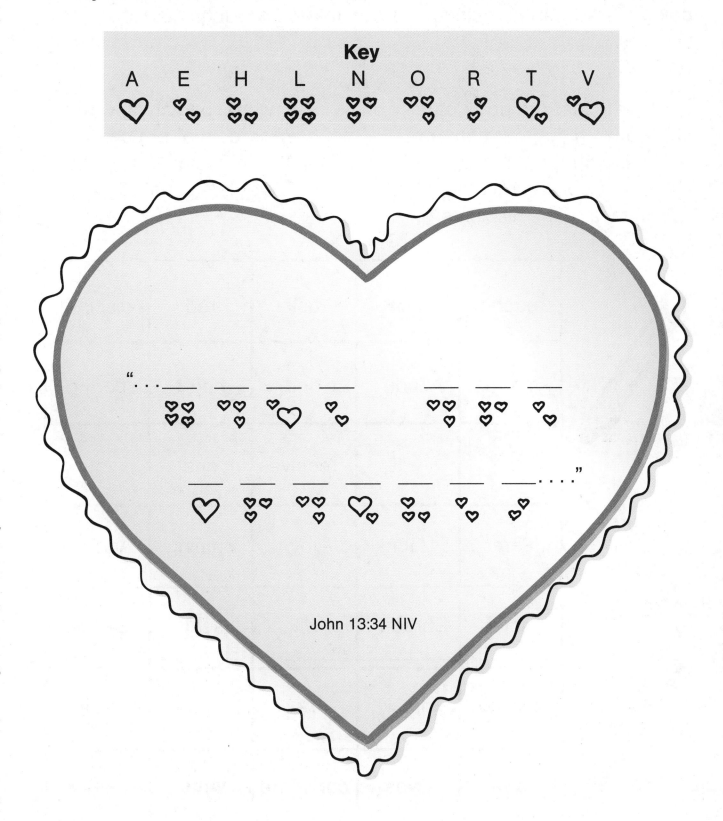

Key

A E H L N O R T V

John 13:34 NIV

Color Coded

Name_____

⭐ Follow the directions below. Color the boxes green that contain the words described below. Color all the remaining boxes yellow. The yellow boxes will reveal a teaching of Jesus taken from John 16:24.

Color these boxes green:

1. words that are parts of the body
2. words in the four corners
3. words that are foods
4. words containing a double t
5. names of the disciples
6. words beginning with S
7. words that are colors
8. New Testament books
9. words ending with ing

teacher	fish	ask	red	disciple
matter	Jude	and	heart	caring
you	will	receive	and	your
Peter	face	joy	coming	Andrew
save	bread	will	seek	better
talking	black	be	going	fruit
love	eyes	complete	Acts	friends

God is Awesome

⭐ Our God is an awesome God! How are we to stand before him? Ecclesiastes 5:1 NIV tells us. Color each of the squares yellow that has a ▲ in the corner. The Bible verse will appear for you to read.

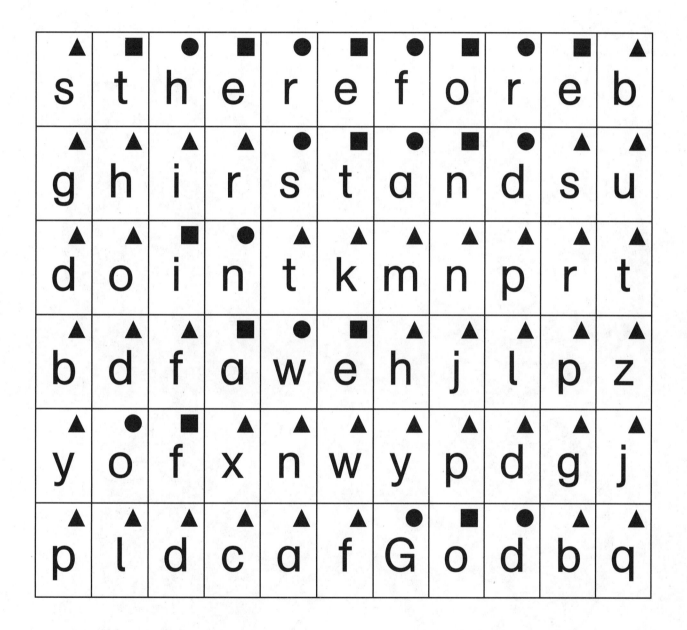

▲	■	●	■	●	■	●	■	●	■	▲
s	t	h	e	r	e	f	o	r	e	b
▲	▲	▲	▲	●	■	●	■	●	▲	▲
g	h	i	r	s	t	a	n	d	s	u
▲	▲	■	●	▲	▲	▲	▲	▲	▲	▲
d	o	i	n	t	k	m	n	p	r	t
▲	▲	▲	■	●	■	▲	▲	▲	▲	▲
b	d	f	a	w	e	h	j	l	p	z
▲	●	■	▲	▲	▲	▲	▲	▲	▲	▲
y	o	f	x	n	w	y	p	d	g	j
▲	▲	▲	▲	▲	▲	●	■	●	▲	▲
p	l	d	c	a	f	G	o	d	b	q

New Creation

Therefore, if anyone is in Christ, he is a new creation; the old has gone, the new has come! 2 Corinthians 5:17 NIV. Starting at the caterpillar, find your way through the maze.

Be Saved

Each word of the Bible verse below is hidden three times in this puzzle. Can you circle each of the words three times? (The words may be hidden diagonally, backwards, across, up or down.)

"Turn to me and be saved, . . ."
Isaiah 45:22 NIV

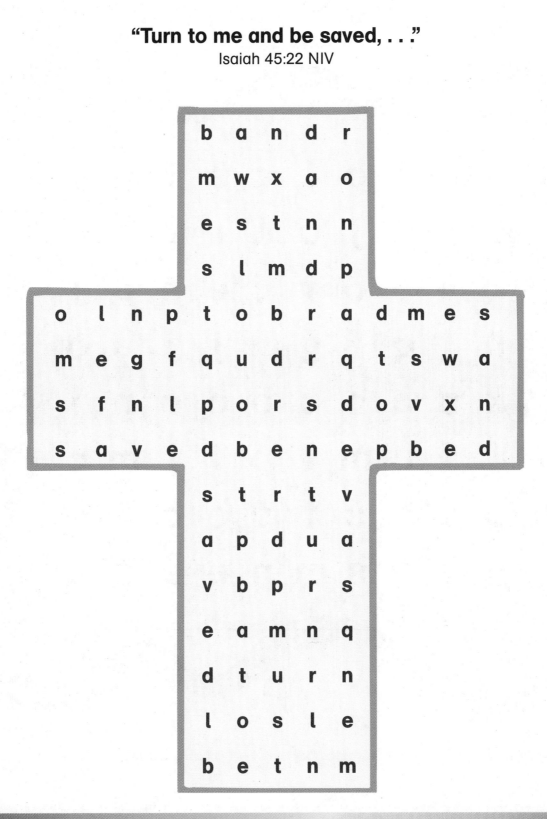

Rejoice Again and Again!

Name_____

Rejoice in the Lord always. (Philippians 4:4 NIV) How many times can you find the word **REJOICE**? Circle the word as you find it.

Serve Each Other

Name_____

⭐ Pick up the words as you go through the maze. Write them in order on the spaces below to complete the Bible verse.

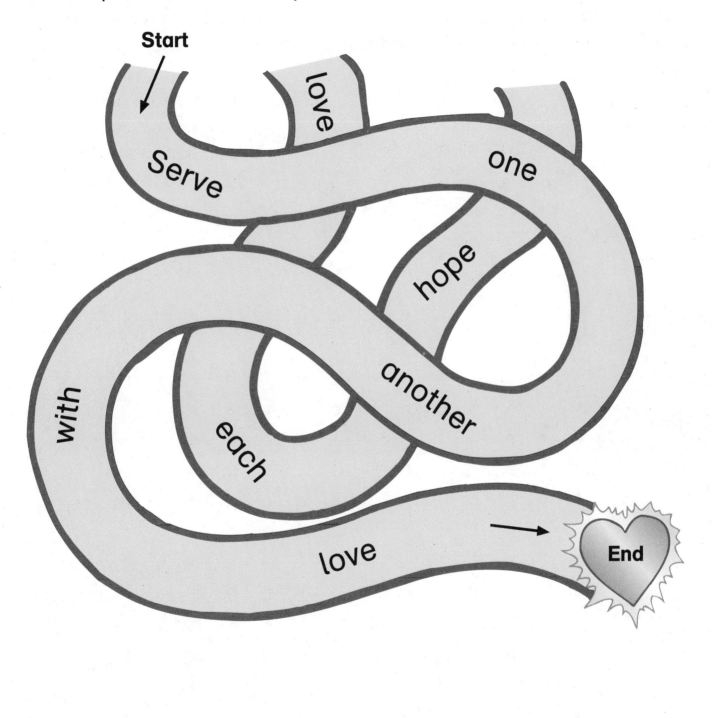

. . . _____ _____ _____

_____ _____. Galatians 5:13 NIV

Good Fruit

Name_____

In Galatians 5:22, we learn about the fruit of the Spirit. As Christians, we should possess these qualities. Search across and diagonally to discover the nine qualities hidden in the apple. Circle the words when you find them. When you are done, see if you can say them in order from memory.

The Fruit of the Spirit Is
love, joy, peace,
patience, kindness,
goodness, faithfulness,
gentleness, self-control

```
n  v  n  t  p  r  j  d  h  s  f  r  e  l
e  f  u  g  s  e  e  o  s  h  f  n  o  s
i  p  a  e  e  o  a  e  y  t  d  r  r  a
m  i  s  i  o  n  n  c  e  v  t  t  s  h
n  d  n  h  t  d  f  i  e  n  f  s  e  u
u  s  h  m  n  h  o  a  o  u  e  i  c  n
r  u  r  i  m  r  f  c  n  n  a  e  e  a
r  s  k  t  i  o  f  u  d  e  e  d  a  l
h  t  s  f  i  l  a  o  l  e  n  d  e  e
a  u  r  m  e  h  o  n  m  n  o  h  o  g
y  n  t  s  h  g  e  a  o  e  e  n  y  o
n  p  p  a  t  i  e  n  c  e  h  s  i  t
m  d  l  o  v  e  d  r  e  s  e  e  s  e
d  y  g  e  n  t  l  e  n  e  s  s  a  l
```

Armor of God

⭐ Paul teaches us about the Armor of God. Do you know what that armor is? Write the letter that comes right before the letter shown in the alphabet. You will learn about the Armor of God.

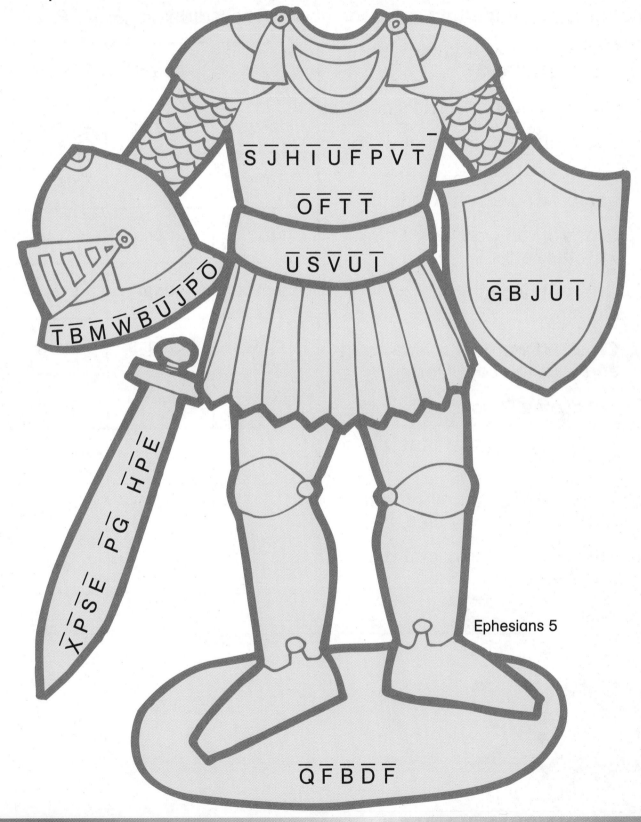

S̄ J̄ H̄ T̄ U̅ F̄ P̄ V̄ T̄

Q̄ F̄ T̄ T̄

Ū S̄ V̄ U̅ T̄

G̅ B̄ J̄ U̅ I̅

T̄ B̄ M̄ W̄ B̄ U̅ J̄ P̄ O̅

X̄ P̄ S̄ E̅   P̄ G̅   H̄ P̄ E̅

Ephesians 5

Q̄ F̄ B̄ D̄ F̄

Pray When?

⭐ Follow the directions by crossing off the indicated words in the columns below. When you are done, the remaining words will spell out two Bible verses. Write the words in the correct order from top to bottom to discover an important message from 1 Thessalonians 5:16–17.

1. Cross off all words that start with the letter M.

2. Cross off every disciple's name.

3. Cross off all three-letter words.

4. Cross off the name of the person who fought Goliath.

5. Cross off all words that start with the letter E.

6. Cross off words that are clothing.

7. Cross off words that start and end with the same letter.

8. Cross off all books of the Bible.

9. Cross off all words that are fruits.

10. Cross off the name of the first person created by God.

11. Cross off all words that begin with the letter F.

John	apple	David
jacket	mother	be
Ruth	was	early
trust	grapes	senses
Thomas	Adam	joyful
can	Romans	many
always	shirt	son
marched	pray	everyone
banana	Peter	continually
forever	Psalms	faith

The verses say:

_____

_____

_____

Little Critters

⭐ Insects, birds, and small animals are mentioned often in the Bible. They were either regarded as pests or were used to teach lessons. Instead of word clues, this puzzle has picture clues of the critters mentioned in the Bible. Put them in the correct squares in the crossword puzzle.

ACROSS

1. Psalm 118:12

3. Job 39:20

4. Matthew 10:29

5. Proverbs 30:28

7. Exodus 8:22

DOWN

1. Leviticus 11:19

2. Luke 11:12

4. Job 8:14

6. Psalm 55:6

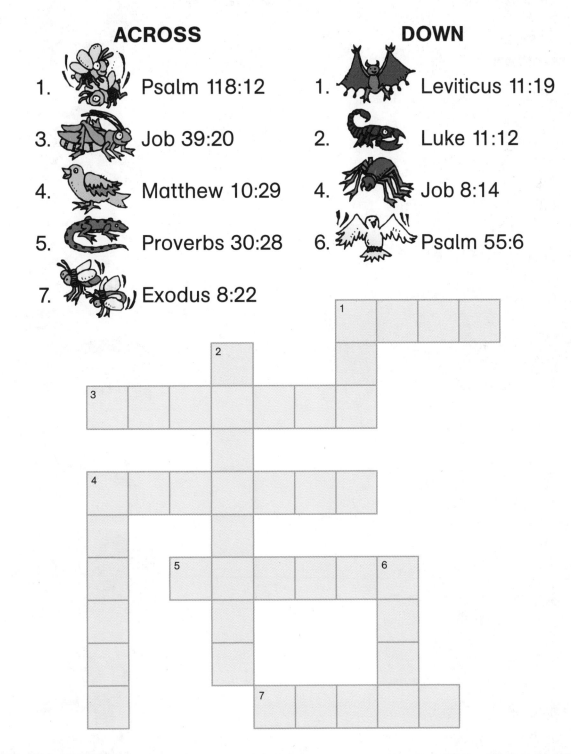

Bible Zoo

★ When we think of certain people in the Bible, we often think of the animals that were part of their stories. Match the person in Column A with the animal that we associate with that person in Column B. Write the matching numbers in the blanks. Read the verses if you need help.

Column A	Column B
1. Jesus (Matthew 3:16)	_____
2. Daniel (Daniel 6:16)	_____
3. Queen of Sheba (1 Kings 10:1–2)	_____
4. Peter (Mark 14:66–72)	_____
5. John the Baptist (Matthew 3:1–4)	_____
6. James and John (Luke 5:9–10)	_____
7. Aaron (Exodus 7:8–10)	_____

Solid Gold

When recording artists have big hits, they receive gold records. The Bible talks about musicians too. Who were some of these musicians? Look them up and write their names on the lines at the bottom of the page.

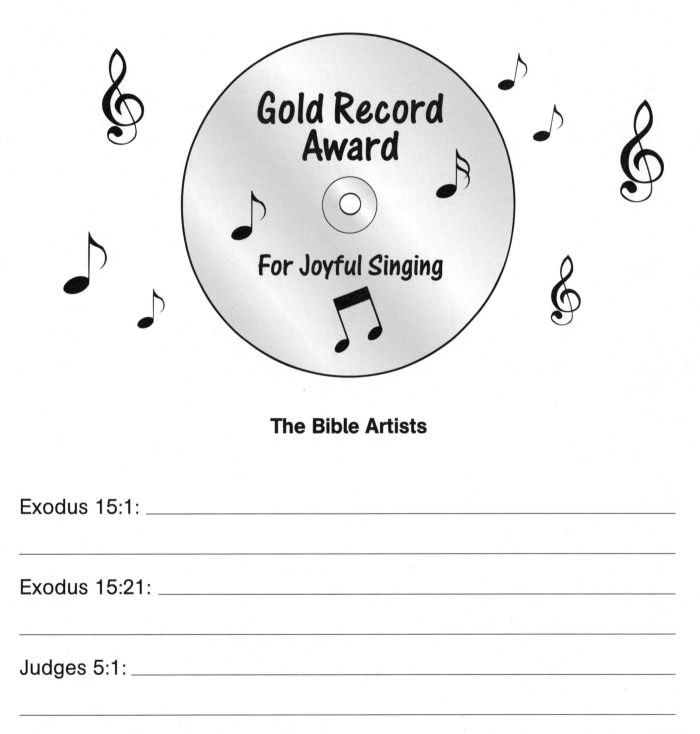

Gold Record Award

For Joyful Singing

The Bible Artists

Exodus 15:1: _____

_____

Exodus 15:21: _____

_____

Judges 5:1: _____

_____

Pizza Scramble

Name_____

⭐ Can you discover the names of some Bible people hidden in the pizzas below? One letter of each person's name is in each slice. To find a name, pick one letter from each slice. The first letter is in the first slice. The second letter is in the second slice and so on. Move clockwise around the circle.

1. Clues for Four-Letter Names

The second book of the New Testament _____

A famous boat builder (Genesis 6:13–14) _____

The first man (1 Corinthians 15:45) _____

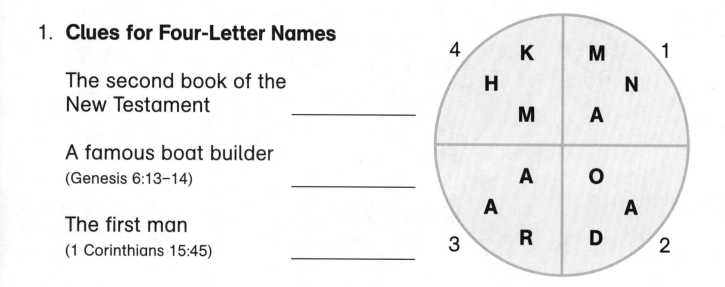

2. Clues for Five-Letter Names

Writer of many psalms (Psalm 23) _____

He was swallowed by a great fish (Jonah 1:17) _____

Abraham's original name (Genesis 17:5) _____

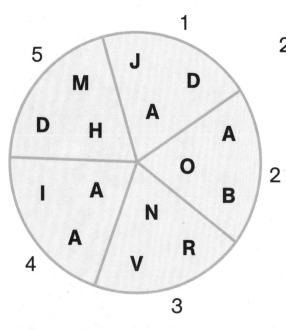

Soccer Balls

⭐ Find out the answer to the statement under each soccer ball. Then write your answer in the five large spaces on the ball, one letter to a space. The first letter goes in the top space, directly under the arrow, as shown in the example. The letters should read clockwise around the ball. All answers are five-letter words.

This bread from heaven fed the Israelites.
(Exodus 16:4, 31)

This is a "fruit of the Spirit."
(Galatians 5:22)

We must have this quality to live as Christians.
(2 Corinthians 5:7)

I commanded King Saul's army.
(1 Samuel 14:50)

Get Connected

⭐ The words on this page are connected. The last letter of one word is the first letter of the next word. Read the clues to discover the names. Begin with clue 1.

1. God spoke to this man through a burning bush (Exodus 3:3–4)

2. God's new name for Abraham's wife (Genesis 17:15)

3. Mother of Ishmael (Genesis 16:15)

4. A name for Jesus (John 1:49)

Who Am I?

⭐ In the box below, cross off all names that appear four times. The name that is left is the answer that fits the description at the bottom of the page.

Moses	Paul	Eve	Job	Ruth
Ezra	Ruth	Hosea	Elijah	Eve
Paul	Job	Ruth	Ezra	Ruth
Ezra	Eve		Moses	Paul
Job	Hosea	Moses	Hosea	Job
Moses	Eve	Ezra	Paul	Hosea

I was the prophet who was carried to heaven in a chariot of fire.

Who am I? _____

2 Kings 2:11

243

Meet My Mom

Name_____

⭐ Match these Bible sons with their mothers. Draw a line from the child listed in column A to his mother in column B. You will find the answers in the verses listed at the bottom of the page. Do you think these children brought flowers to their mothers, just as children do today?

Column A	Column B
Abel	Mary
Isaac	Elizabeth
Jacob	Rachel
Joseph	Hannah
Samuel	Rebekah
John	Eve
Jesus	Sarah

Verses

Genesis 4:1–2

Genesis 21:3

Genesis 27:11

Genesis 30:25

1 Samuel 1:20

Luke 1:57–60

Luke 1:29–31

Draw a flower that you could give to someone you love.

Meet My Dad

⭐ Children and their fathers are a big part of the bible story. Match the child in the left column with his or her father in the right column. Then put the father's name into the puzzle at the bottom. Read the verses listed at the bottom of the page if you need help. You will have to decide how the names fit into the grid.

Children	Dads
_____ 1. Solomon	A. Abraham
_____ 2. James	B. Adam
_____ 3. Miriam	C. Amram
_____ 4. Leah	D. David
_____ 5. Seth	E. Laban
_____ 6. Isaac	F. Zebedee

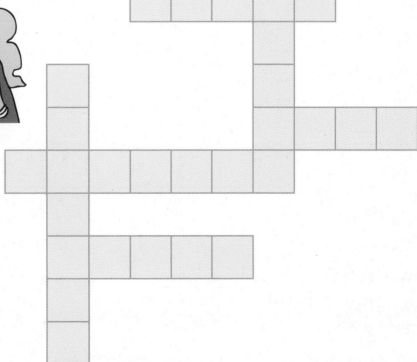

Verses

Genesis 4:25

Genesis 21:3

Genesis 29:16

1 Kings 2:1

1 Chronicles 6:3

Matthew 4:21

Crossings

Each mini-crossword puzzle below has two words that share a letter. The clues provide the two words. You will have to figure out how the words fit together. Find the answers in the verses listed at the bottom of the page.

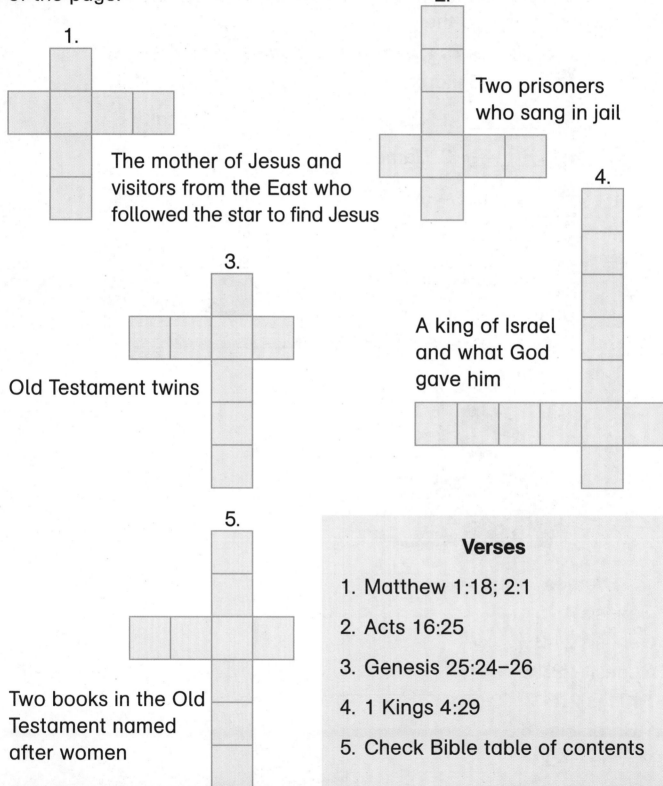

1.

The mother of Jesus and visitors from the East who followed the star to find Jesus

2.

Two prisoners who sang in jail

3.

Old Testament twins

4.

A king of Israel and what God gave him

5.

Two books in the Old Testament named after women

Verses

1. Matthew 1:18; 2:1

2. Acts 16:25

3. Genesis 25:24–26

4. 1 Kings 4:29

5. Check Bible table of contents

Sailing with Paul

Name_____

Paul was a great missionary who sailed to many parts of the world. Read the verses listed below to solve the puzzle and find out some of the places he visited on his three missionary journeys.

Down
1. Acts 19:1
2. Acts 15:4

Across
3. Acts 20:2
4. Acts 13:4
5. Acts 28:14

Sunshine for a Hurt

⭐ Forgiveness is like the sun. We welcome it, and it gives warmth to a hurting heart. Forgiveness brings happiness and peace, both to the forgiver and the one forgiven. Look up the verses on the suns to discover who in the bible forgave. Fill in the blanks below.

_____ forgave his enemies.

_____ forgave Jacob.

_____ forgave his brothers.

_____ forgave those who stoned him.

_____ forgave his son.

Acts
7:54–60

"Forgive, and
you will be
forgiven"
(Luke 6:37).

Genesis
33:1–4

Luke
23:34

Luke
15:11–24

Genesis
45:1–15

Who . . . ?

⭐ The answers to these questions are in the box below. Each answer is the name of a person. Read the questions. Then fill in the blanks with the correct name from the box below. Pictures take the place of key words.

Peter	Jesus	Job
Balaam	Ezekiel	Benaiah

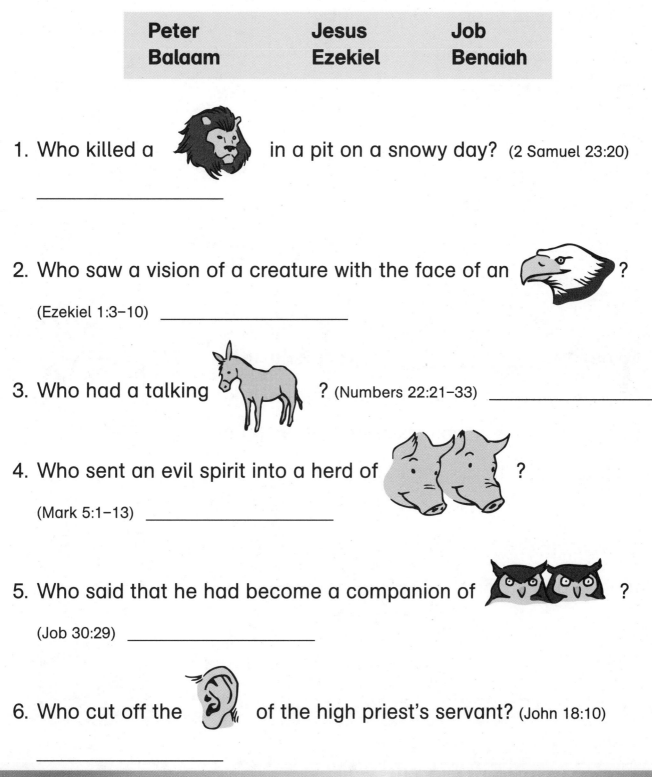

1. Who killed a 🦁 in a pit on a snowy day? (2 Samuel 23:20)

_____

2. Who saw a vision of a creature with the face of an 🦅 ?

(Ezekiel 1:3–10) _____

3. Who had a talking 🐴 ? (Numbers 22:21–33) _____

4. Who sent an evil spirit into a herd of 🐖 ?

(Mark 5:1–13) _____

5. Who said that he had become a companion of 🦉 ?

(Job 30:29) _____

6. Who cut off the 👂 of the high priest's servant? (John 18:10)

_____

Weather Report

⭐ People often plan activities around the weather. The Bible contains many references to weather. Look at the picture clues on the right that show weather conditions. Decide which picture fits in the Bible verse on the left and fill in the blank. Words may be used more than once.

1. "Like _____ in summer or

   _____ in harvest, honor is not fitting

   for a fool" (Proverbs 26:1).

2. "He makes _____ rise from the ends

   of the earth; he sends _____ with the

   _____ and brings out the wind from his

   storehouses" (Psalm 135:7).

3. "When the _____ was setting, the

   people brought to Jesus all who had various kinds

   of sickness, and laying his hands on each one,

   he healed them" (Luke 4:40).

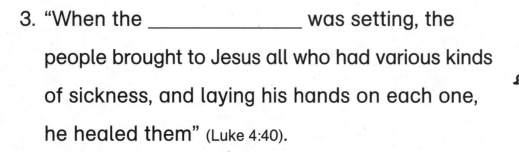

4. "As a north wind brings _____, so a sly

   tongue brings angry looks" (Proverbs 25:23).

5. "The _____ stopped in the middle of

   the sky and delayed going down about a full day"

   (Joshua 10:13).

PSALM 23

⭐ Find and circle the familiar words of the 23rd Psalm in the puzzle below. Remember, the words can appear backwards, across, and up and down.

Words to find:

The Lord is

my shepherd.

Psalm 23

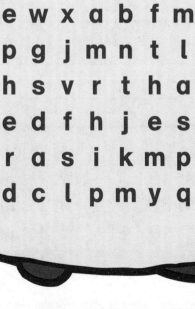

```
s  r  q  l  u  v  3
h  b  l  o  r  d  2
e  w  x  a  b  f  m
p  g  j  m  n  t  l
h  s  v  r  t  h  a
e  d  f  h  j  e  s
r  a  s  i  k  m  p
d  c  l  p  m  y  q
```

Names for God

The Book of Psalms uses a variety of names for God. Each gives us a different picture of what God is like. This crossword puzzle contains some of those names. Look up the verses and put each name in the correct place in the puzzle.

The Lord God Is a Sun.
Psalm 84:11

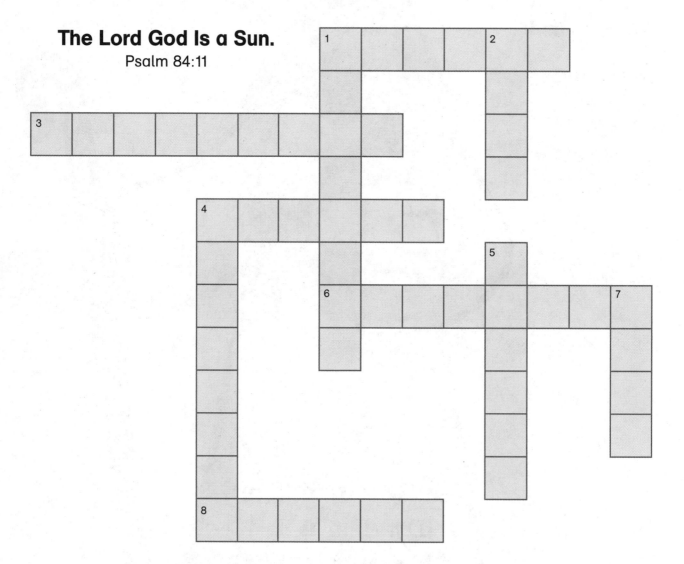

Across	Down
1. Psalm 3:3	1. Psalm 23:1
3. Psalm 18:2	2. Psalm 30:2
4. Psalm 68:5	4. Psalm 144:2
6. Psalm 19:14	5. Psalm 62:8
8. Psalm 25:5	7. Psalm 42:9

Name_____

⭐ Color this verse from Psalm 95:1.

Deciphering

Name_____

⭐ Using the code below, discover an inspiring verse from Psalm 121:8.

Code

1 l	2 w	3 t	4 b	5 g	6 i	7 c
8 d	9 f	10 y	11 h	12 u	13 m	14 r
15 n	16 v	17 a	18 o	19 e		

___ ___ ___   ___ ___ ___ ___   ___ ___ ___ ___
3   11 19   1   18 14 8   2   6   1   1

___ ___ ___ ___ ___   ___ ___ ___ ___
2   17 3   7   11   18 16 19 14

___ ___ ___ ___   ___ ___ ___ ___ ___ ___
10 18 12 14   7   18 13 6   15 5

___ ___ ___   ___ ___ ___ ___ ___
17 15 8   5   18 6   15 5

___ ___ ___ ___   ___ ___ ___   ___ ___ ___
4   18 3   11   15 18 2   17 15 8

___ ___ ___ ___ ___ ___ ___ ___ ___ ___ ___ .
9   18 14 19 16 19 14 13 18 14 19

Whose Job Is It?

People had jobs or occupations in biblical times, just as we do today. Look up the verses and find out who worked at each job pictured.

I was a shepherd.
(Amos 1:1)

_____

I was a queen.
(Esther 2:17)

_____

I was a judge.
(Judges 4:4–5)

_____

I was a carpenter.
(Mark 6:1–3)

_____

I was a tax collector.
(Luke 19:2)

_____

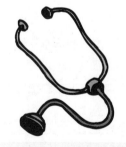

I was a doctor.
(Colossians 4:14)

_____

Reminders

The Bible is brimful of good advice. A clipboard is a handy way to keep ideas in front of you and is easy to carry around. Look up the verses below and write them on the clipboard.

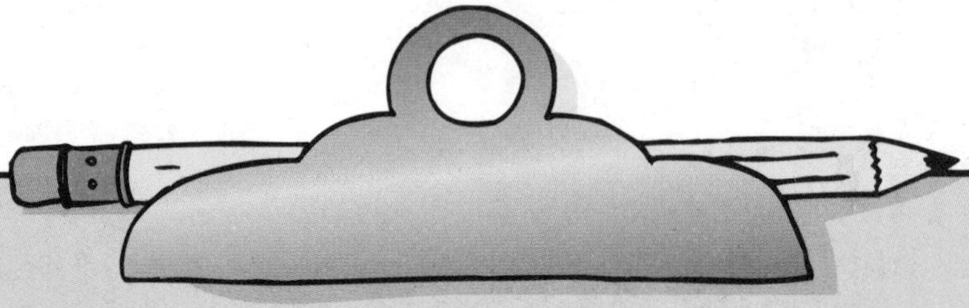

Good Advice to Remember

✔ John 14:1 _____

_____

_____

_____

✔ Psalm 34:14 _____

_____

_____

_____

✔ 1 Thessalonians 5:15 _____

_____

_____

_____

Friendship

⭐ Jesus taught us about friendship. Connect the letters in order on the telephone wires to complete the Bible verse below.

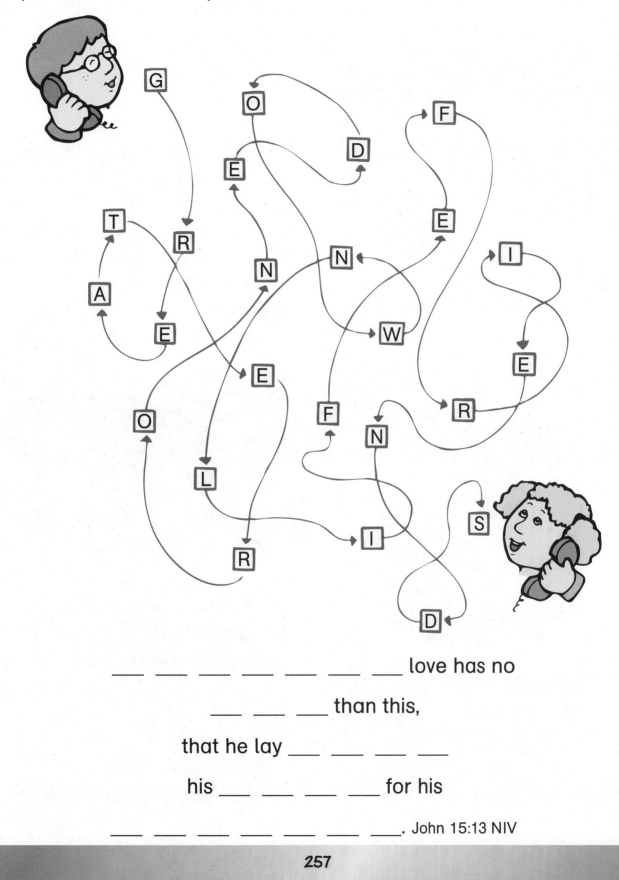

__ __ __ __ __ __ __ love has no

__ __ __ than this,

that he lay __ __ __ __

his __ __ __ __ for his

__ __ __ __ __ __ __. John 15:13 NIV

My Friend

Friends are very important in our lives. They were important for Bible people, too. Look up these friends' names and write them on the lines below.

I was called "God's friend."
(James 2:23)

_____

I was David's friend.
(1 Samuel 20:42)

_____

My husband and I were friends of Paul and risked our lives to help him.
(Romans 16:3–4)

_____

I was a friend to Paul while he was in prison.
(2 Timothy 1:16–17)

_____

Love Is . . .

Name_____

⭐ Look up the verses below, then write these verses of love in the hearts.

1 Peter 4:8

1 Corinthians 16:14

1 John 4:8

Grocery Shopping

Name_____

⭐ Today when we go to the grocery store, we buy food that we like to eat. What kinds of food did people in biblical times eat and drink? Find out the answer to that question by reading the verses below. Write the foods mentioned in the verses on the grocery list to discover what people ate long ago.

🍎 Numbers 11:5

🍎 Deuteronomy 23:24

🍎 1 Samuel 14:25

🍎 2 Samuel 17:28

🍎 Proverbs 27:18

🍎 Proverbs 27:27

🍎 Isaiah 17:6

Grocery List

In High Places

Discover the names of several mountains mentioned in the Bible. Using one of the boxed letters in the word *mountains* as the first letter in your answer, put a mountain's name in the squares. Clues are listed below.

CLUES

The mountain where Jesus prayed before he was arrested by the soldiers. (Luke 22:39–42)

The mountain where Moses died. (Deuteronomy 32:48–50)

The mountain where Noah's ark came to rest at the end of the flood. (Genesis 8:4)

The mountain where Moses received the Ten Commandments from God. (Numbers 3:1)

The Flood

During the flood God stayed with Noah and kept him safe. God is always with you, too. Fill in the crossword puzzle below. The first word has been filled in to get you started.

| rain | promise | animals |
| rainbow | Noah | flood |

10 Plagues

⭐ Pharaoh would not let Moses and the Israelites leave Egypt! So, God sent ten plagues upon the people. Find and circle the ten plagues listed below in the puzzle.

blood	frogs	gnats	flies	livestock
boils	hail	locusts	darkness	firstborn

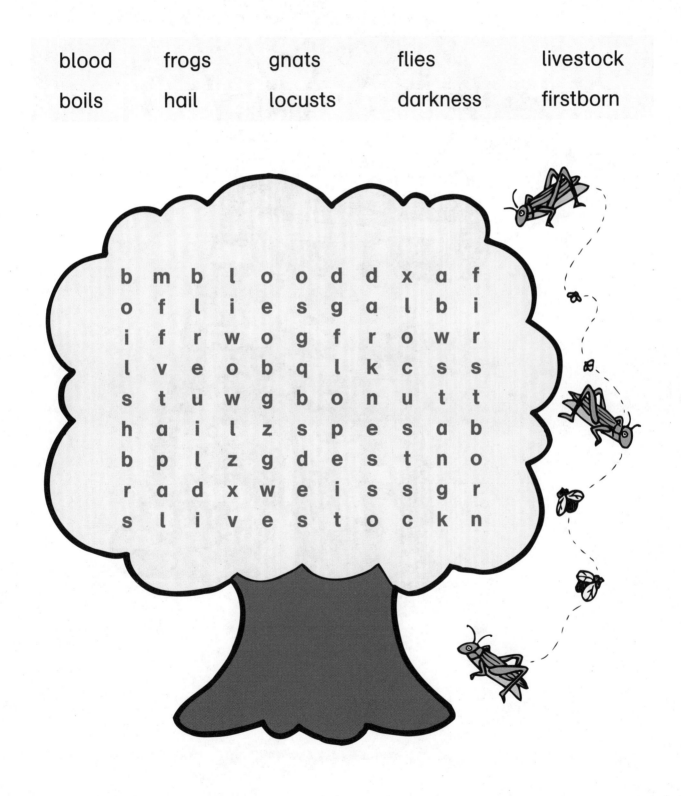

Praise God!

⭐ Start with the letter P and write each letter in the spaces below as you come to them in the maze.

START

P _ _ _ _ _ _ _ _ _ _ _

_ _ _ _ .

Name_____

⭐ King Nebuchadnezzar wanted people to worship false gods. Three Jews refused because they loved God. Using the key below, decode their names. Remember to capitalize the first letter of each name.

Name_____

⭐ God was very pleased with Jesus. When John baptized Jesus, something very special happened. Beginning with the letter "H", go around the dove and write every other letter on the spaces provided.

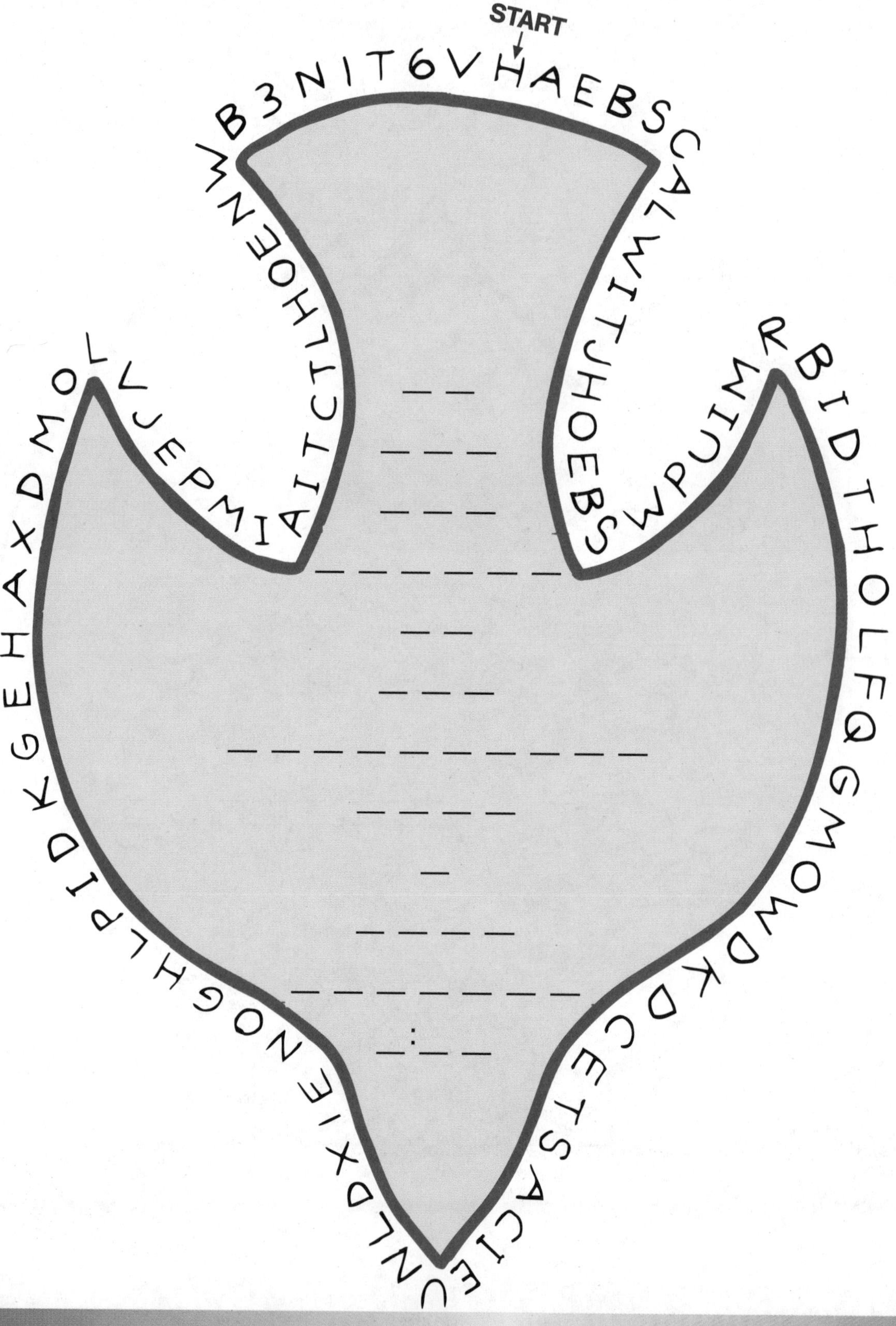

START
↓

H A E B S
C A L W I T H O E B S
W P U I M R
R B I D T H O L F Q G M O W D K D C E T S A C I E
N L X I E U N O
G H L P I D K G E H A X D M O L
V J E P M I A I T C T L H O E N W
B 3 N I T 6 V

— —

— — —

— — —

— — — — — —

— —

— — — —

—

— — — —

— — — — —

— : — —

God Can Do

⭐ Many people wonder what God can really do. What does Luke teach us about God? Using the key below, decode the message to find out what the Bible says God can do.

KEY

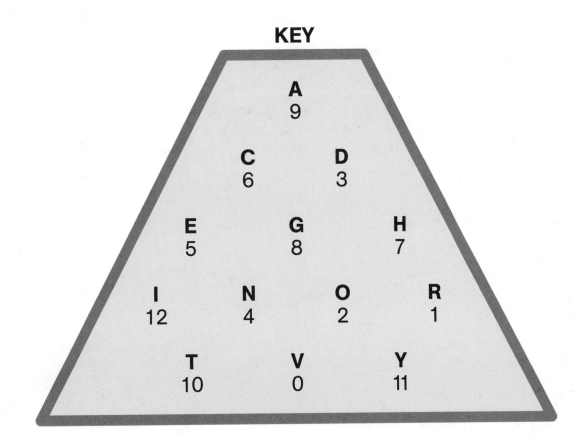

	A 9	
C 6		D 3
E 5	G 8	H 7
I 12	N 4	O 2	R 1
T 10	V 0	Y 11

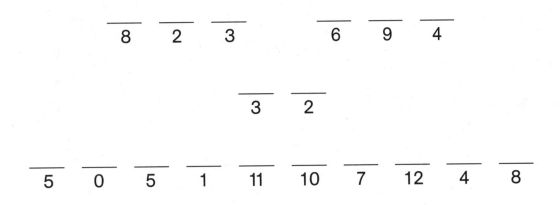

$\overline{8}$ $\overline{2}$ $\overline{3}$ $\overline{6}$ $\overline{9}$ $\overline{4}$

$\overline{3}$ $\overline{2}$

$\overline{5}$ $\overline{0}$ $\overline{5}$ $\overline{1}$ $\overline{11}$ $\overline{10}$ $\overline{7}$ $\overline{12}$ $\overline{4}$ $\overline{8}$

Galatians 5:22

⭐ But the fruit of the spirit is love, joy, peace, patience, kindness, goodness, faithfulness, gentleness and self-control. Paul tells us how to live in the Spirit of God. Fill in the words from the verse above in the spaces below.

Jesus Loves Me

Name_____

⭐ This familiar song is the key to completing this crossword puzzle. Use the missing words from the song to complete the puzzle.

Jesus loves me this I _____ (5)

For the Bible tells me _____ (6)

Little ones to Him _____ (1 down)

They are weak, but He is _____ (7)

Yes, _____ loves me (3)

Yes, Jesus _____ me (2)

Yes, Jesus loves _____ (4)

The _____ tells me so (1 across)

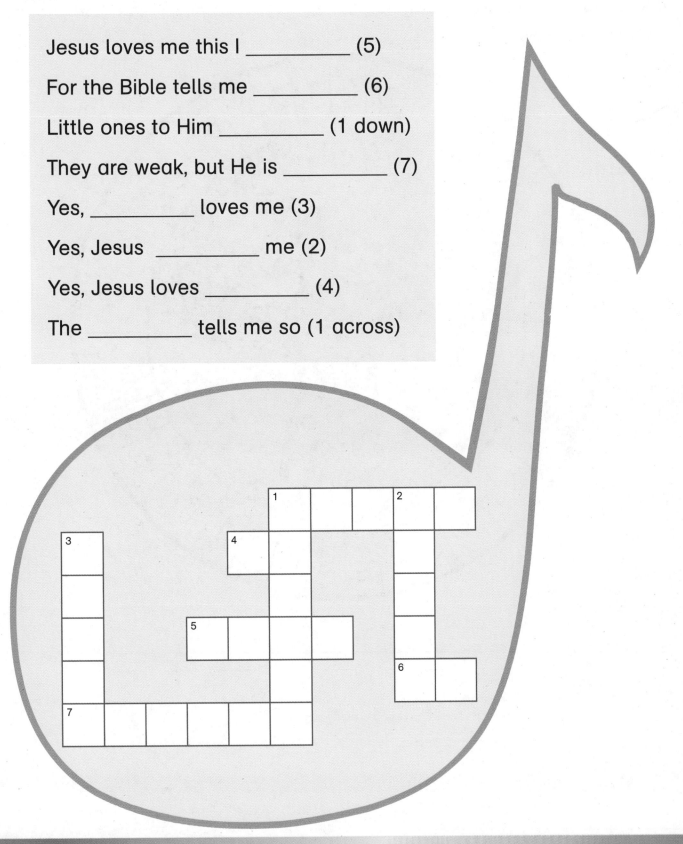

Talk to God

⭐ Wherever you are or whatever you are doing, you can always talk to God. Beginning at the arrow and moving clockwise, write every other letter on the spaces below.

START
↓

__ __ __ __ __ __ __ __ __

__ __ __ __ __ __ __ __

__ __ __ __ __ .

My Heart Belongs to Jesus

Name_____

To find the message, start with the letter "G" and follow the maze through the heart. Write the letters in the order you come to them in the spaces below.

__ __ __ __ __ __ __ __

__ __ __ __ __ __ __ __ .

A Family Tree

Everyone has relatives. Jesus did too. When we name and list our relatives for many generations back, we call that a "family tree." Jesus' family tree is listed in Matthew 1. Find out who some of Jesus' relatives were. Their names are hidden below. They can be found horizontally, diagonally, and vertically. Use the list of names to help you.

Jesus' Relatives

ABRAHAM	AHAZ	ASA	BOAZ	DAVID
ISAAC	JACOB	JEHORAM	JESSE	JOSEPH
JOSIAH	JUDAH	MARY	OBED	PEREZ
RAHAB	RAM	RUTH	SOLOMON	

```
B S E T E E L A L I K A H A Z S N R
S W T R I H M F A E M O J U L R D O
E I V E L A O O P P E A O U T O Y E
Y N C T R N N L N E R U F F D E N O
I E I O F I H H D O R T I N O A E E
E S H R A H A B H S N E H I I E H L
T E A A C D T E H O H R Z T T T M L
J C I A E B A S A L J I D O A A E R
T D W D C A I J I O A I R K H V O H
A J O S I A H E M M C R L A E N P D
C P V F T C P S O O O E R W E E L I
S A R T T G L S E N B B A O S E R H
Y Y A A A O X E L R A T O O D O R N
N B O E M M O P R O O B J D O H C W
O M N E E F N T R A O M O I A E R N
B E A L H S R E E E R Y B A I V D A
E E H R D E T U R U T H R T Z A I U
D E I F Y I B D N H E N L P I T E D
```

Name_____

God has given us so many wonderful things. We should be happy and rejoice. How many words can you make from the letters found in the word **CELEBRATION**? Write the words on the stars.

CELEBRATION

Twisters

⭐ If you enjoy challenges, this word search is for you! Hidden in the puzzle grid are the names of 12 books of the bible. The names are twisted and curved—not in a straight line. The letters in a word may be found next to each other in any direction. The letters in one word will never cross or be joined with another word. One has been done for you.

Books of the Bible

AMOS	JOB	NUMBERS
DANIEL	JOEL	PROVERBS
GENESIS	MALACHI	REVELATION
HEBREWS	MATTHEW	TITUS

Bible Ticktacktoe

★ For 2 or more players

★ A quick and easy game that tests Bible knowledge!

How to play:
If there are more than two players, divide the players evenly into teams.

- Cut out the markers, then have each player or team pick either the fish or crosses as their markers.

- Tear out the quiz card pages and cut out the cards. Divide them, giving half of the cards to each player or team.

- Lay the ticktacktoe game grid out in front of both players or teams, within easy reach.

- One player or team draws a card from their stack and reads a question to the other player or team. If the player or team answers correctly, that player or team places a marker on the game grid in one of the open squares. If the question is answered incorrectly, play moves to the other player or team.

- Play continues until one of the players or teams has three of its markers in a row, diagonally, up and down, or across. If all of the squares are full with no ticktacktoes, the game is considered a tie and a new game begins.

- If desired, score may be kept on a separate sheet of paper.

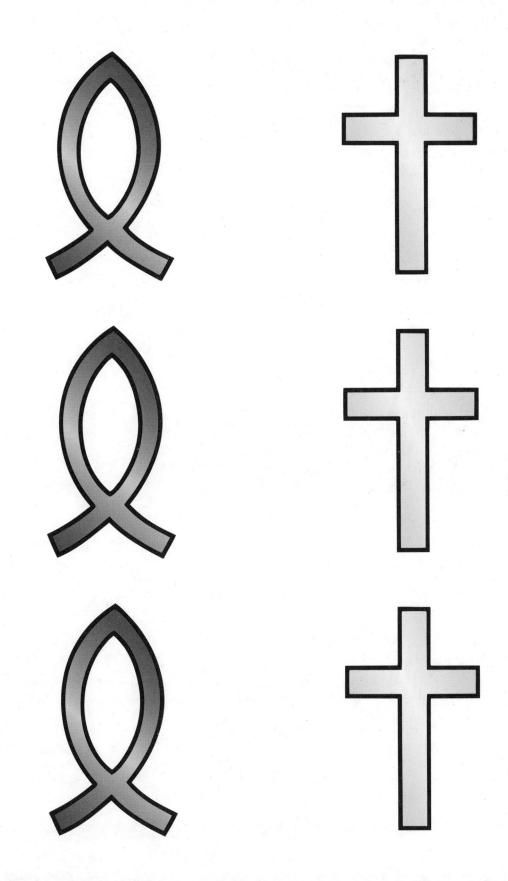

Bible Ticktacktoe Quiz Cards

Q. How is Jesus related to God? A. He's the Son of God.	Q. How many disciples did Jesus have? A. twelve
Q. In what town was Jesus born? A. Bethlehem	Q. Who were Jesus' earthly mother and father? A. Mary and Joseph
Q. Who was Abraham's wife? A. Sarah	Q. What was the name of the garden where Eve ate the forbidden fruit? A. Eden
Q. Who was the boy who defeated a giant with a slingshot? A. David	Q. What was the name of the giant who David killed? A. Goliath
Q. A big fish swallowed me. Who am I? A. Jonah	Q. In Jesus' first miracle, he turned water into what? A. wine

Bible Ticktacktoe Quiz Cards

Q. Jesus used what to feed 5,000 people? A. five loaves of bread and two fish	Q. Who did Jesus heal? Jairus's son or his daughter? A. daughter
Q. Where did Jesus teach when he was only 12 years old? A. the temple	Q. There was no room here for Mary and Joseph. A. the inn
Q. Who told the shepherds about Jesus' birth? A. an angel	Q. What did the wise men from the east follow to find Jesus? A. a star
Q. Where did the wise men find Jesus? A. in a manger/stable	Q. Who is the King of Kings? A. Jesus
Q. I heard God speak trough a burning bush. Who am I? A. Moses	Q. My brothers hated me and sold me as a slave. Who am I? A. Joseph

Bible Ticktacktoe Quiz Cards

Q. To what town did God want Jonah to go?

A. Nineveh

Q. Who was taken up into heaven in a whirlwind?

A. Elijah

Q. Who took Elijah's place as a prophet?

A. Elisha

Q. What king ordered the temple repaired and in the process discovered a lost book of the Bible?

A. King Josiah

Q. Who was the youngest king to rule in Judah?

A. Joash (He was seven.)

Q. I hid two spies on my roof. Because of this, my family was spared when Jericho fell. Who am I?

A. Rahab

Q. What king prayed for wisdom?

A. Solomon

Q. What king committed adultery and had the woman's husband murdered?

A. David

Q. Which Moabite woman was the great-grandmother of King David?

A. Ruth

Q. Which king danced for joy when the Ark of the Covenant was brought into Jerusalem?

A. David

Bible Ticktacktoe Quiz Cards

Q. Moses' people made a false idol while he was on Mt. Sinai. What was it?

A. a golden calf

Q. For a time, what did Paul do for a living?

A. tent making

Q. Who got his strength from his hair?

A. Samson

Q. Who tricked Samson into revealing the source of his strength?

A. Delilah

Q. Who led the army that destroyed Jericho by shouting and blowing trumpets?

A. Joshua

Q. What is the name given to the laws that Moses brought down from the mountain?

A. the Ten Commandments

Q. How did Moses and his people get across the Red Sea?
A. God parted the water for them, and they walked across.

Q. How many plagues did the Egyptians suffer before Pharaoh set the Israelites free?

A. ten

Q. How many years did Moses and his people wander through the desert?

A. forty years

Q. Who became a great ruler in Egypt because he interpreted Pharaoh's dreams?

A. Joseph

Bible Ticktacktoe Quiz Cards

Q. During the Last Supper, what did Jesus say represents his body?

A. bread

Q. What words were posted on Jesus' cross?

A. This is Jesus, the King of the Jews.

Q. Who carried Jesus' cross to Golgotha?

A. Simon of Cyrene

Q. What was Jesus' body laid in after his death?

A. a tomb

Q. Who rolled the stone away from the entrance of Jesus' tomb?

A. an angel

Q. Who looked on and approved of Stephen's stoning?

A. Saul

Q. How many other people were crucified with Jesus?

A. two criminals

Q. Jesus said of me, "On this rock I will build my church." Who am I?

A. Peter

Q. Like Joseph, what skill did Jesus learn?

A. carpentry

Q. What two good friends of Paul worked with him in both tent making and the ministry?

A. Aquila and Priscilla

Bible Ticktacktoe Quiz Cards

Q. What was the first plague that struck the Egyptians?

A. water into blood

Q. Who was the baby placed in a basket in the River Nile?

A. Moses

Q. What were the names of Noah's sons? Name one.

A. Shem, Ham, and Japheth

Q. How long did it rain during the big flood?

A. forty days and nights

Q. Why was Daniel thrown to the lions?

A. because he prayed to God

Q. What did Nehemiah do to the walls of Jerusalem?

A. rebuilt them

Q. Jesus raised me from the dead. My sisters and I were friends of Jesus. Who am I?

A. Lazarus

Q. Who climbed a tree in order to see Jesus?

A. Zacchaeus

Q. I was the forerunner of Jesus. He came to me to be baptized. Who am I?

A. John the Baptist

Q. What did Jesus say represents his blood?

A. wine

Answer Key

God is With You
Name_____

Joshua struggled just like we do at times. What were God's comforting words to him? We can use these words in our lives today. Fill in the missing vowels using the code to read the Bible verse.

A E I O U

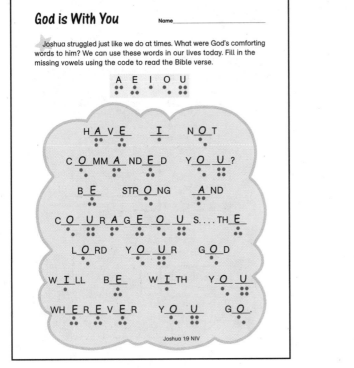

HAVE I NOT
COMMANDED YOU?
BE STRONG AND
COURAGEOUS....THE
LORD YOUR GOD
WILL BE WITH YOU
WHEREVER YOU GO.

Joshua 1:9 NIV

7

Gimme an "E"
Name_____

Several people mentioned in the Bible have names that begin with the letter **E**. Some of the names have several **E**'s in them. The names are listed below. Fit them into the correct lines below. Use a Bible dictionary to discover who these people were.

Ebenezer	Enos	Eli	Ephesians	Elijah
Esther	Elizabeth	Eve	Elisha	Eunice

E u n i c e
E l i z a b e t h
E n o s
E l i s h a (or Elijah)
E b e n e z e r
E v e
E s t h e r
E p h e s i a n s
E l i
E l i j a h (or Elisha)

8

Silly Sarah
Name_____

Look at how silly Sarah dressed today. Fill in the blanks with the missing short vowels to spell what she is wearing.

1. b i g s U ngl a ss e s
2. s i lly n e cklace
3. y e llow r i bb o n
4. dr e ss w i th f a t c a ts
5. ch e ckered s O cks

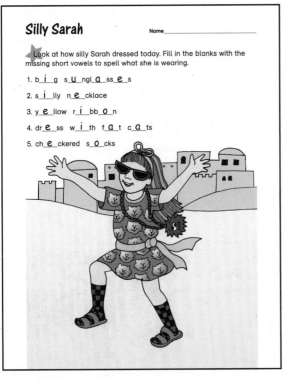

9

Mary Remembers
Name_____

Say the sounds of **ar**, **er**, **ir**, **or**, and **ur**. Then read the story.

Mary will always remember Jesus' birth and the events that followed. After Jesus was born, a bright star shone in the dark sky above the stable. Shepherds followed the star and were the first to see baby Jesus, who lay still, not stirring, curled in the arms of his mother. Mary lay Jesus in the manger and covered him with furs. Later, wise doctors called magi came from far away bringing gifts: a bag of gold, a jug of incense, and a jar of myrrh. Mary was amazed at all that occurred.

List the words from the story that have these letters.

ar	er	ir
Mary	remember	birth
star	After	first
dark	Shepherds	stirring
arms	were	**or**
far	mother	born
jar	manger	doctors
	covered	**ur**
	later	curled
		furs
		occurred

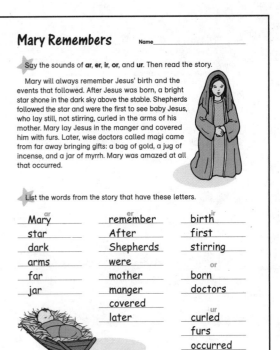

10

Answer Key

M-m-m . . . Good

Name_____

Do you know any people from the Bible whose names begin with the letter **M**? The clues below provide information about some of them. Write their names on the lines below. Can you think of any others?

Clues
I am an archangel. (Jude 9)
I was thrown into a fiery furnace and survived. (Daniel 3:26–27)
I was a disciple of Jesus. (Matthew 10:2–3)
I was a prophet and wrote the last book in the Old Testament.
My sister and I were friends of Jesus. (There will be two names.) (John 11:1)
My mother made a papyrus basket to put me in. (Exodus 2:1–10)

Michael (amhicle)

Meshach (hhemsac)

Matthew (thwemat)

Malachi (iaahclm)

Martha (htaarm)

Mary (ramy)

Moses (smseo)

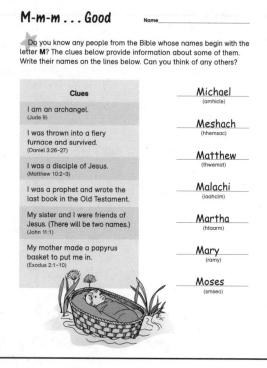

11

Simply S

Name_____

Can you list the six people below whose names begin with the letter **S**? Read the Bible verses if you are stumped. Write each name in the section under the correct description.

The Names		
Genesis 5:32	Luke 2:34–35	1 Samuel 3:1–4
Luke 6:15	1 Samuel 11:15	Acts 5:1–10

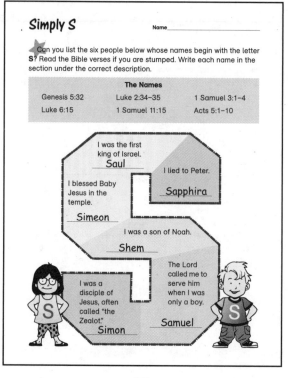

I was the first king of Israel. **Saul**

I lied to Peter. **Sapphira**

I blessed Baby Jesus in the temple. **Simeon**

I was a son of Noah. **Shem**

I was a disciple of Jesus, often called "the Zealot." **Simon**

The Lord called me to serve him when I was only a boy. **Samuel**

12

A Gift from God

Name_____

Every day is a beautifully wrapped gift from God—just look around you. Write the missing blend for each word. Then color the bow the correct color.

Suggested answers below.

bl (red)	tr (green)	pr (blue)	st (yellow)	fl (orange)	cl (pink)	dr (purple)

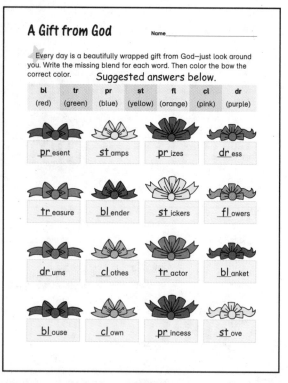

present **st**amps **pr**izes **dr**ess

treasure **bl**ender **st**ickers **fl**owers

drums **cl**othes **tr**actor **bl**anket

blouse **cl**own **pr**incess **st**ove

13

Seeing Doubles

Name_____

Use the clues to write the correct double consonants (**ff**, **ss**, **ll**, or **zz**) at the end of each word.

1. che **s s** = a game
2. hi **l l** = a small mountain
3. le **s s** = not more
4. hi **s s** = snake noise
5. cu **f f** = bottom of sleeve
6. fi **z z** = bubbles in a drink
7. se **l l** = opposite of buy
8. gu **l l** = a sea bird
9. me **s s** = clutter
10. ye **l l** = to scream
11. gla **s s** = holds something to drink
12. du **l l** = not sharp
13. sni **f f** = to smell
14. we **l l** = not sick
15. bu **z z** = bee's sound
16. dre **s s** = gown

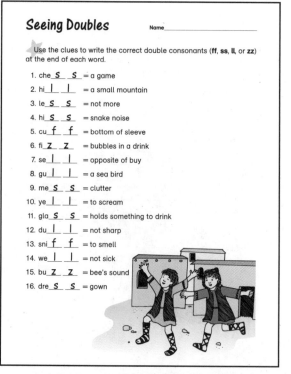

14

Answer Key

Jesus Fed 5,000
Name_____

Write the missing consonant blend.

ph	ck
sh	rt
ct	st
nt	nd
ld	ch

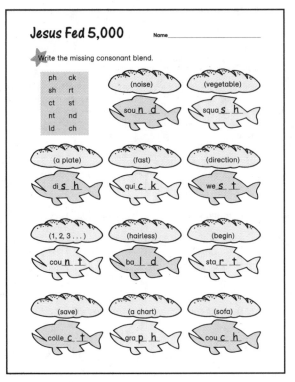

(noise) — sou **n d**

(vegetable) — squa **s h**

(a plate) — di **s h**

(fast) — qui **c k**

(direction) — we **s t**

(1, 2, 3 . . .) — cou **n t**

(hairless) — ba **l d**

(begin) — sta **r t**

(save) — colle **c t**

(a chart) — gra **p h**

(sofa) — cou **c h**

15

Ernest the Elephant
Name_____

Ernest kept busy on the ark learning the words below. Can you help him? Write the final consonant blend for each word. Color each toe by blending the colors shown on Ernest's Color Chart. **Suggested answers below.**

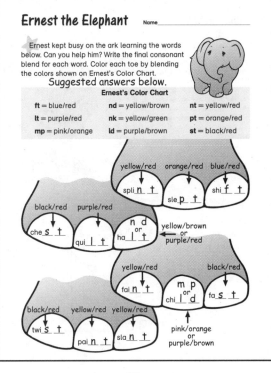

Ernest's Color Chart

ft = blue/red	**nd** = yellow/brown	**nt** = yellow/red
lt = purple/red	**nk** = yellow/green	**pt** = orange/red
mp = pink/orange	**ld** = purple/brown	**st** = black/red

yellow/red — spli **n t**

orange/red — sle **p t**

blue/red — shi **f t**

black/red — che **s t**

purple/red — qui **l t**

yellow/brown or purple/red — ha **l t** / **n d**

yellow/red — fai **n t**

black/red — fa **s t**

pink/orange or purple/brown — chi **l d** / **m p**

black/red — twi **s t**

yellow/red — pai **n t**

yellow/red — sla **n t**

16

Show and Tell
Name_____

Say the **sh** sound. Read the story. Then circle each **sh** in the story.

Shannon's teacher, Mrs. Sheldon, had things to share. She had just come back from the seashore. "Look at the shiny seashell," she said. "I also have a scallop shell. God made them both."

After she shared with the children, she thanked God for sharing his creation. Then she put the shells on the shelf.

"I'm thankful I didn't see a shark with sharp teeth at the seashore," said Mrs. Sheldon.

Write the **sh** words in the puzzle.

Across
1. ship
4. shirt
3. sharp
5. shadow

Down
1. shop
shower
she

17

Paul in Chains
Name_____

Say the **ch** sound. Read the story. Then circle each **ch** in the story.

The church was still as the children sat in their chairs listening to the story of Paul in prison. The teacher told them that God chose Paul to show charity to the Gentiles by telling them about the champion of the world, Jesus. For preaching the gospel, Paul was thrown in a chilly cell and locked in chains. Even in chains, Paul was cheerful and suffered gladly. He continued to spread the good news from his prison cell.

Write a **ch** word from the story for each picture.

chairs   church   chains

18

289

Answer Key

Don't Be Afraid!

Name_____

⭐ Say the **th** sound. Read the story. Then circle each **th** in the story.

Elizabe(th) loved Jesus. Every night she said her prayers wi(th) her mo(ther) and fa(ther). She (th)anked God for her parents, who bo(th) loved her very much. She also (th)anked God for her bro(ther) and her (th)ree best friends. Sometimes she prayed (th)at God would help her wi(th) her ma(th) and o(ther) homework.

One night while Elizabe(th) lay in bed, it began to (th)under. She was afraid until she remembered (th)at God was always wi(th) her, watching over her. She whispered, "(Th)ank you, God," and fell asleep.

⭐ Circle the **th** words in the wordsearch below.

| father |
| mother |
| thunder |
| both |
| brother |
| three |
| other |
| with |
| math |
| that |
| thanked |

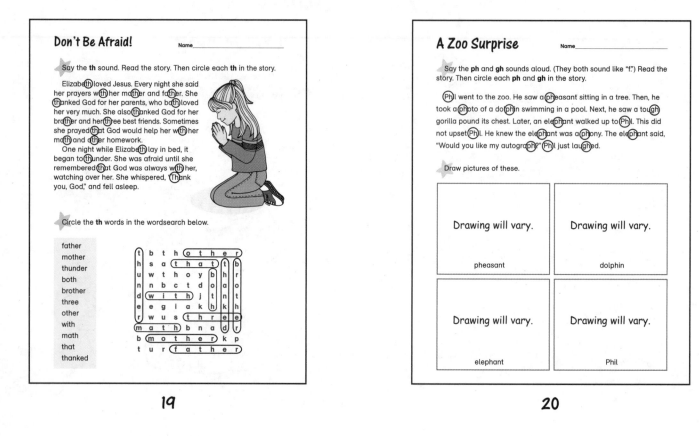

19

A Zoo Surprise

Name_____

⭐ Say the **ph** and **gh** sounds aloud. (They both sound like "f.") Read the story. Then circle each **ph** and **gh** in the story.

(Ph)il went to the zoo. He saw a (ph)easant sitting in a tree. Then, he took a (ph)oto of a dol(ph)in swimming in a pool. Next, he saw a tou(gh) gorilla pound its chest. Later, an ele(ph)ant walked up to (Ph)il. This did not upset (Ph)il. He knew the elephant was a (ph)ony. The ele(ph)ant said, "Would you like my autogra(ph)?" (Ph)il just lau(gh)ed.

⭐ Draw pictures of these.

Drawing will vary.	Drawing will vary.
pheasant	dolphin
Drawing will vary.	Drawing will vary.
elephant	Phil

20

Bible Nouns

Name_____

⭐ Color each Bible blue if the word in it is a noun. Put an **X** on each word that is not a noun.

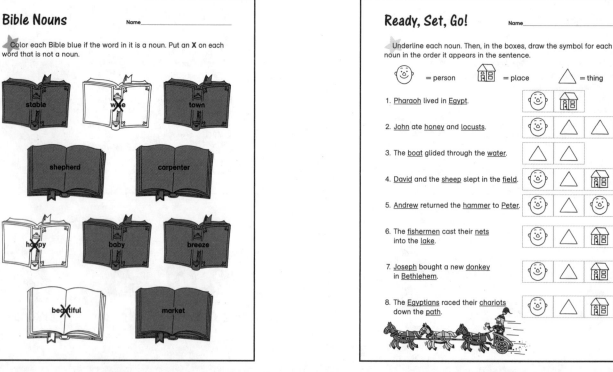

stable · w(X)se · town · shepherd · carpenter · ha(X)py · baby · breeze · bea(X)tiful · market

---

21

Ready, Set, Go!

Name_____

⭐ Underline each noun. Then, in the boxes, draw the symbol for each noun in the order it appears in the sentence.

😊 = person　🏠 = place　△ = thing

1. <u>Pharaoh</u> lived in <u>Egypt</u>.　😊 🏠

2. <u>John</u> ate <u>honey</u> and <u>locusts</u>.　😊 △ △

3. The <u>boat</u> glided through the <u>water</u>.　△ △

4. <u>David</u> and the <u>sheep</u> slept in the <u>field</u>.　😊 △ 🏠

5. <u>Andrew</u> returned the <u>hammer</u> to <u>Peter</u>.　😊 △ 😊

6. The <u>fishermen</u> cast their <u>nets</u> into the <u>lake</u>.　😊 △ 🏠

7. <u>Joseph</u> bought a new <u>donkey</u> in <u>Bethlehem</u>.　😊 △ 🏠

8. The <u>Egyptians</u> raced their <u>chariots</u> down the <u>path</u>.　😊 △ 🏠

22

Answer Key

Reflections

Name_____

⭐ Mirrors are like copy machines. Write the plural for each noun. Then draw each reflection in the mirror.

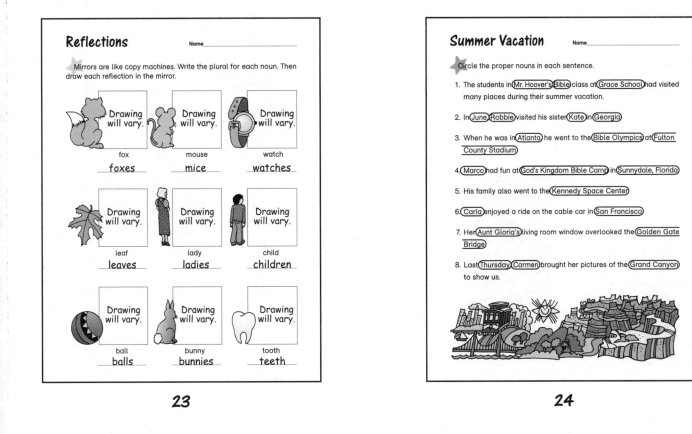

fox	mouse	watch
Drawing will vary.	Drawing will vary.	Drawing will vary.
foxes	mice	watches

leaf	lady	child
Drawing will vary.	Drawing will vary.	Drawing will vary.
leaves	ladies	children

ball	bunny	tooth
Drawing will vary.	Drawing will vary.	Drawing will vary.
balls	bunnies	teeth

23

Summer Vacation

Name_____

⭐ Circle the proper nouns in each sentence.

1. The students in (Mr. Hoover's) (Bible) class at (Grace School) had visited many places during their summer vacation.

2. In (June) (Robbie) visited his sister (Kate) in (Georgia).

3. When he was in (Atlanta) he went to the (Bible Olympics) at (Fulton County Stadium).

4. (Marco) had fun at (God's Kingdom Bible Camp) in (Sunnydale, Florida).

5. His family also went to the (Kennedy Space Center).

6. (Carla) enjoyed a ride on the cable car in (San Francisco).

7. Her (Aunt Gloria's) living room window overlooked the (Golden Gate Bridge).

8. Last (Thursday) (Carmen) brought her pictures of the (Grand Canyon) to show us.

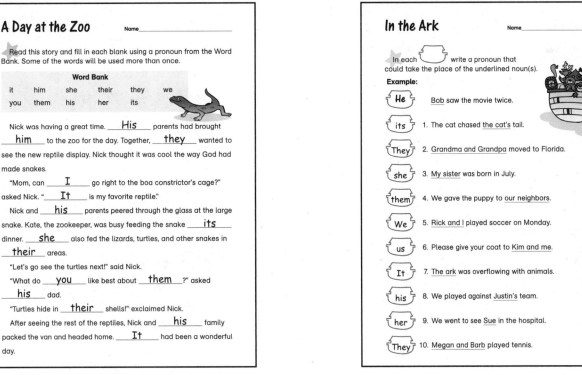

24

A Day at the Zoo

Name_____

⭐ Read this story and fill in each blank using a pronoun from the Word Bank. Some of the words will be used more than once.

Word Bank

it	him	she	their	they	we
you	them	his	her	its	

Nick was having a great time. ___His___ parents had brought ___him___ to the zoo for the day. Together, ___they___ wanted to see the new reptile display. Nick thought it was cool the way God had made snakes.

"Mom, can ___I___ go right to the boa constrictor's cage?" asked Nick. "___It___ is my favorite reptile."

Nick and ___his___ parents peered through the glass at the large snake. Kate, the zookeeper, was busy feeding the snake ___its___ dinner. ___she___ also fed the lizards, turtles, and other snakes in ___their___ areas.

"Let's go see the turtles next!" said Nick.

"What do ___you___ like best about ___them___?" asked ___his___ dad.

"Turtles hide in ___their___ shells!" exclaimed Nick.

After seeing the rest of the reptiles, Nick and ___his___ family packed the van and headed home. ___It___ had been a wonderful day.

25

In the Ark

Name_____

⭐ In each ⬚ write a pronoun that could take the place of the underlined noun(s).

Example:

He — <u>Bob</u> saw the movie twice.

its 1. The cat chased <u>the cat's</u> tail.

They 2. <u>Grandma and Grandpa</u> moved to Florida.

she 3. <u>My sister</u> was born in July.

them 4. We gave the puppy to <u>our neighbors</u>.

We 5. <u>Rick and I</u> played soccer on Monday.

us 6. Please give your coat to <u>Kim and me</u>.

It 7. <u>The ark</u> was overflowing with animals.

his 8. We played against <u>Justin's</u> team.

her 9. We went to see <u>Sue</u> in the hospital.

They 10. <u>Megan and Barb</u> played tennis.

26

Answer Key

Soar Like Eagles

Name_____

Verbs are words that show action. Find and underline the verb in each sentence.

1. Eagles <u>soar</u> among the mountain's cliffs.
2. From tree to tree, a monkey <u>swings</u>.
3. A caterpillar <u>wriggles</u> out of its old skin.
4. Porpoises <u>dive</u> through the ocean spray.
5. Snakes <u>slither</u> on the hot desert sand.
6. Prairie dogs <u>burrow</u> in underground holes.
7. Deer <u>leap</u> through open fields.
8. Woodpeckers <u>drill</u> holes in hollow trees.

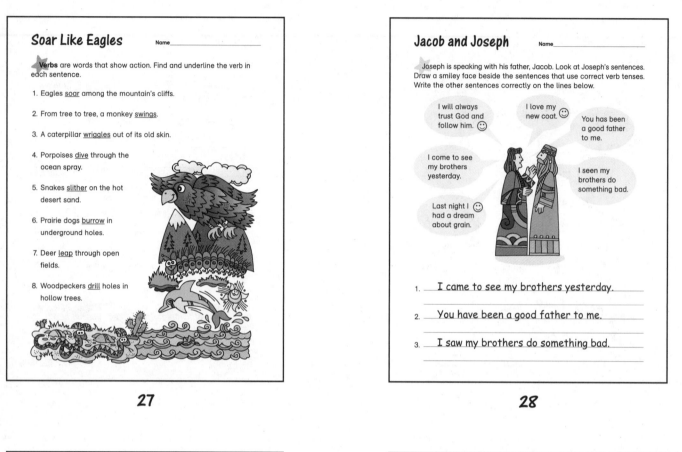

27

Jacob and Joseph

Name_____

Joseph is speaking with his father, Jacob. Look at Joseph's sentences. Draw a smiley face beside the sentences that use correct verb tenses. Write the other sentences correctly on the lines below.

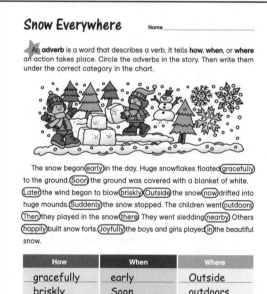

- I will always trust God and follow him. ☺
- I love my new coat. ☺
- You has been a good father to me.
- I come to see my brothers yesterday.
- I seen my brothers do something bad.
- Last night I ☺ had a dream about grain.

1. _I came to see my brothers yesterday._
2. _You have been a good father to me._
3. _I saw my brothers do something bad._

28

Spiders

Name_____

To help explore God's world of spiders, Mrs. Cline's third grade class had an outdoor science lab. Afterwards, the class wrote about their experience and posted the results near the science table. The children used past tense verbs in each sentence. Find and underline each past tense verb. Then write the verbs in the puzzle boxes below.

1. We <u>went</u> on a nature walk.
2. We <u>searched</u> for spider webs.
3. We <u>viewed</u> the webs through magnifying glasses.
4. We <u>looked</u> for bugs in the webs.
5. The spiders <u>caught</u> many bugs.
6. We <u>took</u> photographs of the spider webs.
7. We <u>shared</u> information about spiders with each other.
8. We <u>wrote</u> about spiders and their webs.
9. Mrs. Cline <u>mounted</u> our photos and writing on the bulletin board.
10. We <u>enjoyed</u> our study of spider webs.

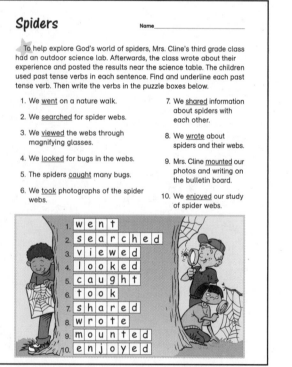

1. w e n t
2. s e a r c h e d
3. v i e w e d
4. l o o k e d
5. c a u g h t
6. t o o k
7. s h a r e d
8. w r o t e
9. m o u n t e d
10. e n j o y e d

29

Snow Everywhere

Name_____

An **adverb** is a word that describes a verb. It tells **how**, **when**, or **where** an action takes place. Circle the adverbs in the story. Then write them under the correct category in the chart.

The snow began (early) in the day. Huge snowflakes floated (gracefully) to the ground. (Soon) the ground was covered with a blanket of white. (Later) the wind began to blow (briskly) (Outside) the snow (now) drifted into huge mounds. (Suddenly) the snow stopped. The children went (outdoors) (Then) they played in the snow (there) They went sledding (nearby) Others (happily) built snow forts. (Joyfully) the boys and girls played (in) the beautiful snow.

How	When	Where
gracefully	early	Outside
briskly	Soon	outdoors
Suddenly	Later	there
happily	now	nearby
Joyfully	Then	in

30

Answer Key

Habits and Habitats

Name_____

A sentence is a group of words that tells a complete thought. Write **yes** if the group of words make a sentence and write **no** if they do not. Punctuate the groups of words that are sentences.

__no__ 1. The rain-drenched forest

__yes__ 2. Mountain goats can climb steep cliffs.

__yes__ 3. Sharks never stop swimming.

__no__ 4. Migrate to lower areas

__yes__ 5. God created all types of animals.

__no__ 6. Leave in the winter

__yes__ 7. Insects reside all over the world.

__no__ 8. Favorite nighttime activity

__yes__ 9. Backyards attract many animals.

__no__ 10. Burrow in the ground

__no__ 11. Spinning silken webs

__yes__ 12. Oceans are miles deep in some places.

31

A Trip to the Circus

Name_____

Some people use their special gifts by performing in the circus! Draw a line from the **subject** (peanut) to the **predicate** (elephant) that makes a complete sentence.

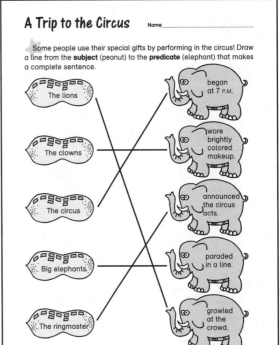

The lions — growled at the crowd.
The clowns — wore brightly colored makeup.
The circus — began at 7 P.M.
Big elephants — paraded in a line.
The ringmaster — announced the circus acts.

32

Pet Parade

Name_____

Circle the 19 words in the story that need to begin with a capital letter.

Remember:
1. All special names for people, places, and things begin with a capital letter. Don't forget that "I" is a special name, too.
2. The first word of a sentence always begins with a capital letter.

(I) took my dog, (max,) to a parade for pets. (there) we met lots of other pets and their owners. (sammy's) pet monkey, (kong,) held onto (sammy's) neck. (rachel) walked with her pet kitten named (fluffy.) (freddie's) frog, (hopalong,) jumped beside him. (even) (sara) came with her pet snake, (slinky.) (each) pet owner thought his or her pet was the best.

(the) other children asked me why (max) was wearing a watch. (I) told them that (max) is a "watch dog." (they) smiled as they looked at my little dog.

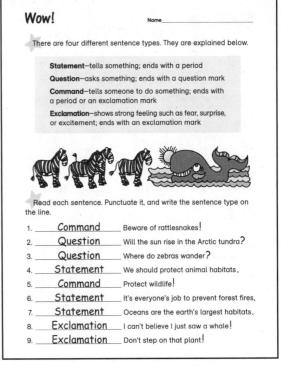

33

Wow!

Name_____

There are four different sentence types. They are explained below.

Statement—tells something; ends with a period
Question—asks something; ends with a question mark
Command—tells someone to do something; ends with a period or an exclamation mark
Exclamation—shows strong feeling such as fear, surprise, or excitement; ends with an exclamation mark

Read each sentence. Punctuate it, and write the sentence type on the line.

1. __Command__ Beware of rattlesnakes!
2. __Question__ Will the sun rise in the Arctic tundra?
3. __Question__ Where do zebras wander?
4. __Statement__ We should protect animal habitats.
5. __Command__ Protect wildlife!
6. __Statement__ It's everyone's job to prevent forest fires.
7. __Statement__ Oceans are the earth's largest habitats.
8. __Exclamation__ I can't believe I just saw a whale!
9. __Exclamation__ Don't step on that plant!

34

293

Answer Key

Calling All Commas

Name_____

Commas are used to make the meaning of a sentence clearer. Use commas to separate a series of three or more words. Place the last comma just before the word *and*. Rewrite each sentence and add commas where they are needed.

1. In the stable, Mary saw hay cows and sheep.

   In the stable, Mary saw hay, cows, and sheep.

2. In Sunday school, we studied Matthew Mark Luke and John.

   In Sunday school, we studied Matthew, Mark, Luke, and John.

3. Kindergartners used scissors magazines and glue to create collages.

   Kindergartners used scissors, magazines, and glue to create collages.

4. The fourth grade made Christian symbol pins cards and magnets.

   The fourth grade made Christian symbol pins, cards, and magnets.

5. The second grade's mosaics featured fish doves and crosses.

   The second grade's mosaics featured fish, doves, and crosses.

6. The Praise Band sang played instruments and prayed.

   The Praise Band sang, played instruments, and prayed.

7. The Bible tells us to love trust and obey.

   The Bible tells us to love, trust, and obey.

35

Protect Our Oceans

Name_____

Read Jamie's letter to the editor. Help him by adding punctuation marks and capitals. (To capitalize a letter, draw three lines under it.) Then circle the six words that are misspelled and write them correctly on the numbered lines.

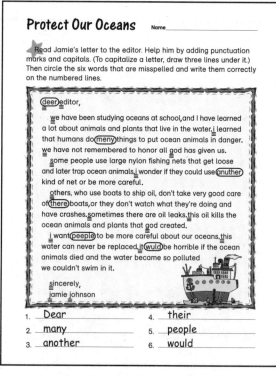

dear editor,

we have been studying oceans at school, and I have learned a lot about animals and plants that live in the water. i learned that humans do meny things to put ocean animals in danger. we have not remembered to honor all god has given us.

some people use large nylon fishing nets that get loose and later trap ocean animals. i wonder if they could use anuther kind of net or be more careful.

others, who use boats to ship oil, don't take very good care of there boats, or they don't watch what they're doing and have crashes. sometimes there are oil leaks. this oil kills the ocean animals and plants that god created.

i want peeple to be more careful about our oceans. this water can never be replaced. it wuld be horrible if the ocean animals died and the water became so polluted we couldn't swim in it.

sincerely,
jamie johnson

1. Dear   4. their
2. many   5. people
3. another   6. would

36

Dear Grandma

Name_____

Letters require correct spelling, capitalization, and punctuation. Help Mark correct his letter by placing capital letters where they belong and adding any necessary punctuation. (To capitalize a letter, draw three lines under it.) Then circle the six words that are misspelled and write the words correctly on the lines below the letter.

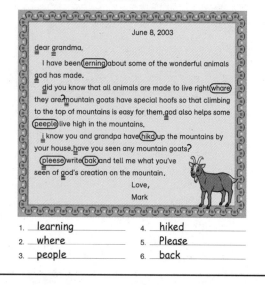

June 8, 2003

dear grandma,

I have been lerning about some of the wonderful animals god has made.

did you know that all animals are made to live right whare they are? mountain goats have special hoofs so that climbing to the top of mountains is easy for them. god also helps some peeple live high in the mountains.

i know you and grandpa have hikd up the mountains by your house. have you seen any mountain goats? pleese write bak and tell me what you've seen of god's creation on the mountain.

Love,
Mark

1. learning   4. hiked
2. where   5. Please
3. people   6. back

37

A Whale of a Tale

Name_____

Jonah had quite a story to tell his friends. If the pair of words on the whale rhyme, color the whale. If the words do not rhyme, put an **X** on the whale.

38

294

Answer Key

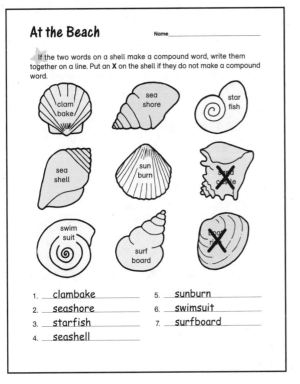

At the Beach

Name_____

If the two words on a shell make a compound word, write them together on a line. Put an **X** on the shell if they do not make a compound word.

1. clambake
2. seashore
3. starfish
4. seashell
5. sunburn
6. swimsuit
7. surfboard

39

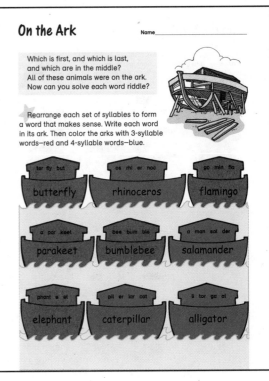

On the Ark

Name_____

Which is first, and which is last, and which are in the middle? All of these animals were on the ark. Now can you solve each word riddle?

Rearrange each set of syllables to form a word that makes sense. Write each word in its ark. Then color the arks with 3-syllable words—red and 4-syllable words—blue.

butterfly   rhinoceros   flamingo

parakeet   bumblebee   salamander

elephant   caterpillar   alligator

40

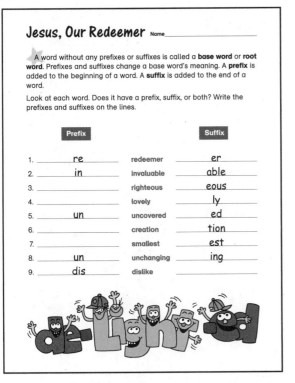

Jesus, Our Redeemer

Name_____

A word without any prefixes or suffixes is called a **base word** or **root word**. Prefixes and suffixes change a base word's meaning. A **prefix** is added to the beginning of a word. A **suffix** is added to the end of a word.

Look at each word. Does it have a prefix, suffix, or both? Write the prefixes and suffixes on the lines.

Prefix		Suffix
1. re	redeemer	er
2. in	invaluable	able
3.	righteous	eous
4.	lovely	ly
5. un	uncovered	ed
6.	creation	tion
7.	smallest	est
8. un	unchanging	ing
9. dis	dislike	

41

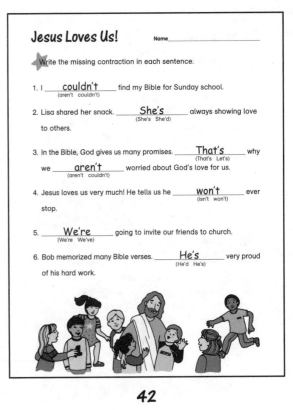

Jesus Loves Us!

Name_____

Write the missing contraction in each sentence.

1. I ___couldn't___ find my Bible for Sunday school.
   (aren't couldn't)

2. Lisa shared her snack. ___She's___ always showing love to others.
   (She's She'd)

3. In the Bible, God gives us many promises. ___That's___ why we ___aren't___ worried about God's love for us.
   (That's Let's) (aren't couldn't)

4. Jesus loves us very much! He tells us he ___won't___ ever stop.
   (isn't won't)

5. ___We're___ going to invite our friends to church.
   (We're We've)

6. Bob memorized many Bible verses. ___He's___ very proud of his hard work.
   (He'd He's)

42

295

Answer Key

Find the Twins

Name_____

Even though twins may look identical, God made each twin unique. Words that have the same meaning are **synonyms**. Think of them as twins. Using the words in the Word Bank, find each pair of synonyms and write them on the box below the twin.

Word Bank

weary	watch	present	evening
gift	tired	night	observe
hurt	tale	injured	fable

1. weary / tired
2. gift / present
3. hurt / injured
4. watch / observe
5. tale / fable
6. night / evening

43

Go to the Ant!

Name_____

Words that have opposite meanings are **antonyms**. Find the matching antonym for each word listed under the anthills. Then draw the correct number of ants on each anthill to show the number of the matching antonym.

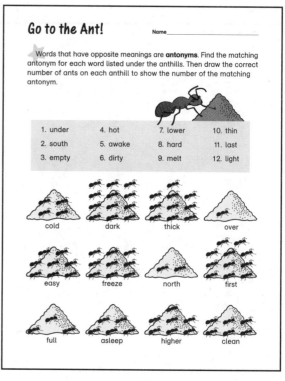

1. under	4. hot	7. lower	10. thin
2. south	5. awake	8. hard	11. last
3. empty	6. dirty	9. melt	12. light

cold   dark   thick   over

easy   freeze   north   first

full   asleep   higher   clean

44

Prickly Cactus

Name_____

Antonyms are words with opposite meanings. Write each word from the Word Bank next to its antonym.

Word Bank

difficult	moist	day
chilly	dull	largest

1. dry — moist
2. smallest — largest
3. sharp — dull
4. night — day
5. easy — difficult
6. warm — chilly

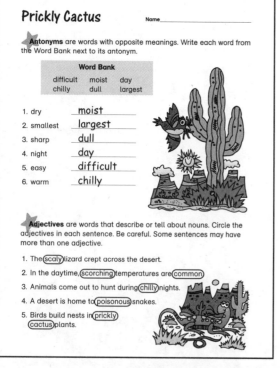

Adjectives are words that describe or tell about nouns. Circle the adjectives in each sentence. Be careful. Some sentences may have more than one adjective.

1. The (scaly) lizard crept across the desert.
2. In the daytime, (scorching) temperatures are (common)
3. Animals come out to hunt during (chilly) nights.
4. A desert is home to (poisonous) snakes.
5. Birds build nests in (prickly) (cactus) plants.

45

Baby Talk

Name_____

Did you know that God loved you before you were even born? Read the sentences describing some baby animals. Then write each baby animal's name under its picture.

1. An elephant has a baby **calf**.
2. The **tadpole** looks very different from its mother, a frog. Its tail helps it swim.
3. A **kid** eats lots of things, just as grown-up goats do.
4. A mother bear takes care of its **cub**.
5. A **piglet** says, "Oink."
6. This **colt** is white with black stripes.

kid   cub   colt

calf   tadpole   piglet

46

Answer Key

Two for One

Name_____

⭐ Some words have more than one meaning. Look at each pair of pictures. Unscramble the word that can be used for both pictures.

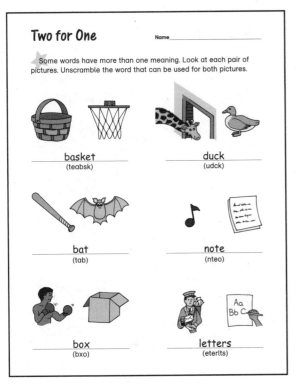

basket
(teabsk)

duck
(udck)

bat
(tab)

note
(nteo)

box
(bxo)

letters
(eterlts)

47

Ask, Seek, Knock

Name_____

⭐ Fill in the missing words from the Bible verse below. Use the words in the Word Bank to help you.

Word Bank			
seek	knock	ask	open

Jesus said,

"_A_ _s_ _k_ and it will be given to you;

_s_ _e_ _e_ _k_ and you will find;

_k_ _n_ _o_ _c_ _k_

and the door will be

_o_ _p_ _e_ _n_ to you."

Matthew 7:7 NIV

48

That's a Pizza!

Name_____

Papa Luigi was having a bad day. He forgot to order some things that he used to make his very special pizza. Then he asked Jesus to help him have a good day anyway.

A man walked into the restaurant. "I'd like to order your 'Papa Luigi's Pizza Supremo,'" he stated.

"I'm sorry, but I do not have all of the toppings," explained Papa Luigi. "However, I can make you a large surprise pizza at a special price of $5.00."

"Okay, I'll try it," said the man.

Luigi had a great day. He sold lots of "surprise pizzas"!

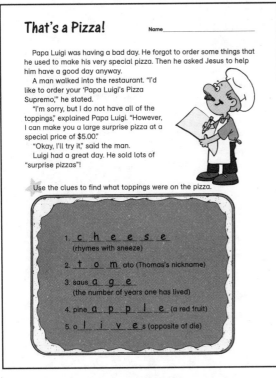

Use the clues to find what toppings were on the pizza.

1. _c_ _h_ _e_ _e_ _s_ _e_
   (rhymes with sneeze)

2. _t_ _o_ _m_ ato (Thomas's nickname)

3. saus _a_ _g_ _e_
   (the number of years one has lived)

4. pine _a_ _p_ _p_ _l_ _e_ (a red fruit)

5. o _l_ _i_ _v_ _e_ s (opposite of die)

49

Jesus Said . . .

Name_____

⭐ Jesus taught us many things about how we should live as his followers. Some of his teachings are listed here, but important words are missing. Fill in the blanks to complete the ideas using the words from the Word Bank. If you need a clue, you will find the answers in the verses listed at the bottom of the page.

Word Bank				
always	forgiven	hearts	money	clothes
judge	neighbor	forgive	judged	others

1. "Love your ___neighbor___ as yourself."

2. "You cannot serve both God and ___money___."

3. "Why do you worry about ___clothes___?"

4. "Do not let your ___hearts___ be troubled. Trust in God; trust also in me."

5. "Do not ___judge___, or you too will be ___judged___."

6. "___Forgive___, and you will be ___forgiven___."

7. "Do to ___others___ as you would have them do to you."

8. "And surely I am with you ___always___, to the very end of the age."

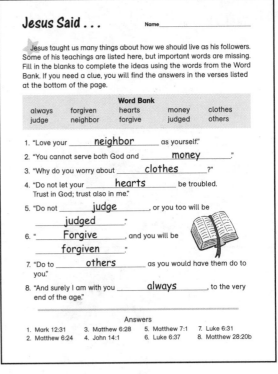

Answers

1. Mark 12:31	3. Matthew 6:28	5. Matthew 7:1	7. Luke 6:31
2. Matthew 6:24	4. John 14:1	6. Luke 6:37	8. Matthew 28:20b

50

Answer Key

Danger!

Name_____

Read the news release below. Then use the words from the Word Bank to fill in the blanks.

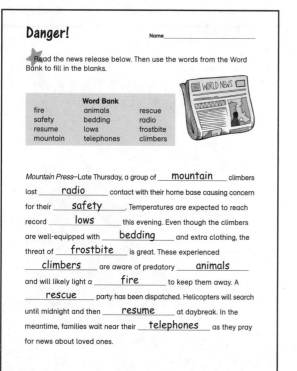

Word Bank

fire	animals	rescue
safety	bedding	radio
resume	lows	frostbite
mountain	telephones	climbers

Mountain Press–Late Thursday, a group of ___mountain___ climbers lost ___radio___ contact with their home base causing concern for their ___safety___. Temperatures are expected to reach record ___lows___ this evening. Even though the climbers are well-equipped with ___bedding___ and extra clothing, the threat of ___frostbite___ is great. These experienced ___climbers___ are aware of predatory ___animals___ and will likely light a ___fire___ to keep them away. A ___rescue___ party has been dispatched. Helicopters will search until midnight and then ___resume___ at daybreak. In the meantime, families wait near their ___telephones___ as they pray for news about loved ones.

51

Picture Gallery

Name_____

Each Bible verse below is missing a word(s). Look at the pictures below each verse. Choose the picture that fits in the verse. Write the word represented by the picture on the line.

1. The prophet Jeremiah went to a potter's house. He saw the potter working at a ___wheel___. (Jeremiah 18:3)

2. Jesus told his disciples: "You are the ___light___ of the world." (Matthew 5:14)

3. In the Parable of the Lost Son, the older brother complained that his father had never given him even a ___kid (goat)___ so he could celebrate with his friends. (Luke 15:28–29)

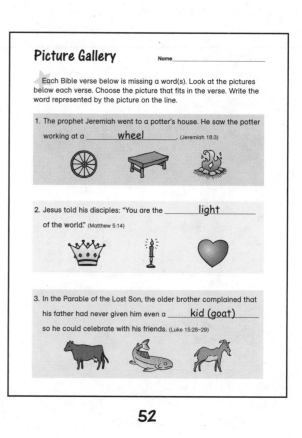

52

Seekers

Name_____

Fill in the missing words from the Bible verse below. Use the words in the Word Bank to help you.

Word Bank

love	those	seek	find

I ___love___ those who love me.

And ___those___ who ___seek___

me ___find___ me.

(Proverbs 8:17)

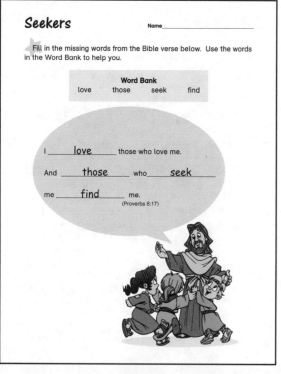

53

Marine Life

Name_____

In each blank, write a word from the paragraph below that matches the meaning given in parentheses.

The ocean contains a huge variety of marine life. Millions of tiny plantlike organisms and animals called plankton live near the ocean's surface because they need sunlight to make food. Plankton, which can be so small you need a microscope to see them, are eaten by large animals. Blue whales devour up to two tons a day. Another ocean plant, seaweed, is used as shelter for many animals and is eaten by animals and humans. Some ocean animals, such as the sponge, look like plants.

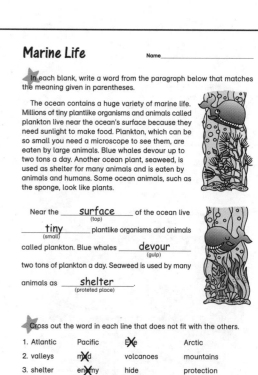

Near the ___surface___ of the ocean live
(top)

___tiny___ plantlike organisms and animals
(small)

called plankton. Blue whales ___devour___
(gulp)

two tons of plankton a day. Seaweed is used by many

animals as ___shelter___.
(proteted place)

Cross out the word in each line that does not fit with the others.

1. Atlantic   Pacific   ~~Erie~~   Arctic
2. valleys   ~~mud~~   volcanoes   mountains
3. shelter   ~~enemy~~   hide   protection

54

298

Answer Key

Back to School

Name_____

Write the missing words. Use words from the Word Bank.

Word Bank

summer	sit	work
new	happy	teacher
prayed	shoes	sleep

My dress is _____**new**_____, and so are my tennis
_____**shoes**_____. This year I get to _____**sit**_____ at a big
desk. I hope that the _____**work**_____ is not too hard. I
_____**prayed**_____ that my _____**teacher**_____ at school is nice.
Last night I could hardly _____**sleep**_____. I got bored during the
_____**summer**_____. So I am really _____**happy**_____ to be going
back to school today!

Read the questions. Underline the correct answers.

1. Who is talking?
   the teacher   <u>a girl</u>   her mother

2. How does she feel?
   <u>glad</u>   sad   lonely

3. When does she go back to school?
   tomorrow   next week   <u>today</u>

55

African Animals

Name_____

Read the paragraph below. Then, using words from the Word Bank,
write a word on each line that matches the meaning given in parentheses.

Word Bank

escape	disappearing	tropical	feed
herds	grazing	offer	quickly

In the grasslands of Africa, _____**herds**_____ of
(large groups)
_____**grazing**_____ animals number more than one million. The
(grass-eating)
_____**tropical**_____ climate is part of God's plan. It provides grass
(hot, muggy)
to _____**feed**_____ the animals. Animals that live in the grasslands
(provide food)
move _____**quickly**_____ to _____**escape**_____ predators.
(fast)   (get away from)
Grasslands are _____**disappearing**_____ as houses and farms take over
(vanishing)
the land. God wants us to _____**offer**_____ animals places to live,
(give)
or they too will disappear.

Choose two of the words from the Word Bank above and use each
one in a sentence.   sample answers:

1. I feed my cat and dog every day.

2. I saw cows grazing at my uncle's farm.

56

Mountain Life

Name_____

Read the paragraph below. Then, using words from the Word Bank,
write a word on each line that matches the meaning given in parentheses.

Word Bank

survive	grip	hibernate	valuable
raise	farm	patches	

God helps animals and people _____**survive**_____ in the mountains.
(manage to live)
He created mountain goats with hoofs that _____**grip**_____ steep
(take hold of)
cliffs. He made North American marmots _____**hibernate**_____ in
(sleep all winter)
underground burrows. People who live in mountain villages
_____**raise**_____ animals and _____**farm**_____ on small
(take care of)   (plant vegetables and grain)
_____**patches**_____ of land. Other people mine _____**valuable**_____
(areas)   (of great worth)
resources.

Alphabetize these mountain words.

1. eagles, sheep, marmots, goats
   eagles
   goats
   marmots
   sheep

2. peaks, predators, prey, plants
   peaks
   plants
   predators
   prey

57

Silly Sandwiches

Name_____

Do you think Jesus ate silly sandwiches when he was little? Write the
foods used in each sandwich in alphabetical order.

nuts
pickles
ham
1. ham
2. nuts
3. pickles

cheese
bananas
liver
1. bananas
2. cheese
3. liver

beans
popcorn
noodles
1. beans
2. noodles
3. popcorn

peas
cookies
beef
1. beef
2. cookies
3. peas

fish
pretzels
lettuce
1. fish
2. lettuce
3. pretzels

candy
olives
apples
1. apples
2. candy
3. olives

58

Answer Key

In Your Cupboard

Name_____

Many spices and flavorings come from the rainforest. Put their names, found in the Word Bank, in alphabetical order.

Word Bank

paprika	chili pepper	black pepper	cardamom
cocoa	cinnamon	cloves	ginger
vanilla	allspice	nutmeg	cayenne

1. allspice
2. black pepper
3. cardamom
4. cayenne
5. chili pepper
6. cinnamon
7. cloves
8. cocoa
9. ginger
10. nutmeg
11. paprika
12. vanilla

Dictionary pronunciations help you learn how to say words correctly. Match the pronunciation to the appropriate word.

1. kĭ-ĕn´ — cardamom
2. pĕp´ ər — cayenne
3. kar´də-məm — pepper
4. pă-prē´ kə — paprika

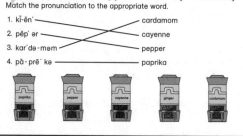

59

God's Awesome Plan

Name_____

Dictionary **guide words** indicate the first and last words on a dictionary page. Show where to look for each word from the Word Bank by writing it on the line beside the correct guide words.

Word Bank

| desert | protection | survive | created |
| scaly | cactus | dunes | predators |

1. save	scamp	scaly
2. surprise	suspender	survive
3. crank	creative	created
4. preach	prefix	predators
5. caboose	cake	cactus
6. describe	desk	desert
7. dump	dwarf	dunes
8. prose	proud	protection

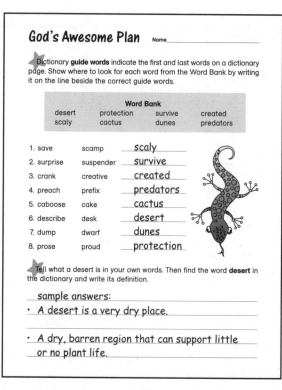

Tell what a desert is in your own words. Then find the word **desert** in the dictionary and write its definition.

sample answers:
- A desert is a very dry place.

- A dry, barren region that can support little or no plant life.

60

Galloping Gazelles

Name_____

Dictionary **guide words** indicate the first and last words on a dictionary page. Show where to look for each word from the Word Bank by writing it on the line beside the correct guide words.

Word Bank

gazelle	giraffes
antelope	grasslands
pummel	release
rodents	rabbits

1. another	antic	antelope
2. pulley	punch	pummel
3. rocket	romp	rodents
4. gill	give	giraffes
5. gather	general	gazelle
6. relate	relic	release
7. grasp	gravy	grasslands
8. rabbi	radar	rabbits

61

Match the Stories

Name_____

Match the people from the Bible with the correct picture.

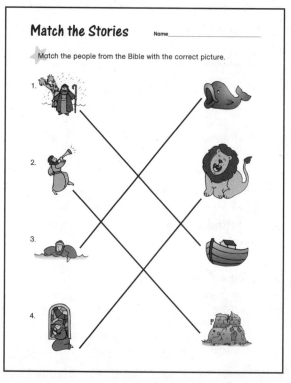

62

Answer Key

The Path

Name_____

Color the picture. Decode the rebus, then write the verse on the lines provided.

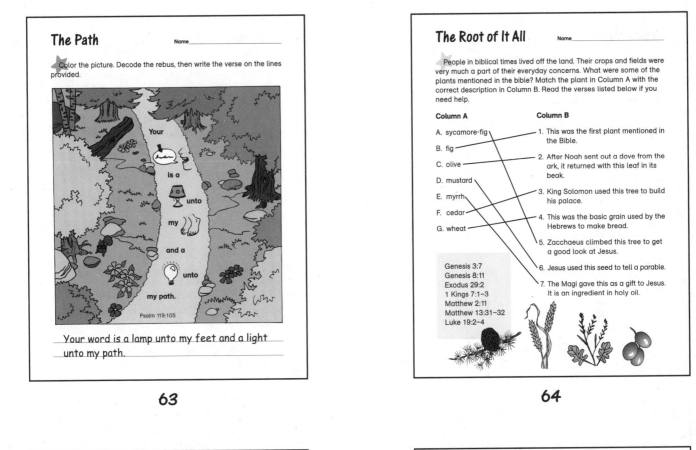

Your [lamp] is a [lamp] unto my [feet] and a [light] unto my path.

Psalm 119:105

Your word is a lamp unto my feet and a light unto my path.

63

The Root of It All

Name_____

People in biblical times lived off the land. Their crops and fields were very much a part of their everyday concerns. What were some of the plants mentioned in the bible? Match the plant in Column A with the correct description in Column B. Read the verses listed below if you need help.

Column A

A. sycamore-fig
B. fig
C. olive
D. mustard
E. myrrh
F. cedar
G. wheat

Column B

1. This was the first plant mentioned in the Bible.
2. After Noah sent out a dove from the ark, it returned with this leaf in its beak.
3. King Solomon used this tree to build his palace.
4. This was the basic grain used by the Hebrews to make bread.
5. Zacchaeus climbed this tree to get a good look at Jesus.
6. Jesus used this seed to tell a parable.
7. The Magi gave this as a gift to Jesus. It is an ingredient in holy oil.

Genesis 3:7
Genesis 8:11
Exodus 29:2
1 Kings 7:1–3
Matthew 2:11
Matthew 13:31–32
Luke 19:2–4

64

Up a Tree

Name_____

A short man wanted to see Jesus, so he climbed a tree. Do you know his name? Read about him in Luke 19:1–10. Then fill in the puzzle.

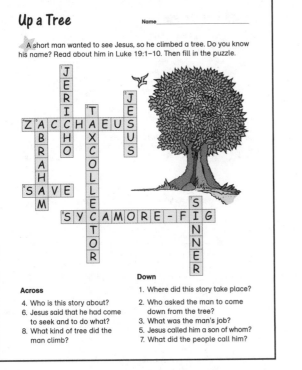

Crossword answers:
J E R I C H O
J E S U S
Z A C C H A E U S
T A X C O L L E C T O R
A B R A H A M
S A V E
S Y C A M O R E - F I G
S I N N E R

Across

4. Who is this story about?
6. Jesus said that he had come to seek and to do what?
8. What kind of tree did the man climb?

Down

1. Where did this story take place?
2. Who asked the man to come down from the tree?
3. What was the man's job?
5. Jesus called him a son of whom?
7. What did the people call him?

65

The Shape of Healing

Name_____

Jesus performed many healing miracles. The Gospel of Luke tells us about some of them. Five stories of healing are listed in the verses below. Read the stories. In each case, discover the illness or condition that Jesus healed. Write it inside the shape. How did the person(s) healed respond to the miracle? Write it on the lines below.

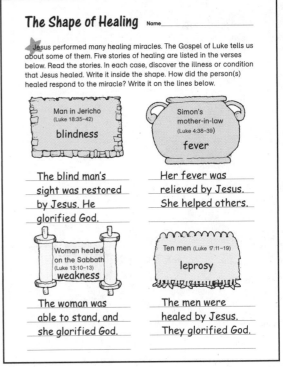

Man in Jericho (Luke 18:35–42)
blindness

The blind man's sight was restored by Jesus. He glorified God.

Simon's mother-in-law (Luke 4:38–39)
fever

Her fever was relieved by Jesus. She helped others.

Woman healed on the Sabbath (Luke 13:10–13)
weakness

The woman was able to stand, and she glorified God.

Ten men (Luke 17:11–19)
leprosy

The men were healed by Jesus. They glorified God.

66

Answer Key

True or False?

Name_____

Read the statements below and decide if they are true or false. Color the **T** red if the statement is true. Color the **F** orange if the statement is false. The Bible verses will give you the answers.

Bethlehem was the town where Jesus was born.
(Matthew 2:1–2) **T** F

Eden was a place where God planted a garden.
(Genesis 2:8) **T** F

Timothy helped Paul and was like a son to him.
(Philippians 1:1; 2:22) **T** F

Revelation is the last book of the Bible.
(Check your Bible's table of contents.) **T** F

Uz is where Job lived.
(Job 1:1) **T** F

Twelve disciples were chosen by Jesus.
(Matthew 10:1) **T** F

Hosea is a book in the New Testament.
(Check your Bible's table of contents.) T **F**

Friendliness is a "fruit of the Spirit."
(Galatians 5:22) T **F**

Ur was Abram's home.
(Genesis 11:31) **T** F

Lot's wife turned into a pillar of salt.
(Genesis 19:26) **T** F

67

What Was That?

Name_____

Read the story, then answer the questions below. Be sure to write your answers in complete sentences.

Kate and Nate walked by the old house. Windows were broken. The walls needed paint. Even the roof had a hole. No one had lived there for a long time. Suddenly Kate saw two big eyes at one window. Then they both heard a sound. It sounded like, "Boo!" The door swung open. Kate and Nate began to run. They looked back, and both children began to laugh. A cow stood in the doorway. It must have walked inside the open door in back.

1. By what did Kate and Nate walk? They walked by the old house.

2. What was wrong with the windows? The windows were broken.

3. What was wrong with the roof? The roof had a hole in it.

4. What did the children see in the window? They saw two big eyes in the window.

5. Why did they laugh? They laughed because they saw a cow in the doorway.

6. How did the cow get inside the house? The cow walked inside the open door in the back.

68

Do What?

Name_____

Draw and color silly pictures for the sentences below.

1. Draw and color two orange zebras with yellow stripes climbing into the ark.

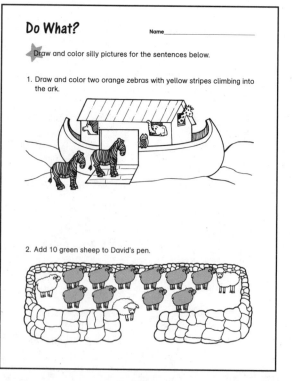

2. Add 10 green sheep to David's pen.

69

Love at First Croak

Name_____

A little, green frog sat alone on a rock in the pond. "I wish I had a friend," he prayed quietly.

Soon a big butterfly flew down to the pond. She landed on a lily pad.

"She is very pretty and can fly," thought the frog.

"Will you be my friend?" asked the butterfly.

"Me?" answered the frog. "I am so ugly. Why do you want to be my friend?"

"You can hop and make croaking sounds. I think you are cute!" she said.

The frog smiled and croaked loudly. He and the butterfly became good friends. The frog thanked God for his new friend.

Read the sentences below and draw a cartoon strip.

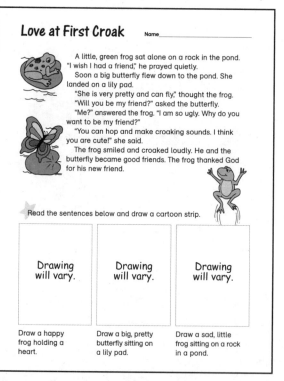

| Drawing will vary. | Drawing will vary. | Drawing will vary. |

Draw a happy frog holding a heart.

Draw a big, pretty butterfly sitting on a lily pad.

Draw a sad, little frog sitting on a rock in a pond.

70

Answer Key

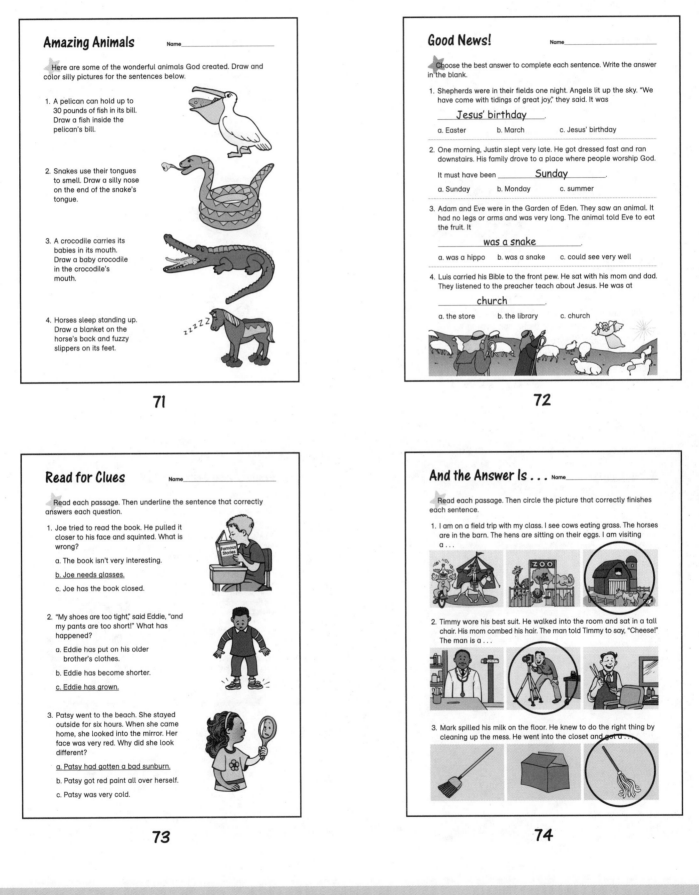

Amazing Animals
Name_____

Here are some of the wonderful animals God created. Draw and color silly pictures for the sentences below.

1. A pelican can hold up to 30 pounds of fish in its bill. Draw a fish inside the pelican's bill.

2. Snakes use their tongues to smell. Draw a silly nose on the end of the snake's tongue.

3. A crocodile carries its babies in its mouth. Draw a baby crocodile in the crocodile's mouth.

4. Horses sleep standing up. Draw a blanket on the horse's back and fuzzy slippers on its feet.

71

Good News!
Name_____

Choose the best answer to complete each sentence. Write the answer in the blank.

1. Shepherds were in their fields one night. Angels lit up the sky. "We have come with tidings of great joy," they said. It was

_____Jesus' birthday_____.

a. Easter   b. March   c. Jesus' birthday

2. One morning, Justin slept very late. He got dressed fast and ran downstairs. His family drove to a place where people worship God.

It must have been _____Sunday_____.

a. Sunday   b. Monday   c. summer

3. Adam and Eve were in the Garden of Eden. They saw an animal. It had no legs or arms and was very long. The animal told Eve to eat the fruit. It

_____was a snake_____.

a. was a hippo   b. was a snake   c. could see very well

4. Luis carried his Bible to the front pew. He sat with his mom and dad. They listened to the preacher teach about Jesus. He was at

_____church_____.

a. the store   b. the library   c. church

72

Read for Clues
Name_____

Read each passage. Then underline the sentence that correctly answers each question.

1. Joe tried to read the book. He pulled it closer to his face and squinted. What is wrong?

a. The book isn't very interesting.

b. Joe needs glasses.

c. Joe has the book closed.

2. "My shoes are too tight," said Eddie, "and my pants are too short!" What has happened?

a. Eddie has put on his older brother's clothes.

b. Eddie has become shorter.

c. Eddie has grown.

3. Patsy went to the beach. She stayed outside for six hours. When she came home, she looked into the mirror. Her face was very red. Why did she look different?

a. Patsy had gotten a bad sunburn.

b. Patsy got red paint all over herself.

c. Patsy was very cold.

73

And the Answer Is . . .
Name_____

Read each passage. Then circle the picture that correctly finishes each sentence.

1. I am on a field trip with my class. I see cows eating grass. The horses are in the barn. The hens are sitting on their eggs. I am visiting a . . .

2. Timmy wore his best suit. He walked into the room and sat in a tall chair. His mom combed his hair. The man told Timmy to say, "Cheese!" The man is a . . .

3. Mark spilled his milk on the floor. He knew to do the right thing by cleaning up the mess. He went into the closet and got a . . .

74

Answer Key

Mountain Climbing

Name_____

⭐ Read each sentence below. Write whether it is fact (**F**) or opinion (**O**).

1. ___O___ Mountains are great places to live.
2. ___F___ Goats have gripping hoofs to help them climb mountains.
3. ___F___ It is harder to breathe at the top of a mountain than at its base.
4. ___O___ Mountain climbers are foolish.
5. ___F___ Valuable rocks and minerals are found in mountains.

⭐ Circle the word that does not belong in each list.

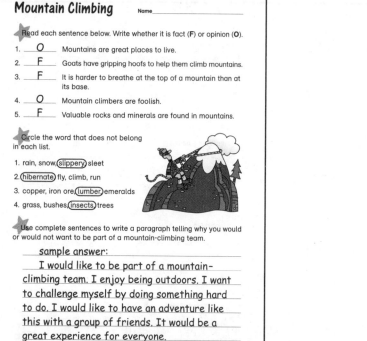

1. rain, snow, (slippery) sleet
2. (hibernate) fly, climb, run
3. copper, iron ore, (lumber,) emeralds
4. grass, bushes, (insects) trees

⭐ Use complete sentences to write a paragraph telling why you would or would not want to be part of a mountain-climbing team.

sample answer:
    I would like to be part of a mountain-climbing team. I enjoy being outdoors. I want to challenge myself by doing something hard to do. I would like to have an adventure like this with a group of friends. It would be a great experience for everyone.

75

Time to Eat!

Name_____

⭐ Are you hungry? If you want to try something different, go to an Arab wedding in the desert. Here is a recipe for a special wedding meal.

1. Cook some eggs.
2. Stuff the eggs into fish.
3. Put the fish inside cooked chickens.
4. Place the chickens into a roasted sheep.
5. Set the sheep inside a whole camel and roast.
6. Enjoy!

Show the recipe order by numbering the ingredients from 1 to 5.

5   1   4

3   2

76

R-r-r-r-ring!

Name_____

⭐ Read the passage, then number the pictures 1, 2, 3, 4, and 5 in order.

The alarm clock rang loudly. Cathy jumped out of bed. She pulled on her clothes and then ran down the steps. She thanked God for her food and ate breakfast. Then she brushed her teeth. When Mom told Cathy that school was cancelled, she moaned. Then she thought of all the fun things she could do.

1   4

3   2

5

77

Emily's Zoo Trip

Name_____

⭐ The order of events in a story is called its **sequence**. Read the passage below. Then number the events listed at the bottom of the page. Look back at the story as you number the events in order.

Emily woke up early and thanked Jesus that it was a beautiful, sunny day. Until now, Emily had only seen zoo animals in books. Today she would visit the zoo with her family.

Emily burst through the zoo gates at 10 A.M., just as the zoo opened. She was eager to visit every display. First she saw the Siberian tigers and the leopards. Emily loved the size of those cats. Next she watched the zookeeper feed three elephants. Then, just before stopping at the Snack Shack for lunch, Emily and her family went to the petting zoo where they fed and touched a variety of barnyard animals.

In the afternoon, Emily saw monkeys, zebras, and giraffes. It was one of the best days Emily could ever remember! That night she thanked God for all the animals she had seen.

___3___ Emily visited the tigers and leopards.
___5___ She visited the petting zoo.
___2___ Emily's family arrived at the zoo at 10 A.M.
___4___ The zookeeper fed the elephants.
___6___ They had lunch at the Snack Shack.
___1___ Emily was excited. She would visit the zoo today.
___7___ She visited the monkeys, zebras, and giraffes.

78

Answer Key

Rainforest Trivia

Name_____

Paraphrasing is stating the same information in new words. Writers use this skill all the time. Read the numbered sentences below and check (✔) the line for the best paraphrase of each statement.

1. Plants thrive in the rainforest.
   - ✔ In the rainforest, plants grow fast and well.
   - ____ Plants grow slowly in the rainforest.

2. Rainforest plants and trees provide many spices, fruits, and vegetables.
   - ____ Grocery stores get supplies from the rainforest.
   - ✔ Rainforests are a source of good foods.

3. About a third of South America is covered by tropical rainforests.
   - ✔ A lot of rainforests are located in South America.
   - ____ South America has many pine forests.

4. The temperature in the rainforest is near 75° Fahrenheit year round.
   - ✔ It is warm all year in the rainforest.
   - ____ Rainforests are hot or cold depending on the rain.

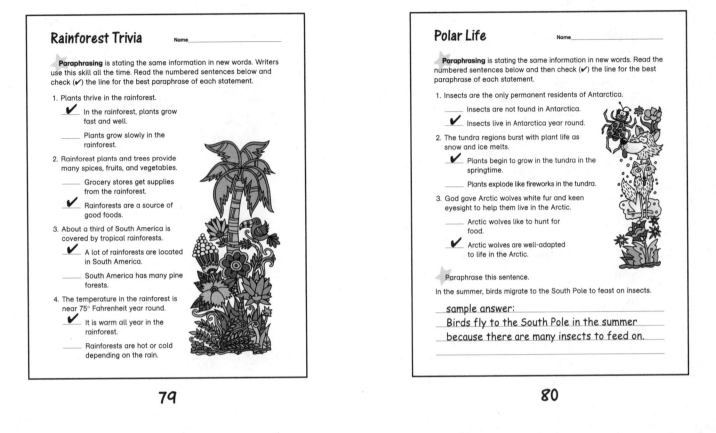

79

Polar Life

Name_____

Paraphrasing is stating the same information in new words. Read the numbered sentences below and then check (✔) the line for the best paraphrase of each statement.

1. Insects are the only permanent residents of Antarctica.
   - ____ Insects are not found in Antarctica.
   - ✔ Insects live in Antarctica year round.

2. The tundra regions burst with plant life as snow and ice melts.
   - ✔ Plants begin to grow in the tundra in the springtime.
   - ____ Plants explode like fireworks in the tundra.

3. God gave Arctic wolves white fur and keen eyesight to help them live in the Arctic.
   - ____ Arctic wolves like to hunt for food.
   - ✔ Arctic wolves are well-adapted to life in the Arctic.

Paraphrase this sentence.

In the summer, birds migrate to the South Pole to feast on insects.

sample answer:
Birds fly to the South Pole in the summer because there are many insects to feed on.

80

Nathan's Backyard

Name_____

Read about Nathan and his backyard. Then complete the story map.

The sky was overcast and gloomy outside Nathan's window. He watched a pair of robins who lived in the maple tree beside his window. He thought of how God cared for them.

For days, the pair of birds had been carrying twigs, string, and grasses to build a nest. Nathan was very thankful he could watch as he kept a close eye on the birds to see what they would do next.

As Nathan watched, the cloudy weather quickly changed to a storm. The old maple tree swayed in the forceful wind. Soon Nathan heard thunder and saw a bolt of lightning dart across the sky and strike the maple tree. All Nathan could think about was the pair of robins and their nest. He prayed that God would protect them and keep them safe.

The storm lasted nearly an hour before Nathan could rush outside to the shattered maple tree. Among the fallen branches, he found the nest. With his father's help, Nathan placed the nest in another tree. He hoped the robins would continue to call the nest home.

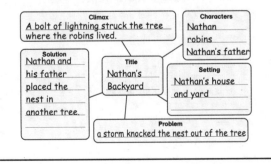

Climax
A bolt of lightning struck the tree where the robins lived.

Characters
Nathan
robins
Nathan's father

Solution
Nathan and his father placed the nest in another tree.

Title
Nathan's Backyard

Setting
Nathan's house and yard

Problem
a storm knocked the nest out of the tree

81

Animal Riddles

Name_____

Imagine all the animals that rode on the ark. Use the animal names in the Word Bank to help you answer the animal riddles below.

Word Bank					
tiger	penguin	snake	monkey	cheetah	elephant

1. I am large and have no fur. My skin is gray and wrinkled. I eat plants and spray myself with my trunk. What animal am I?
   elephant

2. I'm a mammal whose furry coat is covered with spots. I'm known for how fast I can run. I'm a member of the cat family. What animal am I?
   cheetah

3. I am a reptile. My skin is cool and scaly. I am long and slender. I slither on the ground and in trees. What animal am I?
   snake

4. I am covered with a soft, striped fur coat. I live in India and Siberia. My children are called cubs. I am a member of the cat family. What animal am I?
   tiger

5. I have a long, thin tail and am covered with fur. I'm an excellent climber. I can swing from the branches of trees by my tail, hands, or feet. What animal am I?
   monkey

6. I am black and white. I am happy on land or in the water. I cannot fly, but I can swim. My babies hatch from eggs. What animal am I?
   penguin

82

Answer Key

Animal Homes

Name_____

⭐ Look at the Table of Contents below and decide which chapter would contain each sentence listed below.

Table of Contents
Chapter 1 ....What Is an Animal Home?
Chapter 2 ....Homes of Mud
Chapter 3 ....Homes of Grass
Chapter 4 ....Homes of Sticks
Chapter 5 ....Tree Homes
Chapter 6 ....Warrens and Burrows

1. __Chapter 2__   Wasps collect pellets of wet mud that they mold into a ribbon of mud to create nests.

2. __Chapter 4__   Beavers make lodges of sticks and twigs piled on top of one another. These lodges have two or more underwater entrances.

3. __Chapter 1__   Animals build homes from surrounding materials.

4. __Chapter 3__   The harvest mouse builds the strongest grass nest of all.

5. __Chapter 6__   Rabbits build a system of linked burrows that have many different entrances.

83

It's in the Book

Name_____

⭐ Use the table of contents below to help answer the questions.

Table of Contents
Chapter 1 ....Layers of Plant Growth in the Rainforest
Chapter 2 ....Rainfall Records
Chapter 3 ....Critters That Crawl, Climb, and Fly
Chapter 4 ....Rubber and Other Valuable Products
Chapter 5 ....Good Eating in the Rainforest

1. __Chapter 1__   You have been asked to write a report on vegetation in the rainforest. Which chapter will likely have this information?

2. __Chapter 5__   To learn where cashew nuts are found, where should you look?

3. __Chapter 1__   From floor to sky, you must explain the growth of plants and trees in the rainforest. Which chapter, do you think, has this information?

4. __Chapter 3__   With a partner, you must compare animals of the rainforest with those of the desert. Where can you find which animals live in the rainforest?

84

My Pen Pal

Name_____

⭐ Read the passage below, then complete the sentences that follow.

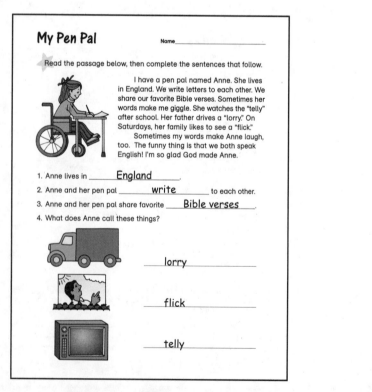

I have a pen pal named Anne. She lives in England. We write letters to each other. We share our favorite Bible verses. Sometimes her words make me giggle. She watches the "telly" after school. Her father drives a "lorry." On Saturdays, her family likes to see a "flick."

Sometimes my words make Anne laugh, too. The funny thing is that we both speak English! I'm so glad God made Anne.

1. Anne lives in __England__.
2. Anne and her pen pal __write__ to each other.
3. Anne and her pen pal share favorite __Bible verses__.
4. What does Anne call these things?

lorry

flick

telly

85

Love One Another

Name_____

⭐ The bible shows us how we should treat one another. What do the three ideas below mean to you: Write your answers in the boxes.

Serve one another. (Galations 5:13)
sample answer:
This idea means that people should help one another and that people should be kind to one another.

Honor one another. (Romans 12:10)
sample answer:
This idea means that people should respect each other.

Instruct one another (Romans 15:14)
sample answer:
This idea means that people can learn from one another.

86

Answer Key

Look Who's Talking

Name_____

Read what each child is saying. Then write in the correct name to complete each sentence below.

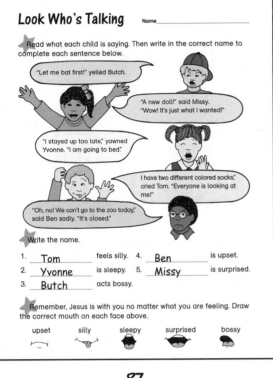

"Let me bat first!" yelled Butch.

"A new doll!" said Missy. "Wow! It's just what I wanted!"

"I stayed up too late," yawned Yvonne. "I am going to bed."

"I have two different colored socks," cried Tom. "Everyone is looking at me!"

"Oh, no! We can't go to the zoo today," said Ben sadly. "It's closed."

Write the name.

1. **Tom** feels silly.   4. **Ben** is upset.
2. **Yvonne** is sleepy.   5. **Missy** is surprised.
3. **Butch** acts bossy.

Remember, Jesus is with you no matter what you are feeling. Draw the correct mouth on each face above.

upset   silly   sleepy   surprised   bossy

87

Who Said It?

Name_____

God made each animal special. Draw a line from the animal to what it might say.

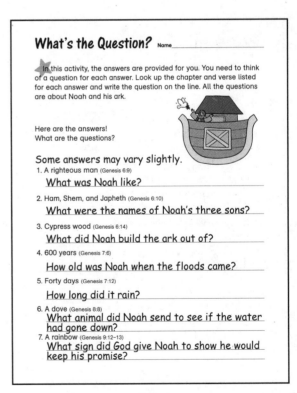

"I live in the forest. Some day I may grow antlers."

"I live in the ocean and have sharp teeth."

"I hop on lily pads in a pond with my webbed feet."

"I save lots of bones and bury them in the yard."

"I slither on the ground because I have no arms or legs."

88

Design It!

Name_____

Most people like to be outdoors enjoying nature. Design a T-shirt that expresses your feelings about the world that God has created for us.

Drawing will vary.

"In the beginning God created the heavens and the earth"

(Genesis 1:1).

89

What's the Question?

Name_____

In this activity, the answers are provided for you. You need to think of a question for each answer. Look up the chapter and verse listed for each answer and write the question on the line. All the questions are about Noah and his ark.

Here are the answers! What are the questions?

Some answers may vary slightly.

1. A righteous man (Genesis 6:9)
   What was Noah like?

2. Ham, Shem, and Japheth (Genesis 6:10)
   What were the names of Noah's three sons?

3. Cypress wood (Genesis 6:14)
   What did Noah build the ark out of?

4. 600 years (Genesis 7:6)
   How old was Noah when the floods came?

5. Forty days (Genesis 7:12)
   How long did it rain?

6. A dove (Genesis 8:8)
   What animal did Noah send to see if the water had gone down?

7. A rainbow (Genesis 9:12–13)
   What sign did God give Noah to show he would keep his promise?

90

Answer Key

God's World

Name_____

Draw a picture in the globe that illustrates the verse at the bottom of the page.

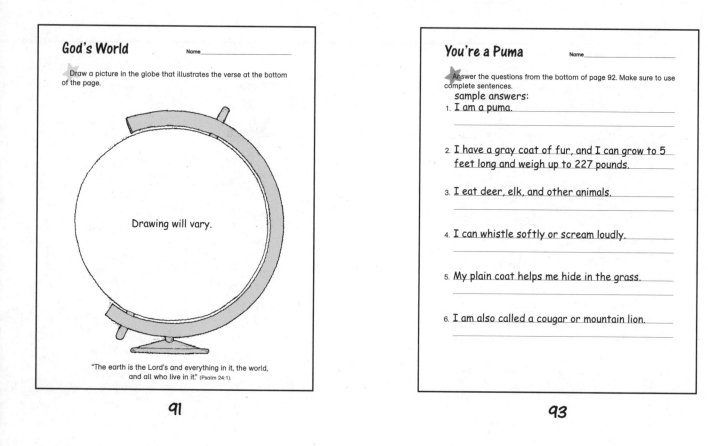

Drawing will vary.

"The earth is the Lord's and everything in it, the world, and all who live in it." (Psalm 24:1).

91

You're a Puma

Name_____

Answer the questions from the bottom of page 92. Make sure to use complete sentences.

sample answers:

1. I am a puma.

2. I have a gray coat of fur, and I can grow to 5 feet long and weigh up to 227 pounds.

3. I eat deer, elk, and other animals.

4. I can whistle softly or scream loudly.

5. My plain coat helps me hide in the grass.

6. I am also called a cougar or mountain lion.

93

Creative Writing

Name_____

Choose a title from the list below. Then write and illustrate a story.

Titles

My Day with Jesus   What Would Jesus Do If . . .
I Was on the Ark   In the Desert

Stories will vary.
Check your child's work for:
– proper punctuation and grammar
– correct spelling
– correct capitalizations
– sentences that relate to the topic and make sense

Illustrations will vary.

94

Dear Noah

Name_____

The ark is crowded, smelly, and damp. The animals got together to talk about how to improve it. Pretend you are one of the animals. Write your letter to Noah below.

Dear _____,
Letters will vary.
Check your child's work for:
– proper punctuation and grammar
– correct spelling
– correct capitalizations
– sentences that relate to the topic and make sense
Also make sure your child included the date, greeting, and closing.

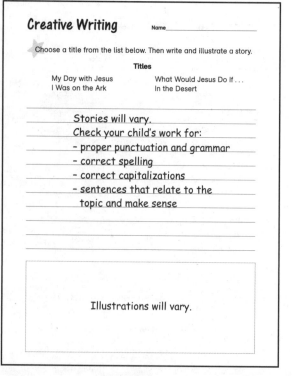

95

Answer Key

Lydia's Ads
Name_____

Lydia was a merchant who sold purple cloth. People who sell products need to advertise. Help Lydia sell her cloth by creating two ads for her. Design a sign in the frame below that she could have used outside a shop. Then create an ad for a flyer she could give to people as they passed. Use your imagination. Read about her in Acts 16:13–15.

> Answers will vary.
> Check your child's work for:
> – proper punctuation and grammar
> – correct spelling
> – correct capitalization
> – sentences that relate to the ad that make sense

96

The Big Story
Name_____

Imagine that you were living during the time of Jesus and were a reporter for the local paper, *The Jerusalem Times*. Your job is to report on the miracle that occurred at Siloam. Read the story in John 9:1–12. Then write your "eye-witness" account of what happened in the space below.

The Jerusalem Times
Miracle at the Pool of Siloam

> Stories will vary.
> Check your child's work for:
> – proper punctuation and grammar
> – correct spelling
> – correct capitalizations
> – sentences that relate to the topic and make sense

97

Cyber Mail
Name_____

Today, we send e-mail messages to people all over the world using our computers and the Internet. Imagine that you could e-mail people who lived in biblical times. Read about Mary Magdalene and John the Baptist in the verses below. Then write them a note on the lines under their imaginary e-mail addresses. What would you like to say to them or ask them about their experiences?

marymagdalene@newtestament.com (John 20:1–18)

> Answers will vary.
> Check your child's work for:
> – proper punctuation and grammar
> – correct spelling
> – correct capitalizations
> – sentences that relate to the topic and make sense

johnthebaptist@newtestament.com (Matthew 3:1–17)

98

In Your Mind's Eye
Name_____

Choose one of your favorite Bible verses. Think about how you could illustrate it. How you illustrate it is all in your mind's eye. Draw your illustration in the light bulb below.

The verse says: Answers will vary.

> Encourage your child to describe his or her drawing to you and ask him or her to tell you why he or she chose the above verse.

99

Answer Key

God's Promise

Name_____

God gave us a promise that He will never flood the earth again. Connect the dots and discover the beautiful image of God's promise.

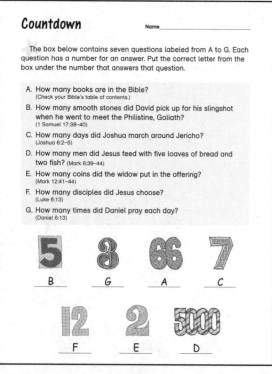

103

In the Beginning

Name_____

God created the world in six days. Each day's creation is pictured. What did God create on each of the days? Read Genesis 1, and then label each picture with the correct day.

fish and birds — Day 5

day and night — Day 1

sun, moon, and stars — Day 4

trees and plants — Day 3

water and sky — Day 2

animals and people — Day 6

104

Countdown

Name_____

The box below contains seven questions labeled from A to G. Each question has a number for an answer. Put the correct letter from the box under the number that answers that question.

A. How many books are in the Bible?
(Check your Bible's table of contents.)

B. How many smooth stones did David pick up for his slingshot when he went to meet the Philistine, Goliath?
(1 Samuel 17:38–40)

C. How many days did Joshua march around Jericho?
(Joshua 6:2–5)

D. How many men did Jesus feed with five loaves of bread and two fish? (Mark 6:39–44)

E. How many coins did the widow put in the offering?
(Mark 12:41–44)

F. How many disciples did Jesus choose?
(Luke 6:13)

G. How many times did Daniel pray each day?
(Daniel 6:13)

5 — B

3 — G

66 — A

7 — C

12 — F

2 — E

5000 — D

105

Words to Count On

Name_____

Draw a line from each numeral to the matching number word.

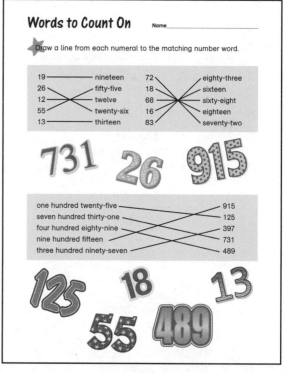

19 — nineteen	72 — eighty-three
26 — fifty-five	18 — sixteen
12 — twelve	68 — sixty-eight
55 — twenty-six	16 — eighteen
13 — thirteen	83 — seventy-two

one hundred twenty-five — 125
seven hundred thirty-one — 731
four hundred eighty-nine — 489
nine hundred fifteen — 915
three hundred ninety-seven — 397

106

Answer Key

How Many Candles?

Name_____

What is the age of each person listed on this cake? Read the Bible verses if you need help.

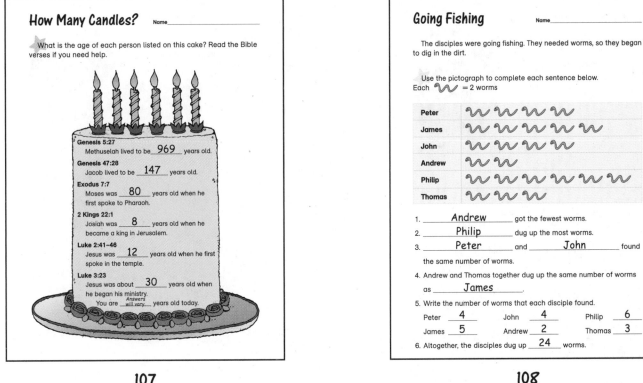

Genesis 5:27
Methuselah lived to be __969__ years old.

Genesis 47:28
Jacob lived to be __147__ years old.

Exodus 7:7
Moses was __80__ years old when he first spoke to Pharaoh.

2 Kings 22:1
Josiah was __8__ years old when he became a king in Jerusalem.

Luke 2:41-46
Jesus was __12__ years old when he first spoke in the temple.

Luke 3:23
Jesus was about __30__ years old when he began his ministry.
You are __Answers will vary__ years old today.

107

Going Fishing

Name_____

The disciples were going fishing. They needed worms, so they began to dig in the dirt.

Use the pictograph to complete each sentence below.
Each 〰 = 2 worms

Peter	〰 〰 〰 〰
James	〰 〰 〰 〰 〰
John	〰 〰 〰 〰
Andrew	〰 〰
Philip	〰 〰 〰 〰 〰 〰
Thomas	〰 〰 〰

1. _____Andrew_____ got the fewest worms.
2. _____Philip_____ dug up the most worms.
3. _____Peter_____ and _____John_____ found the same number of worms.
4. Andrew and Thomas together dug up the same number of worms as _____James_____.
5. Write the number of worms that each disciple found.

Peter __4__   John __4__   Philip __6__
James __5__   Andrew __2__   Thomas __3__

6. Altogether, the disciples dug up __24__ worms.

108

Fundraiser

Name_____

One way to take care of God's world is to recycle. The third-grade classrooms at Valleywood School collected 2-liter soda bottles to help fund a field trip. Each bottle could be returned to the store for a 10-cent refund. This pictograph shows the number of bottles collected by each class. Each 🍶 = 5.

Teacher	Bottles Collected	Total
Townsend	🍶🍶🍶🍶🍶🍶🍶🍶🍶🍶🍶🍶	60
Parks	🍶🍶🍶🍶🍶🍶🍶	35
Beach	🍶🍶🍶🍶🍶🍶🍶🍶🍶	45
Williams	🍶🍶🍶🍶🍶🍶🍶🍶	40
DeGroot	🍶🍶🍶🍶🍶🍶	30
Blue	🍶🍶🍶🍶🍶🍶🍶🍶	40

Count by fives to find out how many bottles each class collected. Fill in the totals on the chart.

1. How many bottles did the third grade collect altogether? __250__

2. Whose class was able to contribute the most money toward the field trip? _____Townsend_____ How much? __$6.00__

3. Whose class contributed the least? __DeGroot__ How much? __$3.00__

4. The third-grade classes needed a total of $20 in order to take their field trip. Did they earn enough money? __yes__

109

Chew on This!

Name_____

God made your jaw bones strong. Color the gumballs with **even** numbers **purple**. Color the gumballs with **odd** numbers **green**.

Remember: Even numbers end with 0, 2, 4, 6, and 8.
Odd numbers end with 1, 3, 5, 7, and 9.

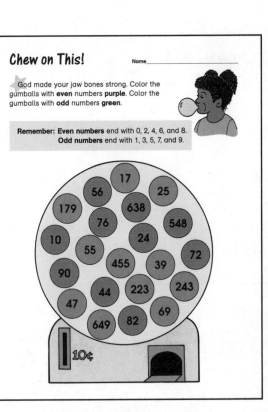

110

Answer Key

Exercise in Addition

Name_____

Solve these problems.

$\begin{array}{r} 4 \\ +2 \\ \hline 6 \end{array}$ E $\begin{array}{r} 0 \\ +0 \\ \hline 0 \end{array}$ S $\begin{array}{r} 2 \\ +2 \\ \hline 4 \end{array}$ M

$\begin{array}{r} 5 \\ +3 \\ \hline 8 \end{array}$ I $\begin{array}{r} 1 \\ +2 \\ \hline 3 \end{array}$ D $\begin{array}{r} 1 \\ +1 \\ \hline 2 \end{array}$ O

$\begin{array}{r} 8 \\ +2 \\ \hline 10 \end{array}$ N $\begin{array}{r} 4 \\ +3 \\ \hline 7 \end{array}$ H $\begin{array}{r} 0 \\ +1 \\ \hline 1 \end{array}$ G $\begin{array}{r} 3 \\ +2 \\ \hline 5 \end{array}$ A $\begin{array}{r} 2 \\ +7 \\ \hline 9 \end{array}$ W

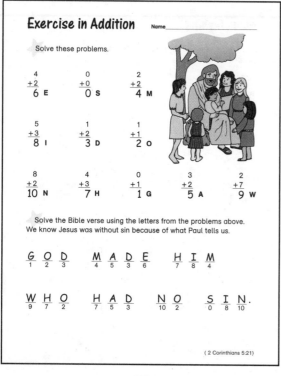

Solve the Bible verse using the letters from the problems above.
We know Jesus was without sin because of what Paul tells us.

G O D   M A D E   H I M
1 2 3   4 5 3 6   7 8 4

W H O   H A D   N O   S I N .
9 7 2   7 5 3   10 2   0 8 10

(2 Corinthians 5:21)

111

Forgive Each Other

Name_____

How many times should we forgive others?
Write the answers on the hearts.

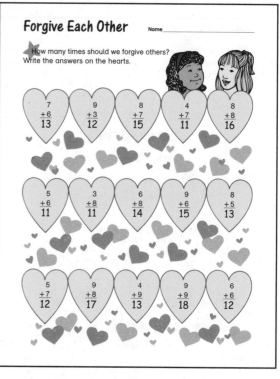

$\begin{array}{r} 7 \\ +6 \\ \hline 13 \end{array}$ $\begin{array}{r} 9 \\ +3 \\ \hline 12 \end{array}$ $\begin{array}{r} 8 \\ +7 \\ \hline 15 \end{array}$ $\begin{array}{r} 4 \\ +7 \\ \hline 11 \end{array}$ $\begin{array}{r} 8 \\ +8 \\ \hline 16 \end{array}$

$\begin{array}{r} 5 \\ +6 \\ \hline 11 \end{array}$ $\begin{array}{r} 3 \\ +8 \\ \hline 11 \end{array}$ $\begin{array}{r} 6 \\ +8 \\ \hline 14 \end{array}$ $\begin{array}{r} 9 \\ +6 \\ \hline 15 \end{array}$ $\begin{array}{r} 8 \\ +5 \\ \hline 13 \end{array}$

$\begin{array}{r} 5 \\ +7 \\ \hline 12 \end{array}$ $\begin{array}{r} 9 \\ +8 \\ \hline 17 \end{array}$ $\begin{array}{r} 4 \\ +9 \\ \hline 13 \end{array}$ $\begin{array}{r} 9 \\ +9 \\ \hline 18 \end{array}$ $\begin{array}{r} 6 \\ +6 \\ \hline 12 \end{array}$

112

Run the Race

Name_____

How far can the runner go in one minute? Write the answers.
After one minute, circle where you are. Then finish the page.

$\begin{array}{r} 2 \\ +8 \\ \hline 10 \end{array}$ $\begin{array}{r} 7 \\ +9 \\ \hline 16 \end{array}$ $\begin{array}{r} 8 \\ +1 \\ \hline 9 \end{array}$ $\begin{array}{r} 9 \\ +4 \\ \hline 13 \end{array}$ $\begin{array}{r} 6 \\ +6 \\ \hline 12 \end{array}$ $\begin{array}{r} 1 \\ +2 \\ \hline 3 \end{array}$

$\begin{array}{r} 8 \\ +5 \\ \hline 13 \end{array}$ $\begin{array}{r} 4 \\ +4 \\ \hline 8 \end{array}$ $\begin{array}{r} 6 \\ +3 \\ \hline 9 \end{array}$ $\begin{array}{r} 7 \\ +3 \\ \hline 10 \end{array}$ $\begin{array}{r} 5 \\ +6 \\ \hline 11 \end{array}$ $\begin{array}{r} 7 \\ +8 \\ \hline 15 \end{array}$

$\begin{array}{r} 7 \\ +6 \\ \hline 13 \end{array}$ $\begin{array}{r} 7 \\ +7 \\ \hline 14 \end{array}$ $\begin{array}{r} 3 \\ +4 \\ \hline 7 \end{array}$ $\begin{array}{r} 8 \\ +6 \\ \hline 14 \end{array}$ $\begin{array}{r} 2 \\ +2 \\ \hline 4 \end{array}$ $\begin{array}{r} 5 \\ +7 \\ \hline 12 \end{array}$

$\begin{array}{r} 0 \\ +0 \\ \hline 0 \end{array}$ $\begin{array}{r} 6 \\ +8 \\ \hline 14 \end{array}$ $\begin{array}{r} 8 \\ +8 \\ \hline 16 \end{array}$ $\begin{array}{r} 3 \\ +4 \\ \hline 7 \end{array}$ $\begin{array}{r} 5 \\ +9 \\ \hline 14 \end{array}$ $\begin{array}{r} 4 \\ +2 \\ \hline 6 \end{array}$

$\begin{array}{r} 9 \\ +9 \\ \hline 18 \end{array}$ $\begin{array}{r} 6 \\ +4 \\ \hline 10 \end{array}$ $\begin{array}{r} 3 \\ +3 \\ \hline 6 \end{array}$ $\begin{array}{r} 8 \\ +9 \\ \hline 17 \end{array}$ $\begin{array}{r} 5 \\ +5 \\ \hline 10 \end{array}$ $\begin{array}{r} 2 \\ +3 \\ \hline 5 \end{array}$

Paul told us to "run in such a way as to
get the prize" (1 Corinthians 9:24)

113

Angels

Name_____

Add the numbers in each problem. Then decode
the verse using the letters from the problems.

A 3 + 2 = 5		H 5 + 2 = 7		R 4 + 2 = 6	
C 2 + 1 = 3		I 8 + 7 = 15		S 9 + 7 = 16	
D 7 + 3 = 10		L 5 + 4 = 9		T 7 + 7 = 14	
E 6 + 5 = 11		M 6 + 6 = 12		U 1 + 1 = 2	
F 9 + 9 = 18		N 8 + 5 = 13		W 8 + 9 = 17	
G 4 + 4 = 8		O 2 + 2 = 4		Y 1 + 0 = 1	

Verse

F O R   H E   W I L L
18 4 6   7 11   17 15 9 9

C O M M A N D   H I S
3 4 12 12 5 13 10   7 15 16

A N G E L S
5 13 8 11 9 16

C O N C E R N I N G
3 4 13 3 11 6 13 15 13 8

Y O U   T O   G U A R D
1 4 2   14 4   8 2 5 6 10

Y O U   I N   A L L
1 4 2   15 13   5 9 9

Y O U R   W A Y S ...
1 4 2 6   17 5 1 16

(Psalm 91:11 NIV)

114

Answer Key

The Missing Sheep

Name_____

An addend in each problem is missing. Write it in the lamb.

1	**8**	6 **3**	**5**
+ 7	+ 2	+	+ 5
8	10	9	10

6 **5**	**6**	8 **8**	9 **9**
+	+ 9	+	+
11	15	16	18

8 **9**	**6**	9 **3**	**7**
+	+ 8	+	+ 6
17	14	12	13

115

How Many Bees?

Name_____

Solve each problem to find the number of bees in each hive.

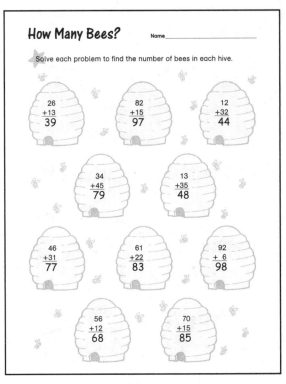

| 26 +13 **39** | 82 +15 **97** | 12 +32 **44** |

| 34 +45 **79** | 13 +35 **48** |

| 46 +31 **77** | 61 +22 **83** | 92 + 6 **98** |

| 56 +12 **68** | 70 +15 **85** |

116

Salvation

Name_____

Add 10 to each number. Write your answers on the lines. Then decode the verse using the letters next to your answers.

23	47	38	51	29	77	34	41
A **33**	B **57**	D **48**	E **61**	H **39**	I **87**	L **44**	N **51**

82	15	25	64	58	86	12	30
O **92**	P **25**	R **35**	S **74**	T **68**	V **96**	W **22**	Z **40**

Verse

"W H O E V E R
22 39 92 61 96 61 35

B E L I E V E S   A N D
57 61 44 87 61 96 61 74   33 51 48

I S   B A P T I Z E D
87 74   57 33 25 68 87 40 61 48

W I L L   B E
22 87 44 44   57 61

S A V E D ..."
74 33 96 61 48   (Psalm 91:11 NIV)

117

"Eggs"tra Work

Name_____

Tommy felt bad because he was always dropping eggs. His mom forgave him and told her she still loved him.

How many unbroken eggs were left in each carton? Finish each number sentence.

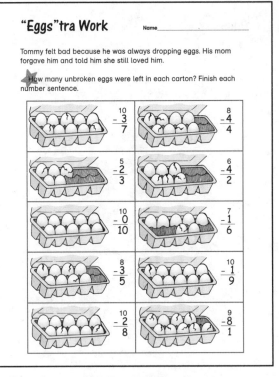

10 - 3 **7**	8 - 4 **4**
5 - 2 **3**	6 - 4 **2**
10 - 0 **10**	7 - 1 **6**
8 - 3 **5**	10 - 1 **9**
10 - 2 **8**	9 - 8 **1**

118

Answer Key

Like Pulling Teeth

Name_____

Draw the total number of teeth in each alligator's mouth. (This is the top number.) Then, color the number of lost teeth black. (This is the bottom number.) Last, write the number of teeth left. (This is the answer.)

Example:

$$\begin{array}{r} 13 \\ -\ 4 \\ \hline 9 \end{array}$$

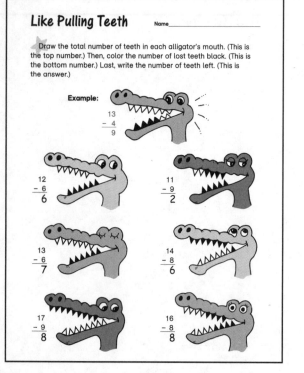

$$\begin{array}{r} 12 \\ -\ 6 \\ \hline 6 \end{array} \qquad \begin{array}{r} 11 \\ -\ 9 \\ \hline 2 \end{array}$$

$$\begin{array}{r} 13 \\ -\ 6 \\ \hline 7 \end{array} \qquad \begin{array}{r} 14 \\ -\ 8 \\ \hline 6 \end{array}$$

$$\begin{array}{r} 17 \\ -\ 9 \\ \hline 8 \end{array} \qquad \begin{array}{r} 16 \\ -\ 8 \\ \hline 8 \end{array}$$

119

The Race is On!

Name_____

How far can the jogger run in one minute? Write the answers. After one minute, circle where you are. Then finish the page.

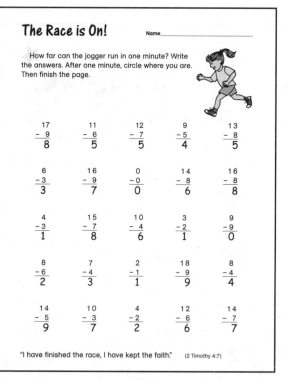

$$\begin{array}{r} 17 \\ -\ 9 \\ \hline 8 \end{array} \quad \begin{array}{r} 11 \\ -\ 6 \\ \hline 5 \end{array} \quad \begin{array}{r} 12 \\ -\ 7 \\ \hline 5 \end{array} \quad \begin{array}{r} 9 \\ -\ 5 \\ \hline 4 \end{array} \quad \begin{array}{r} 13 \\ -\ 8 \\ \hline 5 \end{array}$$

$$\begin{array}{r} 6 \\ -\ 3 \\ \hline 3 \end{array} \quad \begin{array}{r} 16 \\ -\ 9 \\ \hline 7 \end{array} \quad \begin{array}{r} 0 \\ -\ 0 \\ \hline 0 \end{array} \quad \begin{array}{r} 14 \\ -\ 8 \\ \hline 6 \end{array} \quad \begin{array}{r} 16 \\ -\ 8 \\ \hline 8 \end{array}$$

$$\begin{array}{r} 4 \\ -\ 3 \\ \hline 1 \end{array} \quad \begin{array}{r} 15 \\ -\ 7 \\ \hline 8 \end{array} \quad \begin{array}{r} 10 \\ -\ 4 \\ \hline 6 \end{array} \quad \begin{array}{r} 3 \\ -\ 2 \\ \hline 1 \end{array} \quad \begin{array}{r} 9 \\ -\ 9 \\ \hline 0 \end{array}$$

$$\begin{array}{r} 8 \\ -\ 6 \\ \hline 2 \end{array} \quad \begin{array}{r} 7 \\ -\ 4 \\ \hline 3 \end{array} \quad \begin{array}{r} 2 \\ -\ 1 \\ \hline 1 \end{array} \quad \begin{array}{r} 18 \\ -\ 9 \\ \hline 9 \end{array} \quad \begin{array}{r} 8 \\ -\ 4 \\ \hline 4 \end{array}$$

$$\begin{array}{r} 14 \\ -\ 5 \\ \hline 9 \end{array} \quad \begin{array}{r} 10 \\ -\ 3 \\ \hline 7 \end{array} \quad \begin{array}{r} 4 \\ -\ 2 \\ \hline 2 \end{array} \quad \begin{array}{r} 12 \\ -\ 6 \\ \hline 6 \end{array} \quad \begin{array}{r} 14 \\ -\ 7 \\ \hline 7 \end{array}$$

"I have finished the race, I have kept the faith." (2 Timothy 4:7)

120

Open Arms

Name_____

Cross out each heart that has the wrong answer.

$$\begin{array}{r} 26 \\ -15 \\ \hline 11 \end{array}$$

$$\begin{array}{r} 34 \\ -21 \\ \hline 13 \end{array}$$

$$\begin{array}{r} 53 \\ -10 \\ \hline 43 \end{array}$$

$$\begin{array}{r} \cancel{} \\ \cancel{-2} \\ \hline \cancel{54} \end{array} ✗$$

$$\begin{array}{r} 75 \\ -32 \\ \hline 43 \end{array}$$

$$\begin{array}{r} 38 \\ -18 \\ \hline 20 \end{array}$$

$$\begin{array}{r} \cancel{36} \\ \cancel{-23} \\ \hline \end{array} ✗$$

$$\begin{array}{r} 82 \\ -71 \\ \hline 11 \end{array}$$

$$\begin{array}{r} 66 \\ -35 \\ \hline 31 \end{array}$$

$$\begin{array}{r} 70 \\ -60 \\ \hline 10 \end{array}$$

$$\begin{array}{r} 84 \\ -11 \\ \hline 73 \end{array}$$

$$\begin{array}{r} \cancel{57} \\ \cancel{} \\ \hline \cancel{73} \end{array} ✗$$

121

Creation

Name_____

Subtract the numbers in each problem. Then decode the verse using the letters from the problems.

$$\begin{array}{r} 77 \\ -25 \\ \hline 52 \end{array} \text{A} \quad \begin{array}{r} 73 \\ -23 \\ \hline 50 \end{array} \text{D} \quad \begin{array}{r} 96 \\ -15 \\ \hline 81 \end{array} \text{H} \quad \begin{array}{r} 79 \\ -43 \\ \hline 36 \end{array} \text{O} \quad \begin{array}{r} 57 \\ -34 \\ \hline 23 \end{array} \text{T}$$

$$\begin{array}{r} 98 \\ -24 \\ \hline 74 \end{array} \text{B} \quad \begin{array}{r} 67 \\ -32 \\ \hline 35 \end{array} \text{E} \quad \begin{array}{r} 39 \\ -27 \\ \hline 12 \end{array} \text{I} \quad \begin{array}{r} 48 \\ -32 \\ \hline 16 \end{array} \text{R} \quad \begin{array}{r} 99 \\ -35 \\ \hline 64 \end{array} \text{V}$$

$$\begin{array}{r} 46 \\ -25 \\ \hline 21 \end{array} \text{C} \quad \begin{array}{r} 56 \\ -24 \\ \hline 32 \end{array} \text{G} \quad \begin{array}{r} 45 \\ -23 \\ \hline 22 \end{array} \text{N} \quad \begin{array}{r} 86 \\ -25 \\ \hline 61 \end{array} \text{S}$$

Verse

$$\underset{12}{I} \ \underset{22}{N} \qquad \underset{23}{T} \ \underset{81}{H} \ \underset{35}{E}$$

$$\underset{74}{B} \ \underset{35}{E} \ \underset{32}{G} \ \underset{12}{I} \ \underset{22}{N} \ \underset{22}{N} \ \underset{12}{I} \ \underset{22}{N} \ \underset{32}{G} \qquad \underset{32}{G} \ \underset{36}{O} \ \underset{50}{D}$$

$$\underset{21}{C} \ \underset{16}{R} \ \underset{35}{E} \ \underset{52}{A} \ \underset{23}{T} \ \underset{35}{E} \ \underset{50}{D} \qquad \underset{23}{T} \ \underset{81}{H} \ \underset{35}{E}$$

$$\underset{81}{H} \ \underset{35}{E} \ \underset{52}{A} \ \underset{64}{V} \ \underset{35}{E} \ \underset{22}{N} \ \underset{61}{S} \qquad \underset{52}{A} \ \underset{22}{N} \ \underset{50}{D}$$

$$\underset{23}{T} \ \underset{81}{H} \ \underset{35}{E} \qquad \underset{35}{E} \ \underset{52}{A} \ \underset{16}{R} \ \underset{23}{T} \ \underset{81}{H}. \qquad \text{(Genesis 1:1 NIV)}$$

122

Answer Key

King of Kings

Name_____

Who is the King of kings and Lord of lords? Add or subtract. Find out his name by coloring the spaces with answers greater than **12** red. Color the rest of the spaces blue.

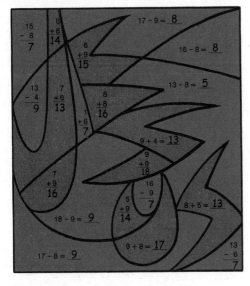

$15 - 8 = 7$ $6 + 8 = 14$ $17 - 9 = 8$

$6 + 9 = 15$ $16 - 8 = 8$

$13 - 4 = 9$ $7 + 6 = 13$ $8 + 8 = 16$ $13 - 8 = 5$

$1 + 6 = 7$

$9 + 4 = 13$

$9 + 9 = 18$

$7 + 9 = 16$ $16 - 9 = 7$

$5 + 9 = 14$ $8 + 5 = 13$

$18 - 9 = 9$

$17 - 8 = 9$ $9 + 8 = 17$ $13 - 6 = 7$

123

The Trumpet Blast

Name_____

Solve the problems on the wall. In the Book of Joshua, the priests blew the trumpets, and Joshua's army shouted. The walls of Jericho fell down.

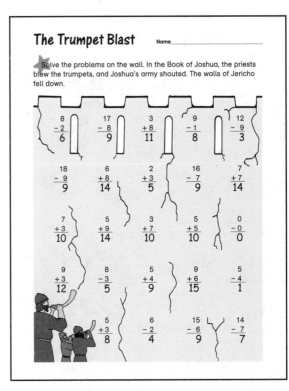

$8 - 2 = 6$ $17 - 8 = 9$ $3 + 8 = 11$ $9 - 1 = 8$ $12 - 9 = 3$

$18 - 9 = 9$ $6 + 8 = 14$ $2 + 3 = 5$ $16 - 7 = 9$ $7 + 7 = 14$

$7 + 3 = 10$ $5 + 9 = 14$ $3 + 7 = 10$ $5 + 5 = 10$ $0 - 0 = 0$

$9 + 3 = 12$ $8 - 3 = 5$ $5 + 4 = 9$ $9 + 6 = 15$ $5 - 4 = 1$

$5 + 3 = 8$ $6 - 2 = 4$ $15 - 6 = 9$ $14 - 7 = 7$

124

In the Desert

Name_____

How far will you get in one minute? Solve the problems in the desert. After one minute, circle where you are. Then finish the page.

$2 + 8 = 10$ $3 + 3 = 6$ $3 + 5 = 8$ $8 + 9 = 17$ $10 - 1 = 9$

$6 - 4 = 2$ $7 + 7 = 14$ $2 + 7 = 9$ $8 - 4 = 4$ $5 + 4 = 9$

$12 - 8 = 4$ $15 - 6 = 9$ $9 - 6 = 3$ $7 - 5 = 2$ $3 + 2 = 5$

$0 + 0 = 0$ $10 - 5 = 5$ $17 - 9 = 8$ $6 + 8 = 14$

$8 + 1 = 9$ $4 - 3 = 1$ $14 - 5 = 9$ $9 + 3 = 12$

125

Weather Wise

Name_____

Meg kept her class's weather chart for two months. Write a number sentence to solve each problem.

1. Meg counted 11 rainy days and 3 foggy days. How many fewer foggy days than rainy days were there?

   $11 - 8 =$ _____   3 days

2. There were 6 rainy days in one week and 3 in the next. How many rainy days were there in 2 weeks?

   $6 + 3 =$ _____   9 days

3. In one week, 5 of the days were snowy. How many days were not snowy?

   $7 - 5 =$ _____   2 days

4. Meg needed 12 stickers to put on the chart for sunny days. She only had 8. How many more stickers did she need?

   $12 - 8 =$ _____   4 days

5. There were 9 days when the temperature was 60° and 5 days when it was 50°. How many more days was the temperature 60°?

   $9 - 5 =$ _____   4 days

126

Answer Key

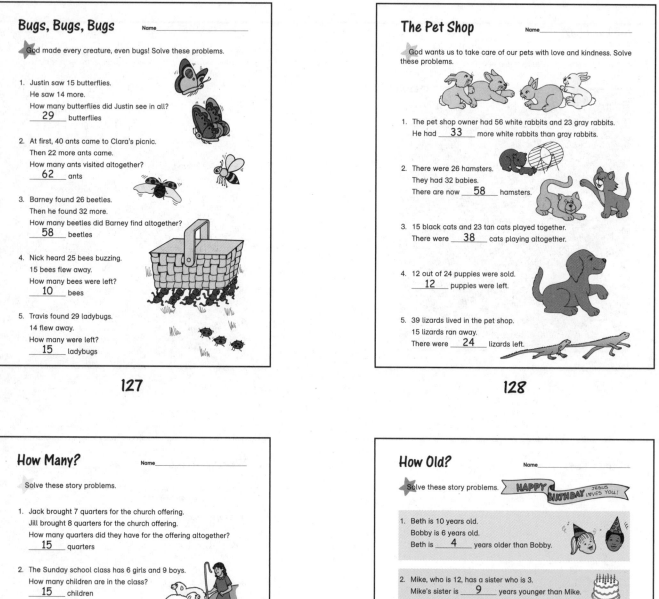

Bugs, Bugs, Bugs   Name_____

⭐ God made every creature, even bugs! Solve these problems.

1. Justin saw 15 butterflies.
   He saw 14 more.
   How many butterflies did Justin see in all?
   ___29___ butterflies

2. At first, 40 ants came to Clara's picnic.
   Then 22 more ants came.
   How many ants visited altogether?
   ___62___ ants

3. Barney found 26 beetles.
   Then he found 32 more.
   How many beetles did Barney find altogether?
   ___58___ beetles

4. Nick heard 25 bees buzzing.
   15 bees flew away.
   How many bees were left?
   ___10___ bees

5. Travis found 29 ladybugs.
   14 flew away.
   How many were left?
   ___15___ ladybugs

127

The Pet Shop   Name_____

⭐ God wants us to take care of our pets with love and kindness. Solve these problems.

1. The pet shop owner had 56 white rabbits and 23 gray rabbits.
   He had ___33___ more white rabbits than gray rabbits.

2. There were 26 hamsters.
   They had 32 babies.
   There are now ___58___ hamsters.

3. 15 black cats and 23 tan cats played together.
   There were ___38___ cats playing altogether.

4. 12 out of 24 puppies were sold.
   ___12___ puppies were left.

5. 39 lizards lived in the pet shop.
   15 lizards ran away.
   There were ___24___ lizards left.

128

How Many?   Name_____

⭐ Solve these story problems.

1. Jack brought 7 quarters for the church offering.
   Jill brought 8 quarters for the church offering.
   How many quarters did they have for the offering altogether?
   ___15___ quarters

2. The Sunday school class has 6 girls and 9 boys.
   How many children are in the class?
   ___15___ children

3. The shepherd had 14 sheep.
   He lost 6 of them.
   How many sheep were still in the pen?
   ___8___ sheep

4. Nancy first grew 9 roses and 2 lilies.
   Then she grew 5 daisies.
   How many flowers does she have altogether?
   ___16___ flowers

5. Mary lit 7 candles.
   Two candles burned out.
   How many candles were still lit?
   ___5___ candles

129

How Old?   Name_____

⭐ Solve these story problems. HAPPY BIRTHDAY JESUS LOVES YOU!

1. Beth is 10 years old.
   Bobby is 6 years old.
   Beth is ___4___ years older than Bobby.

2. Mike, who is 12, has a sister who is 3.
   Mike's sister is ___9___ years younger than Mike.

3. Sally and her twin brother are 8 years old today.
   They will need ___16___ candles altogether for two cakes.

4. It is Ben and Barb's birthday.
   Mom puts up balloons to show their ages.
   If Ben is 6 years old and Barb is 7 years old, Mom will need ___13___ balloons in all.

5. Kathy is 11 years old.
   Carla is 9 years old.
   Kathy is ___2___ years older than Carla.

130

Answer Key

How Many Hearts?   Name_____

Complete each number sentence by writing the number or symbol that is missing. Use small objects or draw pictures to help you solve the problems.

Example: 7 – __4__ = 3	✗✗✗✗ ♡ ♡ ♡

__5__ + 6 = 11	♡♡♡♡♡ ♡♡♡♡♡♡
7 + __6__ = 13	♡♡♡♡♡♡♡ ♡♡♡♡♡♡
4 + __4__ + 1 = 9	♡♡♡♡ ♡♡♡♡ ♡
5 __+__ 4 = 9	♡♡♡♡♡ ♡♡♡♡
__9__ + 5 = 14	♡♡♡♡♡♡♡♡♡ ♡♡♡♡♡
4 + __6__ + 3 = 13	♡♡♡♡ ♡♡♡♡♡♡ ♡♡♡
2 + __5__ + 2 = 9	♡♡ ♡♡♡♡♡ ♡♡
7 – __5__ = 2	✗✗✗✗✗ ♡ ♡
9 __–__ 3 = 6	✗✗✗ ♡ ♡ ♡ ♡ ♡ ♡
7 __–__ 6 = 1	✗✗✗✗✗✗ ♡

"Love the Lord your God with all your heart."   (Mark 12:30a)

131

The Shepherd's Staff   Name_____

Don't be led astray. Follow the numbers from left to right on each staff by adding and subtracting to reach the final answer.

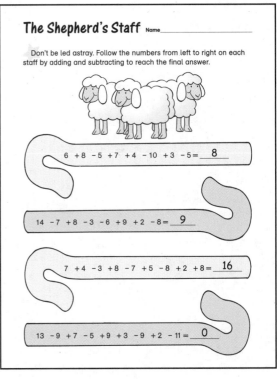

6 + 8 – 5 + 7 + 4 – 10 + 3 – 5 = __8__

14 – 7 + 8 – 3 – 6 + 9 + 2 – 8 = __9__

7 + 4 – 3 + 8 – 7 + 5 – 8 + 2 + 8 = __16__

13 – 9 + 7 – 5 + 9 + 3 – 9 + 2 – 11 = __0__

132

Jesus Loves Kids   Name_____

Draw a red ♡ around the problem if you must add.

Draw a yellow ✝ around the problem if you must subtract.

Solve each problem.

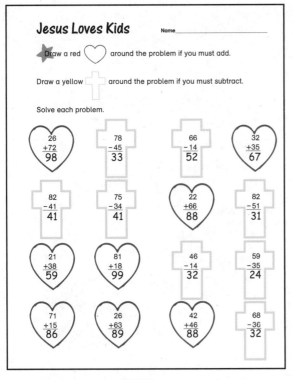

♡ 26 +72 = 98	✝ 78 –45 = 33	✝ 66 –14 = 52	♡ 32 +35 = 67
✝ 82 –41 = 41	✝ 75 –34 = 41	♡ 22 +66 = 88	✝ 82 –51 = 31
♡ 21 +38 = 59	♡ 81 +18 = 99	✝ 46 –14 = 32	✝ 59 –35 = 24
♡ 71 +15 = 86	♡ 26 +63 = 89	♡ 42 +46 = 88	✝ 68 –36 = 32

133

Hop Along Quickly   Name_____

How far can the frog hop in one minute? Solve the problems. After one minute, circle where you are. Then finish the page.

15 +20 = 35	96 –83 = 13	52 +43 = 95	44 +24 = 68	67 –34 = 33
62 –41 = 21	56 –20 = 36	45 +32 = 77	70 +29 = 99	39 –18 = 21
78 –45 = 33	83 +12 = 95	50 +19 = 69	47 +51 = 98	82 –61 = 21
27 –15 = 12	81 +17 = 98	35 –23 = 12	64 +25 = 89	66 –45 = 21

134

Answer Key

A Whale of a Problem
Name_____

Find the sums of these three-digit addition problems.

9 7 +4 **20**	7 3 +8 **18**	4 3 +9 **16**	2 9 +3 **14**

9 2 +1 **12**	5 6 +8 **19**	4 7 +6 **17**	4 5 +2 **11**

2 6 +1 **9**	2 7 +6 **15**	6 3 +4 **13**	7 1 +2 **10**

135

It all Adds Up!
Name_____

Solve the problems.

2 7 +9 **18**	6 5 +4 **15**	7 0 +9 **16**	3 6 +2 **11**

5 5 +2 **12**	4 7 +2 **13**	5 2 +1 **8**	4 3 +7 **14**

6 8 +3 **17**	3 4 +2 **9**	4 5 +1 **10**	3 5 +9 **17**

136

Good Deeds
Name_____

Add the numbers in each problem. Then decode the verse using the letters by the problems.

A 8+8+3= **19**   B 3+9+4= **16**   C 7+7+7= **21**
D 7+4+2= **13**   E 5+9+9= **23**   F 8+9+8= **25**
G 6+2+2= **10**   H 9+9+9= **27**   I 7+3+5= **15**
L 4+4+4= **12**   N 6+5+3= **14**   O 9+7+8= **24**
R 6+5+9= **20**   S 7+6+4= **17**   T 9+9+8= **26**
W 3+3+5= **11**   Y 3+3+3= **9**

Verse

Y E   A R E   T H E
9 23   19 20 23   26 27 23

L I G H T   O F   T H E
12 15 10 27 26   24 25   26 27 23

W O R L D .   A   C I T Y
11 24 20 12 13   19   21 15 26 9

T H A T   I S   S E T
26 27 19 26   15 17   17 23 26

O N   A   H I L L
24 14   19   27 15 12 12

C A N N O T   B E   H I D .
21 19 14 14 24 26   16 23   27 15 13

(Matthew 5:16 NIV)

137

Count On It
Name_____

The king is counting the coins in each pile of gold. He doesn't know that Jesus wants us to store up treasures in heaven, not on Earth. Help the king by writing the missing numbers in the blanks below.

156, **157** , **158** , 159, **160**

241, 242, **243** , **244** , **245**

329 , 330, 331, **332** , **333**

478, **479** , **480** , **481** , 482

501, 502, **503** , **504** , **505**

627, **628** , **629** , 630, **631**

717 , **718** , **719** , 720, 721

838, **839** , **840** , 841, **842**

995 , **996** , **997** , 998, 999

138

318

Answer Key

Chariot Chase

Name_____

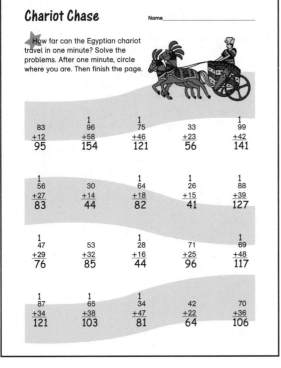

How far can the Egyptian chariot travel in one minute? Solve the problems. After one minute, circle where you are. Then finish the page.

83 +12 **95**	1 96 +58 **154**	1 75 +46 **121**	33 +23 **56**	1 99 +42 **141**
1 56 +27 **83**	30 +14 **44**	1 64 +18 **82**	1 26 +15 **41**	1 88 +39 **127**
1 47 +29 **76**	53 +32 **85**	1 28 +16 **44**	71 +25 **96**	1 69 +48 **117**
1 87 +34 **121**	1 65 +38 **103**	1 34 +47 **81**	42 +22 **64**	70 +36 **106**

139

Seaside Aquarium

Name_____

The town of Seaside attracts thousands of visitors each year. Its aquarium is a wonderful place to see some of the many fish God created. Attendance records are kept for both morning and afternoon visitors. Solve these problems.

Day 1	Day 2	Day 3	Day 4	Day 5
11 247 + 358 **605**	1 502 + 469 **971**	101 + 603 **704**	1 517 + 244 **761**	436 + 304 **740**

Day 6	Day 7	Day 8	Day 9	Day 10
1 185 + 464 **649**	1 327 + 428 **755**	11 299 + 501 **800**	1 316 + 317 **633**	1 402 + 529 **931**

Now answer these questions.

1. Which day had the most visitors? **Day 2**
2. Which day had the least visitors? **Day 1**
3. What is the difference between these two totals? **971 - 605 = 366**

140

Palm Sunday

Name_____

Find each sum. Connect the sums of **83** to make a path for Jesus to follow.

1 17 +66 **83**	1 58 +25 **83**	1 42 +19 **61**	1 38 +25 **63**
1 48 +26 **74**	1 17 +75 **92**	1 57 +26 **83**	1 28 +38 **66**	1 65 +29 **94**
1 58 +37 **95**	64 +24 **88**	1 48 +35 **83**	1 65 +16 **81**	1 37 +39 **76**
1 39 +59 **98**	1 59 +27 **86**	1 55 +28 **83**	1 39 +44 **83**

141

Bird Watching

Name_____

In Matthew 10:29–31, Jesus tells us he watches over the sparrows and, better yet, watches over us!

Joy has a bird feeder in her yard. Help her solve the following problems.

Example: On Monday, she saw 27 robins and 35 chickadees. How many birds did she see?

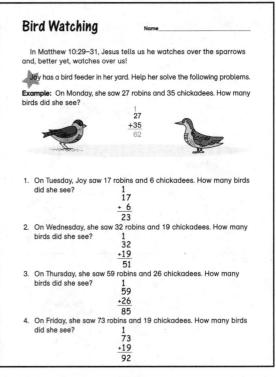

1
 27
 +35
 62

1. On Tuesday, Joy saw 17 robins and 6 chickadees. How many birds did she see?

   1
 17
 + 6
 23

2. On Wednesday, she saw 32 robins and 19 chickadees. How many birds did she see?

   1
 32
 +19
 51

3. On Thursday, she saw 59 robins and 26 chickadees. How many birds did she see?

   1
 59
 +26
 85

4. On Friday, she saw 73 robins and 19 chickadees. How many birds did she see?

   1
 73
 +19
 92

142

Answer Key

Number Crunch

Name_____

Your answers on this page will be numbers. Put the answer to question number 1 in the box marked 1. Put the answer to question number 2 in the box marked 2, and so on. Add up each row across. Read the Bible verses if you need help.

1. How many "great lights" did God create? (Genesis 1:16)
2. How old was Jotham when he became king in Jerusalem? (2 Chronicles 27:1)
3. How many days was Jonah in the huge fish? (Matthew 12:40)
4. How many years did it take Solomon to build his palace? (1 Kings 7:1)
5. How many years did Jacob agree to serve Laban before he could marry Rachel? (Genesis 29:20)
6. How many talents did the first servant receive in the Parable of the Talents? (Matthew 25:15)
7. How old was Joseph when his father gave him a beautiful robe? (Genesis 37:2–3)
8. How many anchors did the sailors put in the water to save Paul's ship from hitting the rocks? (Acts 27:29)
9. After Jesus healed ten lepers, how many did not thank him? (Luke 17:11–19)

1	2	3			
2	25	3	=	30	T
4	5	6			O
13	7	5	=	25	T A
7	8	9			L
17	4	9	=	30	S

143

Unlock This Riddle

Name_____

Add the numbers vertically to find the sum. Then write the letters from the problems in the answer blanks below to solve the riddle.

Riddle:
What did Samson use less of after his encounter with Delilah?

- 24 + 16 + 32 = __72__ R
- 15 + 21 + 9 = __45__ N
- 17 + 26 + 11 = __54__ S
- 36 + 26 + 12 = __74__ S
- 7 + 24 + 19 = __50__ H
- 21 + 24 + 33 = __78__ O
- 17 + 9 + 27 = __53__ Y
- 11 + 31 + 26 = __68__ P
- 30 + 17 + 29 = __76__ E
- 16 + 15 + 32 = __63__ A
- 22 + 39 + 14 = __75__ M
- 9 + 34 + 23 = __66__ O

Answer:

S H A M P O O
74 50 63 75 68 78 66

144

Bound for Bethlehem

Name_____

Work the problems to help Mary and Joseph reach Bethlehem.

1. 409 + 736 = 1,145
921 + 87 = 1,008
562 + 614 = 1,176
11. 824 + 597 = 1,421
11. 536 + 184 = 720
684 + 519 = 1,203
207 + 913 = 1,120
982 + 220 = 1,202
1. 623 + 192 = 815
11. 826 + 95 = 921
1. 462 + 781 = 1,243
547 + 782 = 1,329
284 + 493 = 777
1. 506 + 214 = 720
200 + 489 = 689

145

Baseball Stats

Name_____

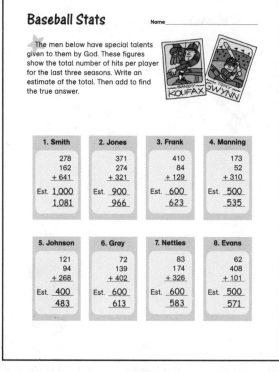

The men below have special talents given to them by God. These figures show the total number of hits per player for the last three seasons. Write an estimate of the total. Then add to find the true answer.

1. Smith	2. Jones	3. Frank	4. Manning
278	371	410	173
162	274	84	52
+ 641	+ 321	+ 129	+ 310
Est. 1,000	Est. 900	Est. 600	Est. 500
1,081	966	623	535

5. Johnson	6. Gray	7. Nettles	8. Evans
121	72	83	62
94	139	174	408
+ 268	+ 402	+ 326	+ 101
Est. 400	Est. 600	Est. 600	Est. 500
483	613	583	571

146

Answer Key

Take a Giant Step

Name_____

How far will the Philistines run? Solve the problems. After one minute, circle where you are. Then finish the page.

98 − 17 **81**	57 − 34 **23**	7 1 8̸2̸ − 69 **13**	35 − 13 **22**	3 1 4̸6̸ − 28 **18**
6 1 7̸2̸ − 56 **16**	67 − 35 **32**	1 1 2̸6̸ − 19 **7**	3 1 4̸7̸ − 28 **19**	4 1 5̸0̸ − 37 **13**
4 1 5̸4̸ − 37 **17**	42 − 31 **11**	5 1 6̸6̸ − 47 **19**	83 − 62 **21**	6 1 7̸5̸ − 38 **37**
74 − 33 **41**	1 1 2̸3̸ − 15 **8**	54 − 21 **33**	8 1 9̸2̸ − 85 **7**	4 1 5̸7̸ − 28 **29**

147

Joseph's Robe

Name_____

Subtract. Regroup as needed. Color the spaces with differences of:

10–19 red	20–29 blue	30–39 green
40–49 yellow	50–59 purple	60–69 orange

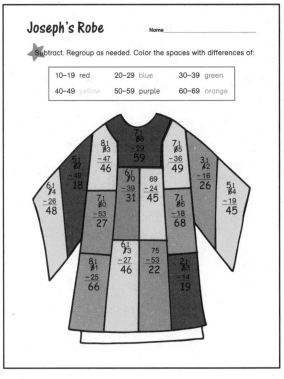

148

Bon Appetit!

Name_____

Jerry and his friends were very hungry! Solve the problems to find out how many leaves were left on each tree after Jerry and his friends ate dinner.

"Give thanks to the Lord of lords . . . who gives food to every creature." (Psalm 136:3, 25)

149

Sports Bonanza

Name_____

Do you think Jesus played games with his friends? Subtract. Regroup as needed.

150

Answer Key

High-Scoring Scoreboards Name_____

Give the difference in points between the team scores on each scoreboard. Show your work.

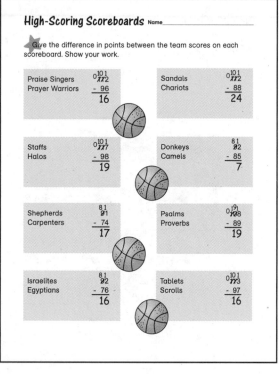

| Praise Singers Prayer Warriors | $\begin{array}{r} 0\,10\,1 \\ \cancel{1}\cancel{1}2 \\ -\ 96 \\ \hline 16 \end{array}$ | Sandals Chariots | $\begin{array}{r} 0\,10\,1 \\ \cancel{1}\cancel{1}2 \\ -\ 88 \\ \hline 24 \end{array}$ |

| Staffs Halos | $\begin{array}{r} 0\,10\,1 \\ \cancel{1}\cancel{1}7 \\ -\ 98 \\ \hline 19 \end{array}$ | Donkeys Camels | $\begin{array}{r} 8\,1 \\ 9\cancel{2} \\ -\ 85 \\ \hline 7 \end{array}$ |

| Shepherds Carpenters | $\begin{array}{r} 8\,1 \\ 9\cancel{1} \\ -\ 74 \\ \hline 17 \end{array}$ | Psalms Proverbs | $\begin{array}{r} 0\,19\,1 \\ \cancel{1}\cancel{0}8 \\ -\ 89 \\ \hline 19 \end{array}$ |

| Israelites Egyptians | $\begin{array}{r} 8\,1 \\ 9\cancel{2} \\ -\ 76 \\ \hline 16 \end{array}$ | Tablets Scrolls | $\begin{array}{r} 0\,10\,1 \\ \cancel{1}\cancel{1}3 \\ -\ 97 \\ \hline 16 \end{array}$ |

151

Let's Weigh In! Name_____

According to God's plan, all baby animals are different. Use the chart below to solve the problems.

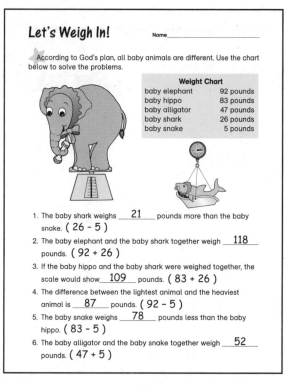

Weight Chart

baby elephant	92 pounds
baby hippo	83 pounds
baby alligator	47 pounds
baby shark	26 pounds
baby snake	5 pounds

1. The baby shark weighs __21__ pounds more than the baby snake. (26 – 5)
2. The baby elephant and the baby shark together weigh __118__ pounds. (92 + 26)
3. If the baby hippo and the baby shark were weighed together, the scale would show __109__ pounds. (83 + 26)
4. The difference between the lightest animal and the heaviest animal is __87__ pounds. (92 – 5)
5. The baby snake weighs __78__ pounds less than the baby hippo. (83 – 5)
6. The baby alligator and the baby snake together weigh __52__ pounds. (47 + 5)

152

Shoot for the Stars Name_____

You are a super math star! How many stars can you catch in one minute? After one minute, stop and circle where you are. Then finish the page.

$\begin{array}{r} 74 \\ +15 \\ \hline 89 \end{array}$	$\begin{array}{r} 52 \\ -10 \\ \hline 42 \end{array}$	$\begin{array}{r} 6\,1 \\ \cancel{7}6 \\ -28 \\ \hline 48 \end{array}$	$\begin{array}{r} 1 \\ 83 \\ +38 \\ \hline 121 \end{array}$
$\begin{array}{r} 4\,1 \\ \cancel{5}4 \\ -28 \\ \hline 26 \end{array}$	$\begin{array}{r} 65 \\ +24 \\ \hline 89 \end{array}$	$\begin{array}{r} 1 \\ 93 \\ +27 \\ \hline 120 \end{array}$	$\begin{array}{r} 39 \\ -12 \\ \hline 27 \end{array}$
$\begin{array}{r} 1 \\ 47 \\ +45 \\ \hline 92 \end{array}$	$\begin{array}{r} 2\,1 \\ \cancel{3}\cancel{2} \\ -24 \\ \hline 8 \end{array}$	$\begin{array}{r} 87 \\ -23 \\ \hline 64 \end{array}$	$\begin{array}{r} 56 \\ +11 \\ \hline 67 \end{array}$
$\begin{array}{r} 6\,1 \\ \cancel{7}1 \\ -19 \\ \hline 52 \end{array}$	$\begin{array}{r} 52 \\ -32 \\ \hline 20 \end{array}$	$\begin{array}{r} 40 \\ +42 \\ \hline 82 \end{array}$	$\begin{array}{r} 1 \\ 65 \\ +99 \\ \hline 164 \end{array}$

153

Fantastic Freckles Name_____

Fred knows that God made him like no one else. During some months, Fred has more freckles. During other months, Fred has fewer freckles. Solve each problem to see how many freckles Fred has each month.

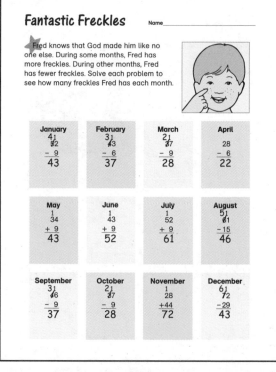

January	February	March	April
$\begin{array}{r} 4\,1 \\ \cancel{5}2 \\ -\ 9 \\ \hline 43 \end{array}$	$\begin{array}{r} 3\,1 \\ \cancel{4}3 \\ -\ 6 \\ \hline 37 \end{array}$	$\begin{array}{r} 2\,1 \\ \cancel{3}7 \\ -\ 9 \\ \hline 28 \end{array}$	$\begin{array}{r} 28 \\ -\ 6 \\ \hline 22 \end{array}$

May	June	July	August
$\begin{array}{r} 1 \\ 34 \\ +\ 9 \\ \hline 43 \end{array}$	$\begin{array}{r} 1 \\ 43 \\ +\ 9 \\ \hline 52 \end{array}$	$\begin{array}{r} 1 \\ 52 \\ +\ 9 \\ \hline 61 \end{array}$	$\begin{array}{r} 5\,1 \\ \cancel{6}1 \\ -15 \\ \hline 46 \end{array}$

September	October	November	December
$\begin{array}{r} 3\,1 \\ \cancel{4}6 \\ -\ 9 \\ \hline 37 \end{array}$	$\begin{array}{r} 2\,1 \\ \cancel{3}7 \\ -\ 9 \\ \hline 28 \end{array}$	$\begin{array}{r} 1 \\ 28 \\ +44 \\ \hline 72 \end{array}$	$\begin{array}{r} 6\,1 \\ \cancel{7}2 \\ -29 \\ \hline 43 \end{array}$

154

Answer Key

Playing with blocks
Name_____

How many blocks? Write the numbers.

Key
□ = one block
⬜⬜⬜⬜ = ten blocks
🔲 = one hundred blocks

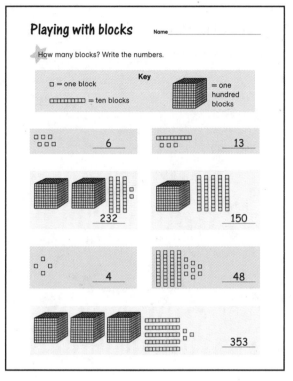

6

13

232

150

4

48

353

155

Numbered
Name_____

Use the Word Bank to complete the crossword puzzle.

Word Bank
one three five seven nine
two four six eight

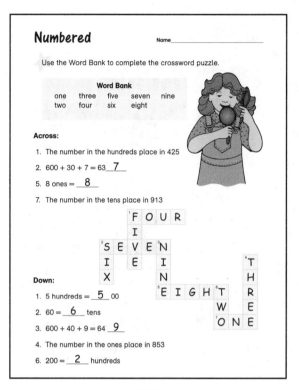

Across:
1. The number in the hundreds place in 425
2. 600 + 30 + 7 = 63 _7_
5. 8 ones = _8_
7. The number in the tens place in 913

Down:
1. 5 hundreds = _5_ 00
2. 60 = _6_ tens
3. 600 + 40 + 9 = 64 _9_
4. The number in the ones place in 853
6. 200 = _2_ hundreds

Crossword answers:
FOUR
I
SEVEN
SIX E N
X THREE
EIGHT TWO
O
ONE

156

Asking
Name_____

Write the numbers described. Then decode the verse using the letters next to your answers.

Three ones A _3_	Seven tens F _70_	One ten N _10_	Three tens U _30_
Five ones B _5_	Two tens H _20_	Seven ones O _7_	Six tens V _60_
Six ones C _6_	Eight ones I _8_	Nine ones P _9_	Zero ones W _0_
Five tens D _50_	Eight tens L _80_	Two ones R _2_	Four tens Y _40_
Nine tens E _90_	Four ones M _4_	One one T _1_	

Verse

"... C A L L   U P O N   M E
6 3 80 80   30 9 7 10   4 90

I N   T H E   D A Y
8 10   1 20 90   50 3 40

O F   T R O U B L E;   I
7 70   1 2 7 30 5 80 90   8

W I L L   D E L I V E R
0 8 80 80   50 90 80 8 60 90 2

Y O U,   A N D   Y O U
40 7 30   3 10 50   40 7 30

W I L L   H O N O R   M E."
0 8 80 80   20 7 10 7 2   4 90

(Psalm 50:15)

157

Communion
Name_____

For each number pair, draw a goblet 🏆 around the smaller number and make an arrow (< or >) pointing to the goblet. If the numbers in the pair are the same draw a loaf of bread 🍞 around both numbers and draw an equal sign (=) between them.

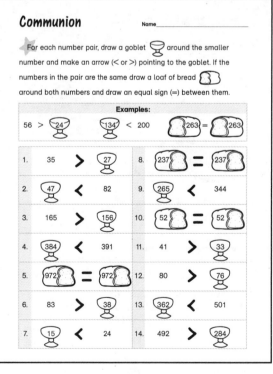

Examples:
56 > (24)   (134) < 200   (263) = (263)

1. 35 > (27)
2. (47) < 82
3. 165 > (156)
4. (384) < 391
5. (972) = (972)
6. 83 > (38)
7. (15) < 24
8. (237) = (237)
9. (265) < 344
10. (52) = (52)
11. 41 > (33)
12. 80 > (76)
13. (362) < 501
14. 492 > (284)

158

Answer Key

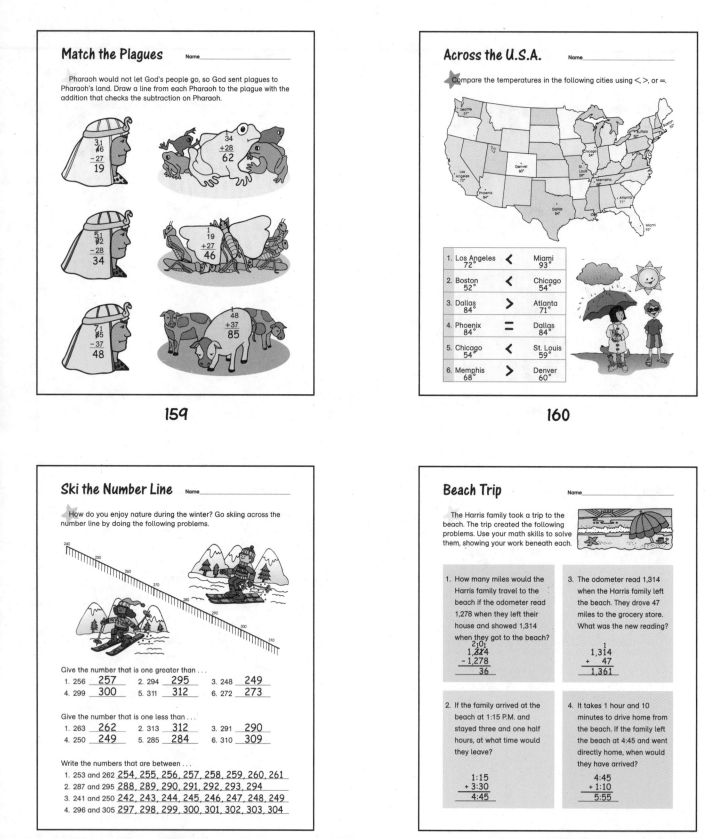

Match the Plagues   Name_____

Pharaoh would not let God's people go, so God sent plagues to Pharaoh's land. Draw a line from each Pharaoh to the plague with the addition that checks the subtraction on Pharaoh.

$$\begin{array}{r} 3\overset{1}{\cancel{4}}6 \\ -\ 27 \\ \hline 19 \end{array}$$

$$\begin{array}{r} 34 \\ +\ 28 \\ \hline 62 \end{array}$$

$$\begin{array}{r} 5\overset{1}{\cancel{6}}2 \\ -\ 28 \\ \hline 34 \end{array}$$

$$\begin{array}{r} \overset{1}{\ }19 \\ +\ 27 \\ \hline 46 \end{array}$$

$$\begin{array}{r} 7\overset{1}{\cancel{8}}5 \\ -\ 37 \\ \hline 48 \end{array}$$

$$\begin{array}{r} \overset{1}{\ }48 \\ +\ 37 \\ \hline 85 \end{array}$$

159

Across the U.S.A.   Name_____

Compare the temperatures in the following cities using <, >, or =.

1. Los Angeles 72°	<	Miami 93°
2. Boston 52°	<	Chicago 54°
3. Dallas 84°	>	Atlanta 71°
4. Phoenix 84°	=	Dallas 84°
5. Chicago 54°	<	St. Louis 59°
6. Memphis 68°	>	Denver 60°

160

Ski the Number Line   Name_____

How do you enjoy nature during the winter? Go skiing across the number line by doing the following problems.

Give the number that is one greater than . . .
1. 256 **257**   2. 294 **295**   3. 248 **249**
4. 299 **300**   5. 311 **312**   6. 272 **273**

Give the number that is one less than . . .
1. 263 **262**   2. 313 **312**   3. 291 **290**
4. 250 **249**   5. 285 **284**   6. 310 **309**

Write the numbers that are between . . .
1. 253 and 262 **254, 255, 256, 257, 258, 259, 260, 261**
2. 287 and 295 **288, 289, 290, 291, 292, 293, 294**
3. 241 and 250 **242, 243, 244, 245, 246, 247, 248, 249**
4. 296 and 305 **297, 298, 299, 300, 301, 302, 303, 304**

161

Beach Trip   Name_____

The Harris family took a trip to the beach. The trip created the following problems. Use your math skills to solve them, showing your work beneath each.

1. How many miles would the Harris family travel to the beach if the odometer read 1,278 when they left their house and showed 1,314 when they got to the beach?

$$\begin{array}{r} 2\ \overset{10}{\cancel{1}}1 \\ 1,3\cancel{1}4 \\ -\ 1,278 \\ \hline 36 \end{array}$$

3. The odometer read 1,314 when the Harris family left the beach. They drove 47 miles to the grocery store. What was the new reading?

$$\begin{array}{r} \overset{1}{\ }\ \\ 1,314 \\ +\ \ \ 47 \\ \hline 1,361 \end{array}$$

2. If the family arrived at the beach at 1:15 P.M. and stayed three and one half hours, at what time would they leave?

$$\begin{array}{r} 1:15 \\ +\ 3:30 \\ \hline 4:45 \end{array}$$

4. It takes 1 hour and 10 minutes to drive home from the beach. If the family left the beach at 4:45 and went directly home, when would they have arrived?

$$\begin{array}{r} 4:45 \\ +\ 1:10 \\ \hline 5:55 \end{array}$$

162

Answer Key

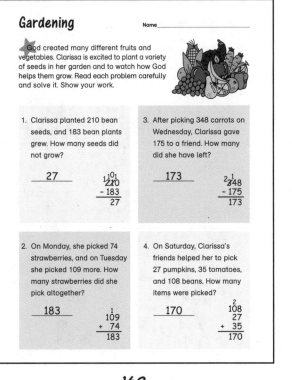

Gardening
Name_____

God created many different fruits and vegetables. Clarissa is excited to plant a variety of seeds in her garden and to watch how God helps them grow. Read each problem carefully and solve it. Show your work.

1. Clarissa planted 210 bean seeds, and 183 bean plants grew. How many seeds did not grow?

   ___27___

   $\begin{array}{r} {}^{1}2{}^{0}\cancel{1}0 \\ -183 \\ \hline 27 \end{array}$

3. After picking 348 carrots on Wednesday, Clarissa gave 175 to a friend. How many did she have left?

   ___173___

   $\begin{array}{r} 2\cancel{3}{}^{1}48 \\ -175 \\ \hline 173 \end{array}$

2. On Monday, she picked 74 strawberries, and on Tuesday she picked 109 more. How many strawberries did she pick altogether?

   ___183___

   $\begin{array}{r} {}^{1} \\ 109 \\ +74 \\ \hline 183 \end{array}$

4. On Saturday, Clarissa's friends helped her to pick 27 pumpkins, 35 tomatoes, and 108 beans. How many items were picked?

   ___170___

   $\begin{array}{r} {}^{2} \\ 108 \\ 27 \\ +35 \\ \hline 170 \end{array}$

163

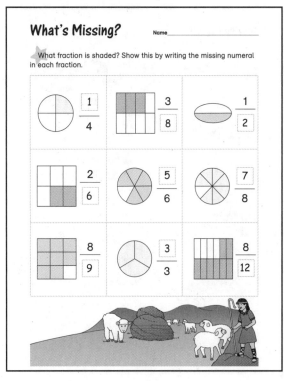

What's Missing?
Name_____

What fraction is shaded? Show this by writing the missing numeral in each fraction.

$\frac{1}{4}$ $\frac{3}{8}$ $\frac{1}{2}$

$\frac{2}{6}$ $\frac{5}{6}$ $\frac{7}{8}$

$\frac{8}{9}$ $\frac{3}{3}$ $\frac{8}{12}$

164

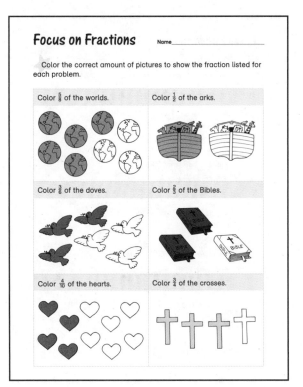

Focus on Fractions
Name_____

Color the correct amount of pictures to show the fraction listed for each problem.

Color $\frac{5}{8}$ of the worlds.

Color $\frac{1}{2}$ of the arks.

Color $\frac{3}{6}$ of the doves.

Color $\frac{2}{3}$ of the Bibles.

Color $\frac{4}{10}$ of the hearts.

Color $\frac{3}{4}$ of the crosses.

165

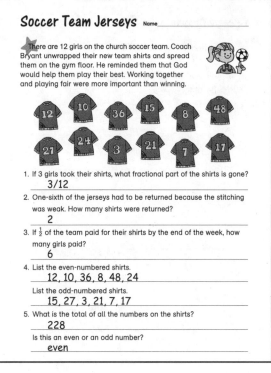

Soccer Team Jerseys
Name_____

There are 12 girls on the church soccer team. Coach Bryant unwrapped their new team shirts and spread them on the gym floor. He reminded them that God would help them play their best. Working together and playing fair were more important than winning.

1. If 3 girls took their shirts, what fractional part of the shirts is gone?
   __3/12__

2. One-sixth of the jerseys had to be returned because the stitching was weak. How many shirts were returned?
   __2__

3. If $\frac{1}{2}$ of the team paid for their shirts by the end of the week, how many girls paid?
   __6__

4. List the even-numbered shirts.
   __12, 10, 36, 8, 48, 24__
   List the odd-numbered shirts.
   __15, 27, 3, 21, 7, 17__

5. What is the total of all the numbers on the shirts?
   __228__
   Is this an even or an odd number?
   __even__

166

Answer Key

Fruity Fractions

Name_____

To help keep our bodies healthy, God has given us fruits and vegetables. Color each fractional part.

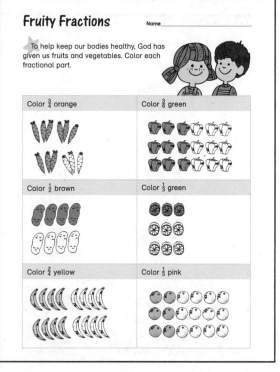

Color $\frac{3}{4}$ orange	Color $\frac{3}{8}$ green
Color $\frac{1}{2}$ brown	Color $\frac{1}{3}$ green
Color $\frac{2}{4}$ yellow	Color $\frac{1}{3}$ pink

167

Sing His Praises

Name_____

The Praise Band celebrated the release of their CD and expressed their thanks to God by giving a concert each night for six days. They also served a chocolate cake each day. The shading shows the portion eaten of each cake. Write a fraction for each shaded portion.

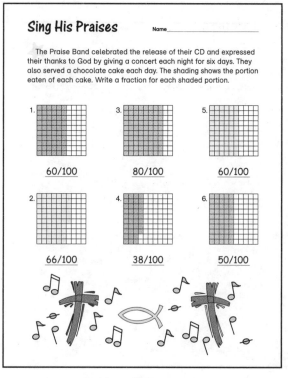

1. 60/100   3. 80/100   5. 60/100

2. 66/100   4. 38/100   6. 50/100

168

Creepy Crawlies

Name_____

Look at a ruler to compare inches and centimeters. Circle the correct answer.

1. The world's shortest snake, the thread snake, is about 4 inches long. This is about _____ long.

   6 centimeters   (10 centimeters)   13 centimeters

2. The smallest frog, the Cuban frog, is less than 1/2 inch long. This is about _____ long.

   (1 centimeter)   3 centimeters   5 centimeters

3. The largest spider, the goliath bird-eating spider, has legs about 28 centimeters long. This is about _____ long.

   10 inches   (11 inches)   12 inches

4. The biggest scorpion, the emperor scorpion, can be over 7 inches long. This is about _____ long.

   16 centimeters   17 centimeters   (18 centimeters)

5. One shark, the spined pygmy shark, grows to be about 15 centimeters long. This is about _____ long.

   5 inches   (6 inches)   7 inches

169

Fishers of Men

Name_____

Peter and Andrew agreed only to keep fish that measured greater than 6 centimeters. One day the brothers caught the fish below. Estimate how many Peter and Andrew will keep. __5__
Then measure to find out the length of each.

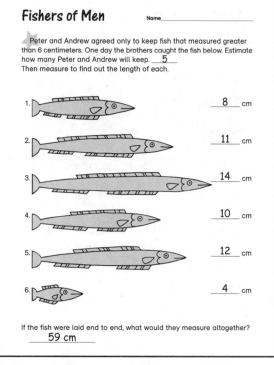

1. __8__ cm
2. __11__ cm
3. __14__ cm
4. __10__ cm
5. __12__ cm
6. __4__ cm

If the fish were laid end to end, what would they measure altogether?
__59 cm__

170

Answer Key

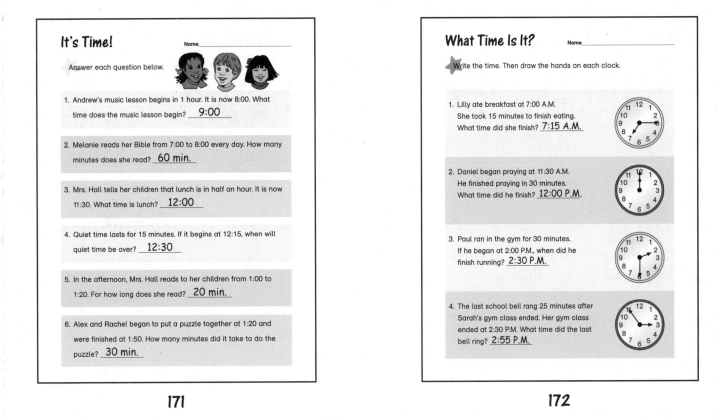

It's Time!

Name_____

⭐ Answer each question below.

1. Andrew's music lesson begins in 1 hour. It is now 8:00. What time does the music lesson begin? **9:00**

2. Melanie reads her Bible from 7:00 to 8:00 every day. How many minutes does she read? **60 min.**

3. Mrs. Hall tells her children that lunch is in half an hour. It is now 11:30. What time is lunch? **12:00**

4. Quiet time lasts for 15 minutes. If it begins at 12:15, when will quiet time be over? **12:30**

5. In the afternoon, Mrs. Hall reads to her children from 1:00 to 1:20. For how long does she read? **20 min.**

6. Alex and Rachel began to put a puzzle together at 1:20 and were finished at 1:50. How many minutes did it take to do the puzzle? **30 min.**

171

What Time Is It?

Name_____

⭐ Write the time. Then draw the hands on each clock.

1. Lilly ate breakfast at 7:00 A.M. She took 15 minutes to finish eating. What time did she finish? **7:15 A.M.**

2. Daniel began praying at 11:30 A.M. He finished praying in 30 minutes. What time did he finish? **12:00 P.M.**

3. Paul ran in the gym for 30 minutes. If he began at 2:00 P.M., when did he finish running? **2:30 P.M.**

4. The last school bell rang 25 minutes after Sarah's gym class ended. Her gym class ended at 2:30 P.M. What time did the last bell ring? **2:55 P.M.**

172

Bible Times

Name_____

⭐ Read each sentence from a Bible story that has a made-up time in it. Write the number of the matching clock by each sentence.

7 Moses saw the burning bush at 10:33.

2 Eve took a bite of the fruit at 1:04.

8 The wise men arrived in Bethlehem at 5:16.

4 The lamb has been missing since 6:30!

1 The wedding banquet began at 9:47.

3 David's suppertime is 5:52.

5 Jesus rode into Jerusalem at 4:39.

6 The disciples threw their nets to the other side of the boat at 8:21.

173

Prayer Time

Name_____

⭐ Jesus hears our prayers any time we pray. Draw the hands on the clock to show the time when you could pray.

10:15   7:27   2:04   5:47

11:58   1:11   9:36   3:22

12:13   8:09   4:41   6:18

174

327

Answer Key

Mark's Busy Schedule — Name_____

Mark had a busy day. Use a clock to help you answer these questions about his schedule.

1. School starts at 8:45. Mark gets up at 7:30. How much time does Mark have before school? __1 hr. 15 min.__

2. Mark eats breakfast ½ hour after he gets out of bed. What time does he eat breakfast? __8:00__

3. After breakfast, Mark and his brother work on their homework for 15 minutes. When are they done with this task? __8:15__

4. Music class starts at 10:20 and ends at 10:50. How long is this class? __30 min.__

5. The afternoon runs from 12:45–3:25. How long is the afternoon session? __2 hrs. 40 min.__

6. After school, Mark has soccer practice. It starts at 4:00 but it takes him 25 minutes to get there. What time must he leave home? __3:35__

7. Mark eats supper at 5:45. It takes him 15 minutes to eat. After supper, he spends 30 minutes doing his homework, two hours playing with his friends, and 30 minutes watching his favorite TV show until bedtime. What time does Mark go to bed? __9:00__

175

Tithes and Offering — Name_____

Everyone in Mrs. Johnson's Sunday school class put money in the offering plate each Sunday. Write the total amount in each offering plate.

nickel dime nickel penny — __21__ ¢

half-dollar penny penny penny — __53__ ¢

nickel quarter nickel dime — __45__ ¢

quarter nickel quarter — __55__ ¢

nickel quarter dime penny — __41__ ¢

dime quarter dime — __45__ ¢

Color the offering plate with the most money green.

Color the offering plate with the least money red.

Color the 2 plates with the same amount yellow.

176

Money Matters — Name_____

Use the work spaces to solve the problems. Write the answers in the blanks.

5¢   10¢   25¢   50¢

Work Space

1. A bowl costs 20¢. Mary paid a quarter. How much change did Mary get back? __5¢__

   25¢
− 20¢
   5¢

2. Sarah spent 3 nickels on a vase and a dime on a basket. How much money did Sarah spend altogether? __25¢__

   15¢
+ 10¢
   25¢

3. A boat ride costs 25¢. Peter had 15¢. How much more money did he need for a boat ride? __10¢__

   25¢
− 15¢
   10¢

4. James and Matthew each spent 30¢ for a ride on a donkey. What was the total amount the two boys spent? __60¢__

   30¢
+ 30¢
   60¢

5. Ruth had 5 nickels. She gave one to Naomi. How much money does Ruth have now? __20¢__

   25¢
− 5¢
   20¢

177

Change Back — Name_____

God wants us to use our money wisely and to not make it the most important thing in our lives. Complete these problems.

1. cheeseburger and cola $2.54
You pay $3.00
Your change = __46¢__

2. 3 pairs of jeans 2 shirts $78.41
You pay $80.50
Your change = __$2.09__

3. movie $5.60
You pay $6.00
Your change = __40¢__

4. 2 large pizzas $16.36
You pay $16.50
Your change = __14¢__

Complete these problems.

$155.75
− 25.75
$130.00

7 11 1
$98.20
− 74.87
$23.33

2 17 1
$328.74
− 71.93
$256.81

178

Answer Key

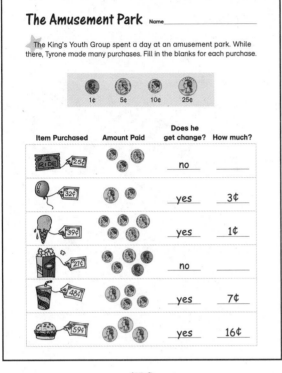

The Amusement Park   Name_____

The King's Youth Group spent a day at an amusement park. While there, Tyrone made many purchases. Fill in the blanks for each purchase.

1¢	5¢	10¢	25¢

Item Purchased	Amount Paid	Does he get change?	How much?
RIDE 25¢		no	
32¢		yes	3¢
39¢		yes	1¢
27¢		no	
48¢		yes	7¢
59¢		yes	16¢

179

Eating Out   Name_____

The youth group went out on Wednesday night. Use the menu to solve the problems.

Menu
Hot Dog . . . . 52¢
Hamburger . . . . .69¢
Milk . . . . 40¢
Cupcake . . . . 47¢
French Fries . . . . 63¢

1. Frank bought a hot dog, French fries, and milk. How much did Frank spend altogether? $1.55
   52¢ + 63¢ + 40¢ = $1.55

2. Greg had five dimes and a nickel. He bought a cupcake. How much money did he have left?   8¢
   55¢ - 47¢ = 8¢

3. Ron decided to get a hamburger and French fries. How much money in all did he need? $1.32
   69¢ + 63¢ = $1.32

4. Doris had 39¢. She really wanted a cupcake. How much more money did she need?   8¢
   47¢ - 39¢ = 8¢

180

Sweet Treats   Name_____

Mr. Morgan owns a candy shop. To share God's love, he gives children a free piece of candy if they can tell him a Bible verse from memory. He has the sweetest treats in town. Use a calculator to work the problems below.

peppermints 12¢   candy hearts 26¢   jellybeans 8¢   lemon drops 28¢   caramels 23¢

licorice 44¢   gum 38¢

cinnamon drops 6¢   gumdrops 35¢   fudge 56¢   sourballs 22¢

Aaron has $1.00 to spend. Show three different ways he can spend that amount. List each treat and its price.

- 2 items: licorice 44¢   fudge 56¢
- 3 items: candy hearts 26¢   gum 38¢
             gum drops 35¢   Answers may vary.
- 4 items: peppermints 12¢   fudge 56¢
             cinnamon drops 6¢   jellybeans 8¢
             Answers may vary.

181

Tally It Up   Name_____

A trip to the grocery store can cost a lot of money. Use a calculator to find the totals for each set of grocery items. Then add the totals to learn the grand total of the grocery bill.

	3 3			1 3
1. English muffin bread	$1.79	4. milk		$2.09
pretzel snacks	2.49	orange juice		1.49
baby carrots	1.99	noodle soup		1.13
flower bouquet	+ 5.99	spaghetti sauce		+ 2.89
	$12.26			$7.60

	1 3			2 2
2. roast beef	$3.44	5. wheat crackers		$2.81
sandwich bags	2.19	bread		.79
cheese slices	1.79	rice cereal		2.19
bleach	+ 1.19	marshmallows		+ .89
	$8.61			$6.68

	2 3			2 3
3. bananas	$1.39	6. salad dressing		$1.79
magazine	1.99	mustard		.83
grape jelly	1.59	broom		6.99
dish soap	+ 1.79	soy sauce		+ 1.29
	$6.76			$10.90

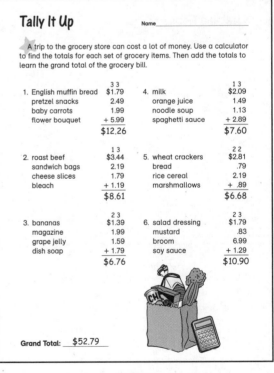

Grand Total: _$52.79_

182

Answer Key

Ned's Grill

Name_____

Sue has been hired at Ned's Grill to wait tables. On her first night, two families order from the children's menu. Help her total these orders and figure the change owed. You may use a calculator.

Kids' Menu

Hot Dog $1.50	Chicken Fingers $2.95
Grilled Cheese . . $1.95	Cheese Nachos $1.50
Hamburger. $2.25	Cheeseburger. $2.50
Cheese Pizza. . . . $1.95	PBJ Sandwich $1.35

Item	# of Items	Amount Per Item	Total
1. Chicken Fingers	2	$2.95	$5.90
Cheese Nachos	1	$1.50	$1.50
PBJ Sandwich	1	$1.35	$1.35
		Total Cost:	$8.75
		Amount Paid:	$10.00
		Change:	$1.25
2. Cheese Pizza	3	$1.95	$5.85
Chicken Fingers	1	$2.95	$2.95
Grilled Cheese	2	$1.95	$3.90
		Total Cost:	$12.70
		Amount Paid:	$15.00
		Change:	$2.30

183

Two by Two

Name_____

Finish numbering the animals 1–20. Color the second animal in each pair red. Then, read the numbers on the red animals aloud.

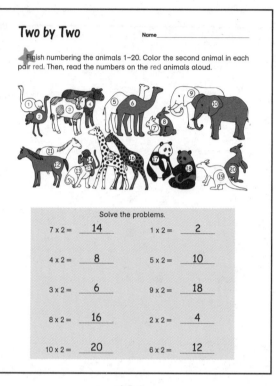

Solve the problems.

7 x 2 =	14	1 x 2 =	2
4 x 2 =	8	5 x 2 =	10
3 x 2 =	6	9 x 2 =	18
8 x 2 =	16	2 x 2 =	4
10 x 2 =	20	6 x 2 =	12

184

Helping Hands

Name_____

Finish numbering the fingers 1–50. Color the fifth finger on each hand brown. Then, read the numbers on the brown fingers aloud.

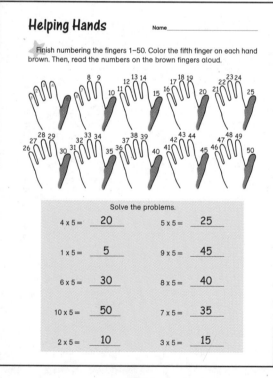

Solve the problems.

4 x 5 =	20	5 x 5 =	25
1 x 5 =	5	9 x 5 =	45
6 x 5 =	30	8 x 5 =	40
10 x 5 =	50	7 x 5 =	35
2 x 5 =	10	3 x 5 =	15

185

Time to Multiply

Name_____

Remember to thank God for your talents. Complete the multiplication grid by writing the products in the boxes.

X	4	9	0	3	8	5	1	7	2	6
2	8	18	0	6	16	10	2	14	4	12
8	32	72	0	24	64	40	8	56	16	48
1	4	9	0	3	8	5	1	7	2	6
6	24	54	0	18	48	30	6	42	12	36
7	28	63	0	21	56	35	7	49	14	42
4	16	36	0	12	32	20	4	28	8	24
0	0	0	0	0	0	0	0	0	0	0
9	36	81	0	27	72	45	9	63	18	54
5	20	45	0	15	40	25	5	35	10	30
3	12	27	0	9	24	15	3	21	6	18

"For nothing is impossible with God."
Luke 1:37

186

Answer Key

Help Moses Up Mt. Sinai

Name_____

Help Moses up Mt. Sinai. Start at the bottom of the boulder and work the problems up to the top!

$\begin{array}{c}8\\ \times 9\\ \hline 72\end{array}$ $\begin{array}{c}7\\ \times 8\\ \hline 56\end{array}$ $\begin{array}{c}0\\ \times 4\\ \hline 0\end{array}$

$9 \times 9 = \underline{81}$ $3 \times 3 = \underline{9}$

$4 \times 8 = \underline{32}$ $\begin{array}{c}4\\ \times 6\\ \hline 24\end{array}$ $3 \times 5 = \underline{15}$

$7 \times 7 = \underline{49}$ $\begin{array}{c}6\\ \times 6\\ \hline 36\end{array}$ $2 \times 8 = \underline{16}$ $\begin{array}{c}9\\ \times 1\\ \hline 9\end{array}$

$6 \times 1 = \underline{6}$ $\begin{array}{c}6\\ \times 7\\ \hline 42\end{array}$ $6 \times 6 = \underline{36}$ $\begin{array}{c}2\\ \times 2\\ \hline 4\end{array}$

$8 \times 6 = \underline{48}$ $\begin{array}{c}8\\ \times 7\\ \hline 56\end{array}$ $7 \times 9 = \underline{63}$ $\begin{array}{c}5\\ \times 5\\ \hline 25\end{array}$

$3 \times 6 = \underline{18}$ $\begin{array}{c}2\\ \times 3\\ \hline 6\end{array}$ $6 \times 7 = \underline{42}$ $\begin{array}{c}3\\ \times 9\\ \hline 27\end{array}$

187

How Many Times?

Name_____

Write each product in the grid as shown.

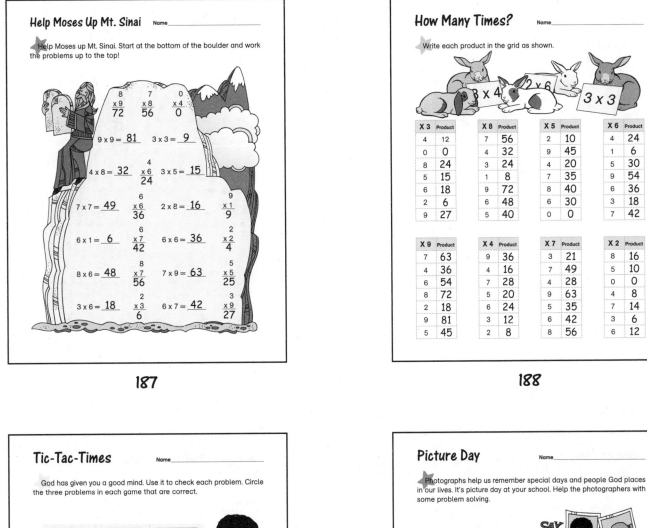

X 3	Product
4	12
0	0
8	24
5	15
6	18
2	6
9	27

X 8	Product
7	56
4	32
3	24
1	8
9	72
6	48
5	40

X 5	Product
2	10
9	45
4	20
7	35
8	40
6	30
0	0

X 6	Product
4	24
1	6
5	30
9	54
6	36
3	18
7	42

X 9	Product
7	63
4	36
6	54
8	72
2	18
9	81
5	45

X 4	Product
9	36
4	16
7	28
5	20
6	24
3	12
2	8

X 7	Product
3	21
7	49
4	28
9	63
5	35
6	42
8	56

X 2	Product
8	16
5	10
0	0
4	8
7	14
3	6
6	12

188

Tic-Tac-Times

Name_____

God has given you a good mind. Use it to check each problem. Circle the three problems in each game that are correct.

(3 x 2 = 6)	(4 x 5 = 20)	(1 x 4 = 4)
1 x 7 = 8	7 x 5 = 2	6 x 5 = 11
3 x 3 = 6	2 x 2 = 0	9 x 5 = 4

8 x 2 = 10	5 x 2 = 7	(5 x 5 = 25)
6 x 3 = 6	(3 x 3 = 9)	9 x 3 = 6
(7 x 2 = 14)	2 x 8 = 10	9 x 1 = 8

3 x 5 = 8	(6 x 2 = 12)	8 x 3 = 11
2 x 7 = 9	(3 x 5 = 15)	4 x 4 = 0
3 x 4 = 7	(1 x 2 = 2)	5 x 6 = 11

189

Picture Day

Name_____

Photographs help us remember special days and people God places in our lives. It's picture day at your school. Help the photographers with some problem solving.

1. If 292 students came to have pictures taken in the a.m. and 373 students in the p.m., how many students came in all? __665__

2. All of the students in the three first-grade classes had pictures taken. There were 26 students per room. How many first-grade students had pictures taken? __78__

3. The 20 kindergarten students each bought a $10 picture packet. How much did they spend in all? __$200__

4. Extra wallet pictures are available for $.50 apiece. How much would 8 extra wallet pictures cost? __$4.00__

5. One student's mother wants three 8" x 10" photos for relatives. They cost $1.85 each. How much money does she need for these pictures? __$5.55__

190

Answer Key

Moses and Manna

Name_____

Read the problems. Then circle the picture that answers each question.

1. The boy ate 2 fish for lunch. He ate 3 times as many fish for dinner. How many did he eat at dinner?

2. Noah loves bananas. He eats them for snacks. Each snack consists of 4 bananas. If Noah has 3 snacks each day, how many bananas does he eat altogether?

3. Moses loves manna. He eats 5 manna cakes each day. Aaron eats twice as many. How many does Aaron eat?

4. Mrs. Smith has twins. Her best friend, Mrs. Jones, has 6 times as many children. How many children does Mrs. Jones have?

191

Everyday Math

Name_____

There are many ways to use math every day. Solve these story problems. Show your work.

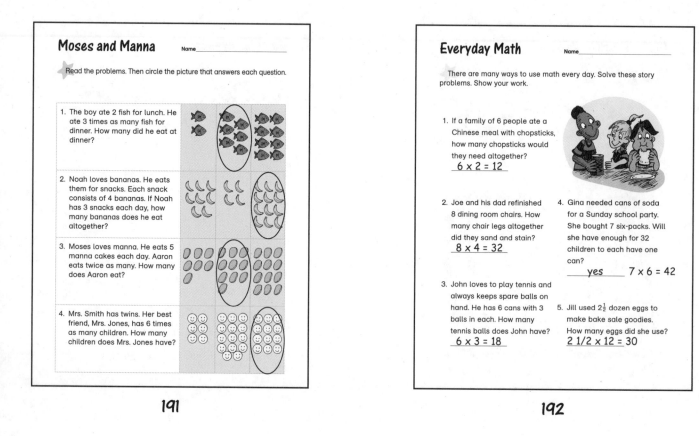

1. If a family of 6 people ate a Chinese meal with chopsticks, how many chopsticks would they need altogether?
   <u>6 x 2 = 12</u>

2. Joe and his dad refinished 8 dining room chairs. How many chair legs altogether did they sand and stain?
   <u>8 x 4 = 32</u>

3. John loves to play tennis and always keeps spare balls on hand. He has 6 cans with 3 balls in each. How many tennis balls does John have?
   <u>6 x 3 = 18</u>

4. Gina needed cans of soda for a Sunday school party. She bought 7 six-packs. Will she have enough for 32 children to each have one can?
   <u>yes</u>   7 x 6 = 42

5. Jill used $2\frac{1}{2}$ dozen eggs to make bake sale goodies. How many eggs did she use?
   <u>2 1/2 x 12 = 30</u>

192

Walls of Jericho

Name_____

Help build this colorful wall of Jericho before Joshua knocks it down! Write each quotient. Then color the bricks according to the code.

1 = black	4 = yellow	7 = green
2 = pink	5 = orange	8 = blue
3 = brown	6 = red	9 = purple

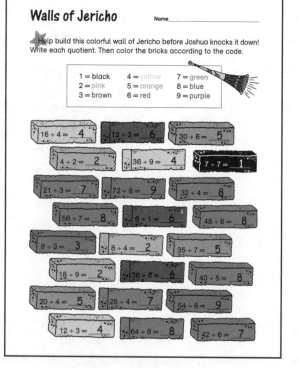

16 ÷ 4 = 4   12 ÷ 2 = 6   30 ÷ 6 = 5

4 ÷ 2 = 2   36 ÷ 9 = 4   7 ÷ 7 = 1

21 ÷ 3 = 7   72 ÷ 8 = 9   32 ÷ 4 = 8

56 ÷ 7 = 8   6 ÷ 1 = 6   48 ÷ 6 = 8

9 ÷ 3 = 3   8 ÷ 4 = 2   35 ÷ 7 = 5

18 ÷ 9 = 2   36 ÷ 6 = 6   40 ÷ 5 = 8

20 ÷ 4 = 5   28 ÷ 4 = 7   54 ÷ 6 = 9

12 ÷ 3 = 4   64 ÷ 8 = 8   42 ÷ 6 = 7

193

Packaging Plants

Name_____

All of the beautiful flowers you see are gifts from God! When packaging plants at a greenhouse, workers put equal amounts of plants in each box. Help the workers divide the plants for packaging. Draw pictures in the boxes to help you solve the problems.

- 15 rose bushes in three boxes. How many are in each box? <u>5</u>

- 20 lilies in four boxes. How many are in each box? <u>5</u>

- 35 tulip bulbs in five boxes. How many are in each box? <u>7</u>

- 42 daisies in 6 boxes. How many are in each box? <u>7</u>

194

Answer Key

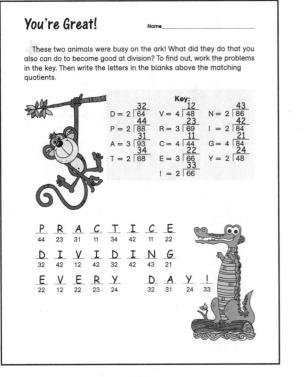
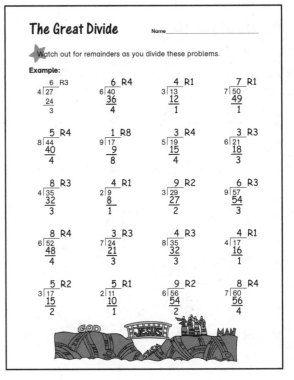
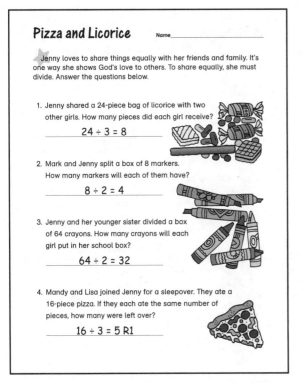
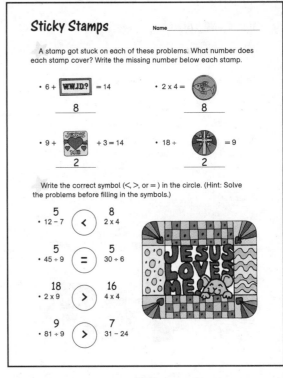
333

Answer Key

The Sticker Club

Name_____

A group of friends formed a sticker club. They bought, sold, traded, and shared stickers. Solve these problems. Show your work.

1. For her birthday, Erin got a set of 8 animal stickers from three different people. How many animal stickers did she recieve? __24__

$$8 \times 3 = 24$$

3. Jeff made a bookmark for each of 7 friends. He put 3 stickers on each bookmark. How many stickers did he use? __21__

$$7 \times 3 = 21$$

2. Erin placed equal amounts of the new animal stickers on 2 pages of her album. How many stickers were on each page? __12__

$$24 \div 2 = 12$$

4. Each time Jeff bought 5 stickers, he recieved 2 free stickers. If he bought 20 stickers, how many total would he recieve? __8__

$$20 \div 5 = 4$$
$$4 \times 2 = 8$$

199

Church Street

Name_____

Jesus knows right where you live. He shines his love on you every day. Fill in the number line to show the addresses on Church Street. Notice that the top numbers are even and the bottom numbers are odd.

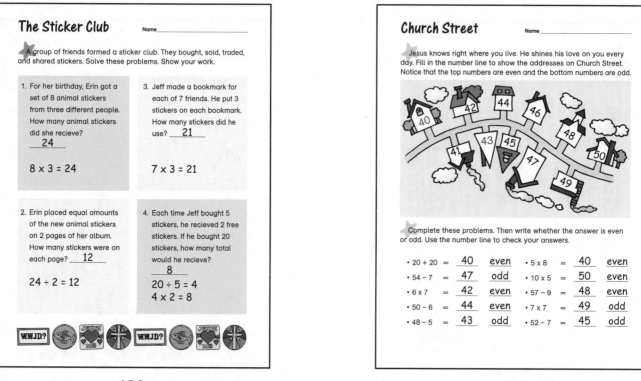

Complete these problems. Then write whether the answer is even or odd. Use the number line to check your answers.

- 20 + 20 = __40__ even
- 54 – 7 = __47__ odd
- 6 x 7 = __42__ even
- 50 – 6 = __44__ even
- 48 – 5 = __43__ odd
- 5 x 8 = __40__ even
- 10 x 5 = __50__ even
- 57 – 9 = __48__ even
- 7 x 7 = __49__ odd
- 52 – 7 = __45__ odd

200

Goose and Gander

Name_____

Work each problem on your calculator. Then, turn the calculator upside down and write the word which should match each clue.

Example: 256 + 362 = __618__   antonym of small   __Big__

	Answer	Clue	Word
• 139 + 524 =	663	a nest occupant	Egg
• 11,862 – 4,757 =	7,105	a synonym for dirt	SOIL
• 29,331 + 5,675 =	35,006	a gander's wife	gOOSE
• 609 x 5 =	3,045	a foot warmer	ShOE
• 12,955 – 9,251 =	3,704	a gopher's home	hOLE
• 323 x 25 =	8,075	a messy, unkempt person	SLOB
• 9,867 + 25,140 =	35,007	an antonym of tight	LOOSE
• 2,428 ÷ 4 =	607	fireplace fuel	LOg
• 918 x 6 =	5,508	an employer	BOSS
• 3,412 + 4,304 =	7,716	a fish uses this to breathe	gILL

201

In My Estimation

Name_____

Sarah's teacher just gave her the following math problems. Help her estimate the answers. To do that, round any numbers greater than 10, and then multiply the numbers in your head. Use that estimate to help you choose the exact answer. Check your work with a calculator.

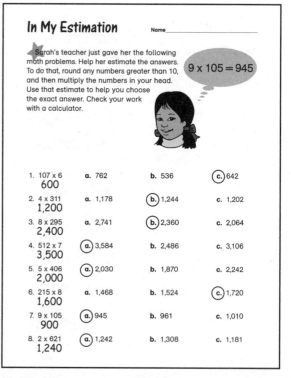

$$9 \times 105 = 945$$

1. 107 x 6
   600
   a. 762   b. 536   c. 642

2. 4 x 311
   1,200
   a. 1,178   b. 1,244   c. 1,202

3. 8 x 295
   2,400
   a. 2,741   b. 2,360   c. 2,064

4. 512 x 7
   3,500
   a. 3,584   b. 2,486   c. 3,106

5. 5 x 406
   2,000
   a. 2,030   b. 1,870   c. 2,242

6. 215 x 8
   1,600
   a. 1,468   b. 1,524   c. 1,720

7. 9 x 105
   900
   a. 945   b. 961   c. 1,010

8. 2 x 621
   1,240
   a. 1,242   b. 1,308   c. 1,181

202

Answer Key

Pleasantville Events

Name_____

The town of Pleasantville hosted many events last year. Help the town newspaper reporter round the attendance figures so that they can be used in headlines to report the events.

Event	Attendance	Round to Nearest 10	Round to Nearest 100	Round to Nearest 1,000
Vacation Bible School	1,246	1,240	1,200	1,000
Family Fun Day	9,367	9,370	9,400	9,000
Prayer Power	4,822	4,820	4,800	5,000
Jesus' Kids Carnival	5,111	5,110	5,100	5,000
Youth Rally	6,781	6,780	6,800	7,000
Bible Bike Ride	3,759	3,760	3,800	4,000
Harvest Festival	2,674	2,670	2,700	3,000
Easter Musical	8,888	8,890	8,900	9,000

203

Going Buggy

Name_____

Each bug has a special shape inside. Draw a line from the shape to its name.

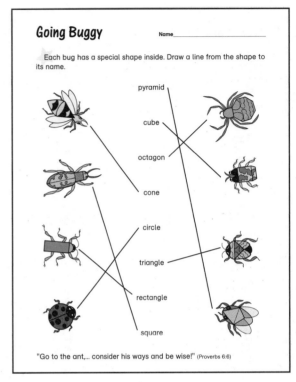

pyramid
cube
octagon
cone
circle
triangle
rectangle
square

"Go to the ant,... consider his ways and be wise!" (Proverbs 6:6)

204

Fun with Shapes

Name_____

Create each object using the geometric shapes indicated.

circle (c) triangle (t) rectangle (r) trapezoid (tr) cylinder(cy) cone (co) square (s)

robot	house	boat
sample answer	Answers will vary.	
	Check to make sure your child used the correct shapes and amounts listed.	
1 cy, 4 r, 1 co, 3 t, 1 c	2 r, 1 t, 3 s	3 t, 2 c, 1 r, 1 tr
lighthouse	**fence**	**scarecrow**
1 cy, 1 co, 1 c, 4 s	4 r, 4 t	1 tr, 2 r, 2 cy, 1 s

205

Hmmm...

Name_____

Perimeter is the distance around an area. **Area** is the space inside a shape. Find the perimeter and area for each shape using each square unit.

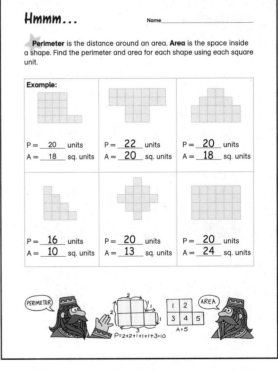

Example:

P = 20 units
A = 18 sq. units

P = 22 units
A = 20 sq. units

P = 20 units
A = 18 sq. units

P = 16 units
A = 10 sq. units

P = 20 units
A = 13 sq. units

P = 20 units
A = 24 sq. units

206

Answer Key

Animal Creations

Name_____

What is your favorite animal that God created? Draw that animal on this grid, using complete squares. When you have finished drawing, write the area of your animal.

Area: _____ boxes

Answers will vary.

207

Looking Good

Name_____

You have 3 T-shirts and 3 pairs of shorts.

Using the different colors of the clothes above, color these 9 outfits so that each one is different.

208

Full Hearts

Name_____

Matthew 22:37 tells us to "Love the Lord your God with all your heart." The Bible contains dozens of other verses that talk about the heart. The hearts on this page may look alike, but they are not. One is slightly different. Can you find which one it is? Look carefully.

209

Symbol Survey

Name_____

The youth group asked 60 church members which Christian symbol they liked best. Show the results of the survey on the graph using a different color for each type of symbol.

Favorite Symbol								
heart								
dove								
fish								
praying hands								
cross								
	0	5	10	15	20	25	30	35

Survey Results

15 chose a fish.
10 chose a cross.
5 chose a dove.
20 chose a heart.
10 chose praying hands.

Read the questions. Then using the graph above, fill in the correct answers.

1. What was the most favorite symbol? ___heart___
2. What was the least favorite symbol? ___dove___
3. Which was more popular—a fish or praying hands?
   ___a fish___
4. How many more people chose a heart than chose a cross?
   ___10___
5. How many more people chose a heart than chose praying hands?
   ___10___

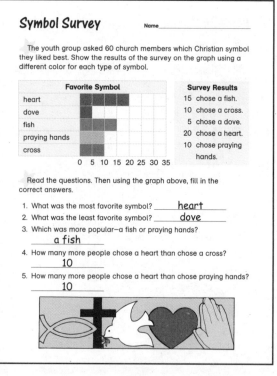

210

336

Answer Key

Faraway Friends

Name_____

Sharing Jesus' love with friends who live far away is fun. Refer to the chart to determine the cost of mailing each package.

If it weighs this amount or less...	5 oz.	10 oz.	15 oz.	1 lb. 4 oz.	1 lb. 9 oz.	1 lb. 14 oz.	2 lb. 3 oz.	2 lb. 8 oz.
It costs	50¢	$1.00	$1.25	$1.50	$1.75	$2.00	$2.25	$2.50

1.
weight: 3 oz.
cost: 50¢

3.
weight: 2 lbs.
cost: $2.25

5.
weight: 2 lbs. 5 oz.
cost: $2.50

2.
weight: 1 lb. 12 oz.
cost: $2.00

4.
weight: 9 oz.
cost: $1.00

6.
weight: 16 oz.
cost: $1.50

211

Summer Earnings

Name_____

The Bethlehem Boys Choir held fundraisers during the summer to raise money for a mission trip to Mexico. The church kept accounts for each boy. The table below shows the money each boy earned. Add the rows to fill in the total column.

Choir Members	June	July	August	Total
Tim	$12.50	$14.00	$10.00	$36.50
Jeff	$19.00	$17.60	$14.75	$51.35
Nick	$16.50	$13.85	$21.00	$51.35
Dan	$11.75	$14.25	$16.50	$42.50
Blake	$9.90	$11.20	$17.80	$38.50
Kyle	$15.00	$15.00	$15.00	$45.00

1. How much altogether did Dan earn? $42.50

2. How much more did Blake earn in August than in June?
$17.80 - $9.90 = $7.90

3. Which two boys earned the same total amount?
Jeff and Nick

4. Boys who were able to raise $45 or more received a prayer journal for the trip. Which boys raised enough funds to receive a prayer journal? Jeff, Nick, and Kyle

212

Cool Collections

Name_____

People love to collect things! Refer to the chart to answer each of the story problems. Show your work.

Sue	Mike	Ryan	Lisa	Mary	Austin
342 shells	425 baseball cards	1,098 coins	1,387 stamps	139 teddy bears	216 rocks

1. If Sue and Mary combined their collections, how many items would they have? 342 + 139 = 481

2. If Lisa gave 248 stamps to a friend, how many stamps would remain in her collection? 1,387 - 248 = 1,139

3. Do the girls or the boys own more items in their collections? How many more? The girls own more items. 1,868 - 1,739 = 129

4. Mike has collected 83 more items than Sue.

5. How many more items are in Mike's collection than in Austin's collection? 425 - 216 = 209

6. If Ryan sold 312 of his coins at a collectors' show, how many coins would remain in his collection? 1,098 - 312 = 786

7. Mary has 77 less items than Austin.

8. Ryan needs 289 more coins to equal the number of items in Lisa's collection. 1,387 - 1,098 = 289

213

Star Bright

Name_____

God promised Abraham that his descendants would be as plentiful as the stars in the sky. You can read this promise in Genesis 15:5. How many stars can you count in the picture below? Write the number in the blank. Color the stars using bright colors.

Coloring will vary.

I see 77 stars in the box.

217

337

Answer Key

Moses

Name_____

Moses brought the commandments down from Mount Sinai. Can you decode the first two commandments using the letter key below?

A	B	D	E	F	G	H	I	L	M	N	O	R	S	T	U	V	Y
4	16	13	3	17	6	10	1	12	11	18	5	7	14	9	2	15	8

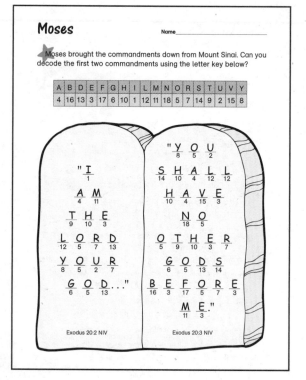

"I
1

AM
4 11

THE
9 10 3

LORD
12 5 7 13

YOUR
8 5 2 7

GOD..."
6 5 13

Exodus 20:2 NIV

"YOU
8 5 2

SHALL
14 10 4 12 12

HAVE
10 4 15 3

NO
18 5

OTHER
5 9 10 3 7

GODS
6 5 13 14

BEFORE
16 3 17 5 7 3

ME."
11 3

Exodus 20:3 NIV

218

Which Disciple?

Name_____

There are many stories about the disciples in the Bible. Read the questions below and look up the Bible verses to find the answers. Then, instead of writing a disciple's name, draw the symbol from the bottom of the page that represents that disciple. Names and symbols can be used more than once.

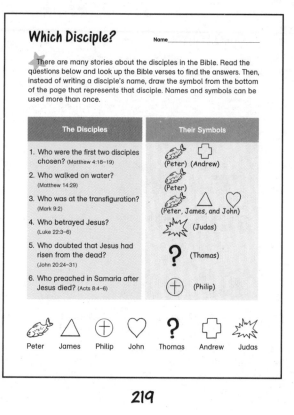

The Disciples	Their Symbols
1. Who were the first two disciples chosen? (Matthew 4:18–19)	(Peter) (Andrew)
2. Who walked on water? (Matthew 14:29)	(Peter)
3. Who was at the transfiguration? (Mark 9:2)	(Peter, James, and John)
4. Who betrayed Jesus? (Luke 22:3–6)	(Judas)
5. Who doubted that Jesus had risen from the dead? (John 20:24–31)	(Thomas)
6. Who preached in Samaria after Jesus died? (Acts 8:4–6)	(Philip)

Peter   James   Philip   John   Thomas   Andrew   Judas

219

Roll Call

Name_____

The crucifixion and the resurrection of Jesus are two of the most important events in Christian history. Many people were part of those stories. Who were they? Some of them are mentioned in the Bible verses below. Fit their names around the word resurrection.

Clues
1. He was set free instead of Jesus. (Mark 15:6–15)
2. He was the Roman governor. (Matthew 27:12–14)
3. He carried the cross for Jesus. (Mark 15:21)
4. He betrayed Jesus. (Luke 22:3–4)
5. They put a crown of thorns on Jesus. (Matthew 27:27–29)
6. This disciple disowned Jesus. (Matthew 26:69–75)
7. He placed Jesus' body in a tomb. (Matthew 27:57–60)
8. He brought spices to bury Jesus. (John 19:39–40)
9. He doubted that Jesus had risen. (John 20:24–25)
10. He was the high priest who tried Jesus. (Matthew 26:57)
11. They went to the tomb on Easter morning. (Luke 24:1)
12. He announced that Jesus had risen. (Matthew 28:5–6)

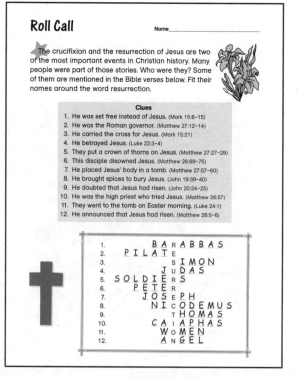

1. BARABBAS
2. PILATE
3. SIMON
4. JUDAS
5. SOLDIERS
6. PETER
7. JOSEPH
8. NICODEMUS
9. THOMAS
10. CAIAPHAS
11. WOMEN
12. ANGEL

220

Matthew 4:10

Name_____

Decode the Bible verse using the key below.

"...WORSHIP
THE LORD
YOUR GOD,
AND SERVE
HIM ONLY."

Matthew 4:10 NIV

221

Answer Key

Fishing for Men

Name_____

Jesus taught his disciples about the importance of believing in God. What did Jesus say when he asked them to be disciples? Catch the fish in order and write the words in the spaces.

"Come, follow me,...
and I will make
you fishers of men."

222

Let Others See Jesus in You

Name_____

Jesus wants us to tell others about Him. Decode the Bible verse using the key below.

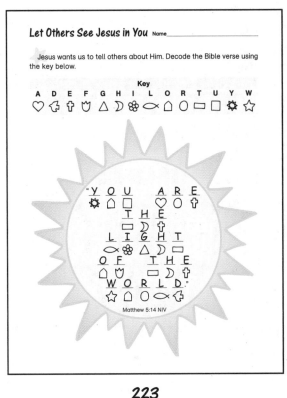

"YOU ARE
THE
LIGHT
OF THE
WORLD."

Matthew 5:14 NIV

223

Squared Off

Name_____

This puzzle reveals a promise that Jesus gave to his disciples before he ascended into heaven. Start with the letter **I** in the upper left corner of the grid. This is the first letter of the quote. Then skip every other letter to discover the message. Follow the direction of the arrows all the way around to the inside of the square. Write the verse on the lines at the bottom.

```
I J A Z M O W S I P T
                    N
H N E R V O E S R    H
Y               G    B
T   H S E Y A   Y    Y
M   D       S   D    G
O   T   E C G   E    O
U   L           L    D
T   F A O W D A N    U
E                    L
S T Y R A O W S L P  A
```

Matthew 28:20

I AM WITH YOU ALWAYS TO THE
VERY END OF THE AGE.
_____

224

Search and Find Mission

Name_____

Jesus told a parable of a man who owned 100 sheep. One sheep was lost, so the man left the other 99 and went searching for it. When he found his sheep, he was so happy he told his friends all about it.

Jesus also told the parable of a woman who lost a coin. After searching everywhere and then finding it, she was so happy that she called her neighbors to rejoice with her.

Jesus told these stories to teach us about God. God searches for sinners to come to him, and when they do, he rejoices.

Search for the lost sheep in the first puzzle. Clue: This sheep is different from the others. Then find the word **coin** hidden in the second puzzle.

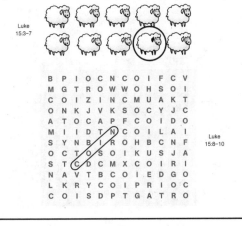

Luke 15:3-7

B P I O C N C O I F C V
M G T R O W W O H S O I
C O I Z I N C M U A K T
O N K J V K S O C Y J C
A T O C A P F C O I D O
M I I D T N C O I L A I
S Y N B I R O H B C N F
O C T O S O I K U S J A
S T C D C M X C O I R I
N A V T B C O I E D G O
L K R Y C O I P R I O C
C O I S D P T G A T R O

Luke 15:8-10

225

Answer Key

I Am

Name_____

Jesus often used the phrase "I am" in describing himself. For example, he said, "I am the way and the truth and the life." Many of these sayings come from the Book of John. Three "I am" phrases are illustrated for you below. Look up the verse to discover what Jesus said about himself and write it on the line by the picture. The last verse is for you to look up and illustrate in the box.

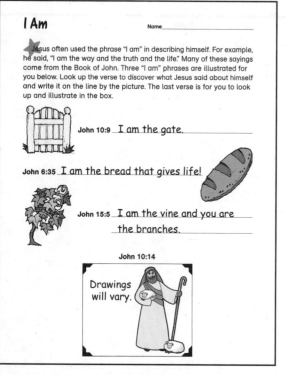

John 10:9 I am the gate.

John 6:35 I am the bread that gives life!

John 15:5 I am the vine and you are the branches.

John 10:14

Drawings will vary.

226

Love

Name_____

Jesus teaches us many things. He gave us a command to live by. Use the key below to find out what Jesus wants us to do.

"...LOVE ONE ANOTHER..."

John 13:34 NIV

227

Color Coded

Name_____

Follow the directions below. Color the boxes green that contain the words described below. Color all the remaining boxes yellow. The yellow boxes will reveal a teaching of Jesus taken from John 16:24.

Color these boxes green:
1. words that are parts of the body
2. words in the four corners
3. words that are foods
4. words containing a double t
5. names of the disciples
6. words beginning with S
7. words that are colors
8. New Testament books
9. words ending with ing

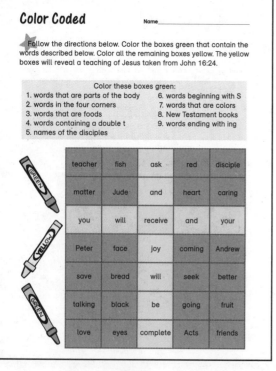

teacher	fish	ask	red	disciple
matter	Jude	and	heart	caring
you	will	receive	and	your
Peter	face	joy	coming	Andrew
save	bread	will	seek	better
talking	black	be	going	fruit
love	eyes	complete	Acts	friends

228

God is Awesome

Name_____

Our God is an awesome God! How are we to stand before him? Ecclesiastes 5:1 NIV tells us. Color each of the squares yellow that has a ▲ in the corner. The Bible verse will appear for you to read.

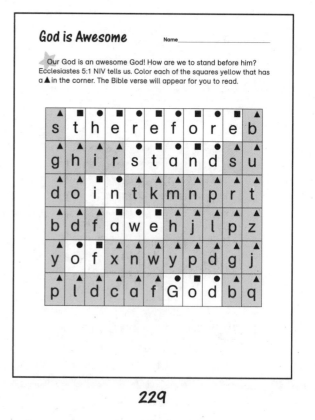

s	t	h	e	r	e	f	o	r	e	b
g	h	i	r	s	t	a	n	d	s	u
d	o	i	n	t	k	m	n	p	r	t
b	d	f	a	w	e	h	j	l	p	z
y	o	f	x	n	w	y	p	d	g	j
p	l	d	c	a	f	G	o	d	b	q

229

Answer Key

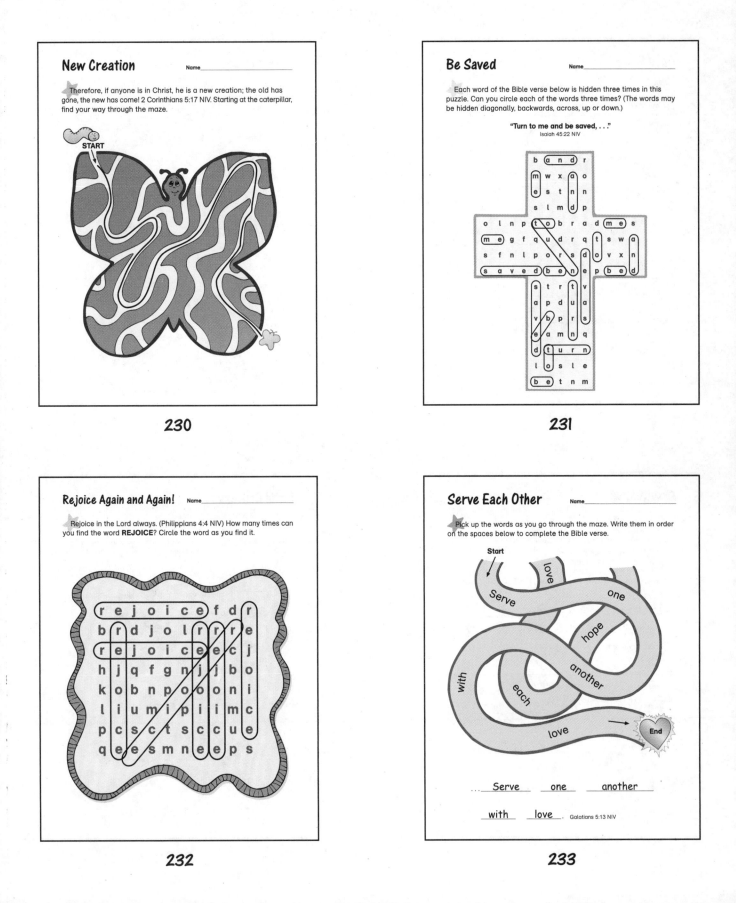

New Creation Name_____

Therefore, if anyone is in Christ, he is a new creation; the old has gone, the new has come! 2 Corinthians 5:17 NIV. Starting at the caterpillar, find your way through the maze.

START

230

Be Saved Name_____

Each word of the Bible verse below is hidden three times in this puzzle. Can you circle each of the words three times? (The words may be hidden diagonally, backwards, across, up or down.)

"Turn to me and be saved, . . ."
Isaiah 45:22 NIV

231

Rejoice Again and Again! Name_____

Rejoice in the Lord always. (Philippians 4:4 NIV) How many times can you find the word **REJOICE**? Circle the word as you find it.

232

Serve Each Other Name_____

Pick up the words as you go through the maze. Write them in order on the spaces below to complete the Bible verse.

Start

End

. . . __Serve__ __one__ __another__

__with__ __love__ . Galatians 5:13 NIV

233

Answer Key

Good Fruit

Name_____

In Galatians 5:22, we learn about the fruit of the Spirit. As Christians, we should possess these qualities. Search across and diagonally to discover the nine qualities hidden in the apple. Circle the words when you find them. When you are done, see if you can say them in order from memory.

The Fruit of the Spirit Is love, joy, peace, patience, kindness, goodness, faithfulness, gentleness, self-control

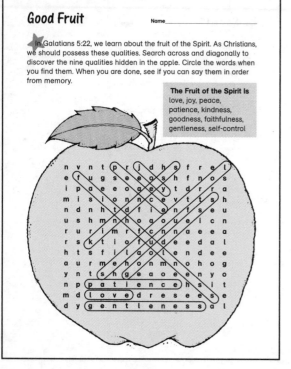

234

Armor of God

Name_____

Paul teaches us about the Armor of God. Do you know what that armor is? Write the letter that comes right before the letter shown in the alphabet. You will learn about the Armor of God.

RIGHTEOUS-
SJHIUFPVT
NESS
OFTT
TRUTH
USVUI
SALVATION
TBMWBUJPO
FAITH
GBJUI
WORD OF GOD
XPSE PG HPE
PEACE
QFBDF

Ephesians 5

235

Pray When?

Name_____

Follow the directions by crossing off the indicated words in the columns below. When you are done, the remaining words will spell out two Bible verses. Write the words in the correct order from top to bottom to discover an important message from 1 Thessalonians 5:16–17.

1. Cross off all words that start with the letter M.
2. Cross off every disciple's name.
3. Cross off all three-letter words.
4. Cross off the name of the person who fought Goliath.
5. Cross off all words that start with the letter E.
6. Cross off words that are clothing.
7. Cross off words that start and end with the same letter.
8. Cross off all books of the Bible.
9. Cross off all words that are fruits.
10. Cross off the name of the first person created by God.
11. Cross off all words that begin with the letter F.

~~John~~	~~apple~~	~~David~~
~~jacket~~	~~mother~~	be
~~Ruth~~	~~was~~	~~eddy~~
~~trust~~	~~grapes~~	~~series~~
~~Thomas~~	~~Adam~~	joyful
~~cat~~	~~Romans~~	~~may~~
always	~~shirt~~	~~so~~
~~married~~	pray	~~everyone~~
~~banana~~	~~Peter~~	continually
~~forever~~	~~Psalms~~	~~faith~~

The verses say:

Be joyful always. Pray
continually.

236

Little Critters

Name_____

Insects, birds, and small animals are mentioned often in the Bible. They were either regarded as pests or were used to teach lessons. Instead of word clues, this puzzle has picture clues of the critters mentioned in the Bible. Put them in the correct squares in the crossword puzzle.

ACROSS

1. Psalm 118:12
3. Job 39:20
4. Matthew 10:29
5. Proverbs 30:28
7. Exodus 8:22

DOWN

1. Leviticus 11:19
2. Luke 11:12
4. Job 8:14
6. Psalm 55:6

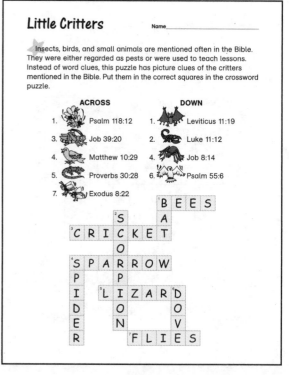

237

342

Answer Key

Bible Zoo

Name_____

When we think of certain people in the Bible, we often think of the animals that were part of their stories. Match the person in Column A with the animal that we associate with that person in Column B. Write the matching numbers in the blanks. Read the verses if you need help.

Column A	Column B
1. Jesus (Matthew 3:16)	4
2. Daniel (Daniel 6:16)	5
3. Queen of Sheba (1 Kings 10:1–2)	6
4. Peter (Mark 14:66–72)	7
5. John the Baptist (Matthew 3:1–4)	1
6. James and John (Luke 5:9–10)	2
7. Aaron (Exodus 7:8–10)	3

Solid Gold

Name_____

When recording artists have big hits, they receive gold records. The Bible talks about musicians too. Who were some of these musicians? Look them up and write their names on the lines at the bottom of the page.

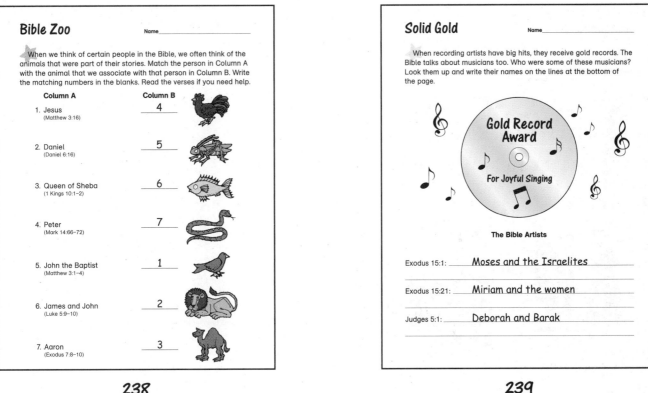

Gold Record Award

For Joyful Singing

The Bible Artists

Exodus 15:1: _Moses and the Israelites_

Exodus 15:21: _Miriam and the women_

Judges 5:1: _Deborah and Barak_

Pizza Scramble

Name_____

Can you discover the names of some Bible people hidden in the pizzas below? One letter of each person's name is in each slice. To find a name, pick one letter from each slice. The first letter is in the first slice. The second letter is in the second slice and so on. Move clockwise around the circle.

1. **Clues for Four-Letter Names**

The second book of the New Testament ___MARK___

A famous boat builder (Genesis 6:13–14) ___NOAH___

The first man (1 Corinthians 15:45) ___ADAM___

2. **Clues for Five-Letter Names**

Writer of many psalms (Psalm 23) ___DAVID___

He was swallowed by a great fish (Jonah 1:17) ___JONAH___

Abraham's original name (Genesis 17:5) ___ABRAM___

Soccer Balls

Name_____

Find out the answer to the statement under each soccer ball. Then write your answer in the five large spaces on the ball, one letter to a space. The first letter goes in the top space, directly under the arrow, as shown in the example. The letters should read clockwise around the ball. All answers are five-letter words.

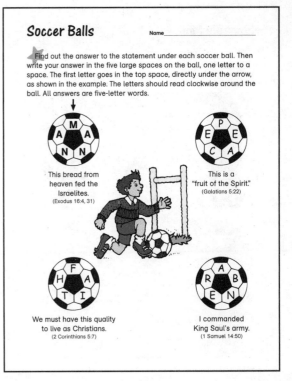

This bread from heaven fed the Israelites. (Exodus 16:4, 31)

This is a "fruit of the Spirit." (Galatians 5:22)

We must have this quality to live as Christians. (2 Corinthians 5:7)

I commanded King Saul's army. (1 Samuel 14:50)

Answer Key

Get Connected

Name_____

The words on this page are connected. The last letter of one word is the first letter of the next word. Read the clues to discover the names. Begin with clue 1.

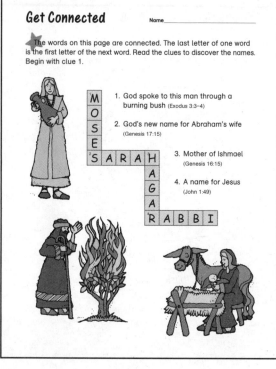

1. God spoke to this man through a burning bush (Exodus 3:3–4)

2. God's new name for Abraham's wife (Genesis 17:15)

3. Mother of Ishmael (Genesis 16:15)

4. A name for Jesus (John 1:49)

```
M
O
S
²S A R A H
    A
    G
    A
    R A B B I
```

242

Who Am I?

Name_____

In the box below, cross off all names that appear four times. The name that is left is the answer that fits the description at the bottom of the page.

~~Moses~~	~~Paul~~	~~Eve~~	~~Job~~	~~Ruth~~
~~Ezra~~	~~Ruth~~	~~Hosea~~	Elijah	~~Eve~~
~~Paul~~	~~Job~~	~~Ruth~~	~~Ezra~~	~~Ruth~~
~~Ezra~~	~~Eve~~		~~Moses~~	~~Paul~~
~~Job~~	~~Hosea~~	~~Moses~~	~~Hosea~~	~~Job~~
~~Moses~~	~~Eve~~	~~Ezra~~	~~Paul~~	~~Hosea~~

I was the prophet who was carried to heaven in a chariot of fire.

Who am I? _____Elijah_____

2 Kings 2:11

243

Meet My Mom

Name_____

Match these Bible sons with their mothers. Draw a line from the child listed in column A to his mother in column B. You will find the answers in the verses listed at the bottom of the page. Do you think these children brought flowers to their mothers, just as children do today?

Column A	Column B
Abel	Mary
Isaac	Elizabeth
Jacob	Rachel
Joseph	Hannah
Samuel	Rebekah
John	Eve
Jesus	Sarah

Verses
Genesis 4:1–2
Genesis 21:3
Genesis 27:11
Genesis 30:25
1 Samuel 1:20
Luke 1:57–60
Luke 1:29–31

Draw a flower that you could give to someone you love.

Drawings will vary.

244

Meet My Dad

Name_____

Children and their fathers are a big part of the bible story. Match the child in the left column with his or her father in the right column. Then put the father's name into the puzzle at the bottom. Read the verses listed at the bottom of the page if you need help. You will have to decide how the names fit into the grid.

	Children	Dads
D	1. Solomon	A. Abraham
F	2. James	B. Adam
C	3. Miriam	C. Amram
E	4. Leah	D. David
B	5. Seth	E. Laban
A	6. Isaac	F. Zebedee

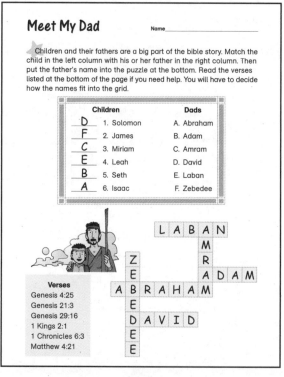

Verses
Genesis 4:25
Genesis 21:3
Genesis 29:16
1 Kings 2:1
1 Chronicles 6:3
Matthew 4:21

```
        L A B A N
              M
              R
              R A D A M
Z E B R A H A M
E
D A V I D
E
E
```

245

Answer Key

Crossings

Name_____

Each mini-crossword puzzle below has two words that share a letter. The clues provide the two words. You will have to figure out how the words fit together. Find the answers in the verses listed at the bottom of the page.

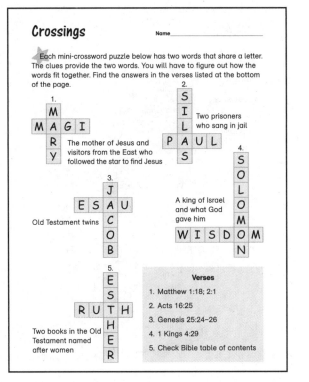

1. MAGI / MARY — The mother of Jesus and visitors from the East who followed the star to find Jesus

2. SILAS / PAUL — Two prisoners who sang in jail

3. ESAU / JACOB — Old Testament twins

4. SOLOMON / WISDOM — A king of Israel and what God gave him

5. ESTHER / RUTH — Two books in the Old Testament named after women

Verses
1. Matthew 1:18; 2:1
2. Acts 16:25
3. Genesis 25:24–26
4. 1 Kings 4:29
5. Check Bible table of contents

246

Sailing with Paul

Name_____

Paul was a great missionary who sailed to many parts of the world. Read the verses listed below to solve the puzzle and find out some of the places he visited on his three missionary journeys.

Down
1. Acts 19:1
2. Acts 15:4

Across
3. Acts 20:2
4. Acts 13:4
5. Acts 28:14

EPHESUS / JERUSALEM / GREECE / CYPRUS / ROME

247

Sunshine for a Hurt

Name_____

Forgiveness is like the sun. We welcome it, and it gives warmth to a hurting heart. Forgiveness brings happiness and peace, both to the forgiver and the one forgiven. Look up the verses on the suns to discover who in the bible forgave. Fill in the blanks below.

___Jesus___ forgave his enemies.

___Esau___ forgave Jacob.

___Joseph___ forgave his brothers.

___Stephen___ forgave those who stoned him.

___A father___ forgave his son.

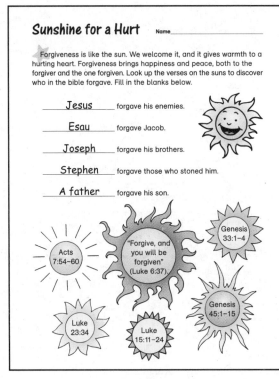

Acts 7:54–60

"Forgive, and you will be forgiven" (Luke 6:37).

Genesis 33:1–4

Luke 23:34

Luke 15:11–24

Genesis 45:1–15

248

Who . . . ?

Name_____

The answers to these questions are in the box below. Each answer is the name of a person. Read the questions. Then fill in the blanks with the correct name from the box below. Pictures take the place of key words.

| Peter | Jesus | Job |
| Balaam | Ezekiel | Benaiah |

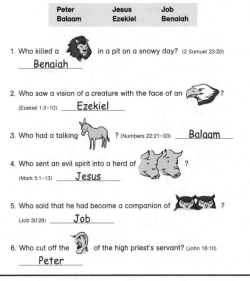

1. Who killed a 🦁 in a pit on a snowy day? (2 Samuel 23:20)
   ___Benaiah___

2. Who saw a vision of a creature with the face of an 🦅?
   (Ezekiel 1:3–10) ___Ezekiel___

3. Who had a talking 🐴? (Numbers 22:21–33) ___Balaam___

4. Who sent an evil spirit into a herd of 🐷?
   (Mark 5:1–13) ___Jesus___

5. Who said that he had become a companion of 🦉?
   (Job 30:29) ___Job___

6. Who cut off the 👂 of the high priest's servant? (John 18:10)
   ___Peter___

249

345

Answer Key

Weather Report

Name_____

People often plan activities around the weather. The Bible contains many references to weather. Look at the picture clues on the right that show weather conditions. Decide which picture fits in the Bible verse on the left and fill in the blank. Words may be used more than once.

1. "Like __snow__ in summer or __rain__ in harvest, honor is not fitting for a fool" (Proverbs 26:1).

2. "He makes __clouds__ rise from the ends of the earth; he sends __lightning__ with the __rain__ and brings out the wind from his storehouses" (Psalm 135:7).

3. "When the __sun__ was setting, the people brought to Jesus all who had various kinds of sickness, and laying his hands on each one, he healed them" (Luke 4:40).

4. "As a north wind brings __rain__, so a sly tongue brings angry looks" (Proverbs 25:23).

5. "The __sun__ stopped in the middle of the sky and delayed going down about a full day" (Joshua 10:13).

250

PSALM 23

Name_____

Find and circle the familiar words of the 23rd Psalm in the puzzle below. Remember, the words can appear backwards, across, and up and down.

Words to find:

The Lord is
my shepherd.
Psalm 23

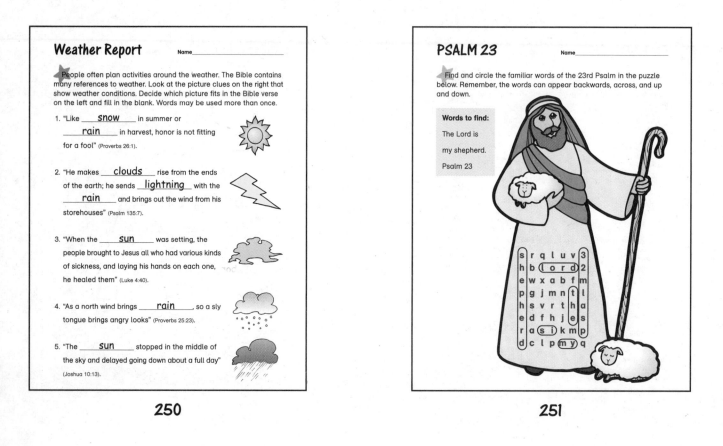

```
s r q l u v 3
h b l o r d 2
e w x a b f m
p g j m n t l
h s v r t h a
e d f h j e s
r a s i k m p
d c l p m y q
```

251

Names for God

Name_____

The Book of Psalms uses a variety of names for God. Each gives us a different picture of what God is like. This crossword puzzle contains some of those names. Look up the verses and put each name in the correct place in the puzzle.

The Lord God Is a Sun.
Psalm 84:11

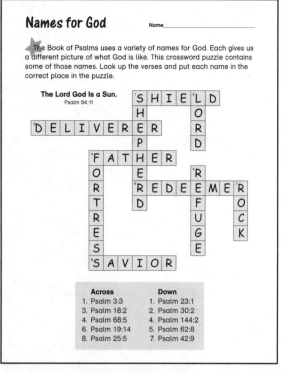

Crossword answers:
- SHIELD
- SHEPHERD
- LORD
- DELIVERER
- FATHER
- FORTRESS
- REDEEMER
- ROCK
- REFUGE
- SAVIOR

Across	Down
1. Psalm 3:3	1. Psalm 23:1
3. Psalm 18:2	2. Psalm 30:2
4. Psalm 68:5	4. Psalm 144:2
6. Psalm 19:14	5. Psalm 62:8
8. Psalm 25:5	7. Psalm 42:9

252

Make a Joyful Noise

Name_____

Color this verse from Psalm 95:1.

COME LET US SING FOR JOY TO THE LORD.

Coloring will vary.

253

Answer Key

Deciphering

Name_____

Using the code below, discover an inspiring verse from Psalm 121:8.

Code

1	2	3	4	5	6	7
l	w	t	b	g	i	c

8	9	10	11	12	13	14
d	f	y	h	u	m	r

15	16	17	18	19
n	v	a	o	e

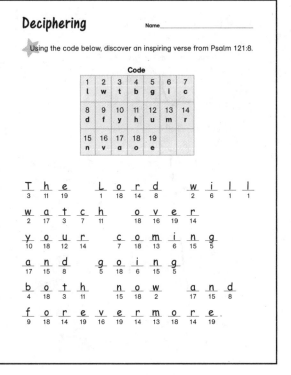

The Lord will
3 11 19 1 18 14 8 2 6 1 1

watch over
2 17 3 7 11 18 16 19 14

your coming
10 18 12 14 7 18 13 6 15 5

and going
17 15 8 5 18 6 15 5

both now and
4 18 3 11 15 18 2 17 15 8

forevermore.
9 18 14 19 16 19 14 13 18 14 19

254

Whose Job Is It?

Name_____

People had jobs or occupations in biblical times, just as we do today. Look up the verses and find out who worked at each job pictured.

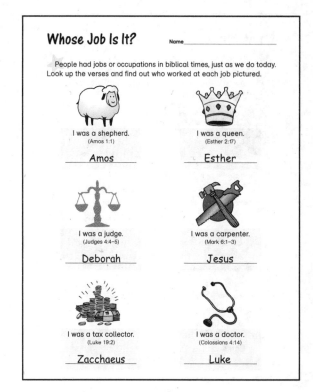

I was a shepherd.
(Amos 1:1)

Amos

I was a queen.
(Esther 2:17)

Esther

I was a judge.
(Judges 4:4–5)

Deborah

I was a carpenter.
(Mark 6:1–3)

Jesus

I was a tax collector.
(Luke 19:2)

Zacchaeus

I was a doctor.
(Colossians 4:14)

Luke

255

Reminders

Name_____

The Bible is brimful of good advice. A clipboard is a handy way to keep ideas in front of you and is easy to carry around. Look up the verses below and write them on the clipboard.

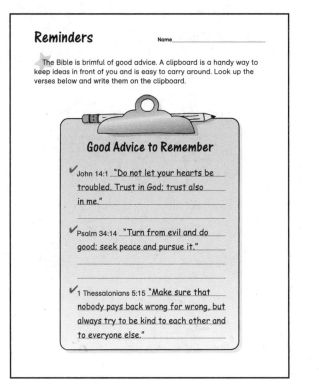

Good Advice to Remember

✔ John 14:1 "Do not let your hearts be troubled. Trust in God; trust also in me."

✔ Psalm 34:14 "Turn from evil and do good; seek peace and pursue it."

✔ 1 Thessalonians 5:15 "Make sure that nobody pays back wrong for wrong, but always try to be kind to each other and to everyone else."

256

Friendship

Name_____

Jesus taught us about friendship. Connect the letters in order on the telephone wires to complete the Bible verse below.

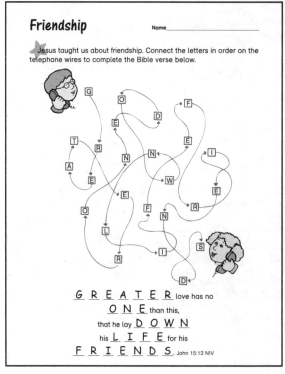

G R E A T E R love has no
O N E than this,
that he lay D O W N
his L I F E for his
F R I E N D S. John 15:13 NIV

257

Answer Key

My Friend
Name

Friends are very important in our lives. They were important for Bible people, too. Look up these friends' names and write them on the lines below.

I was called "God's friend."
(James 2:23)

Abraham

I was David's friend.
(1 Samuel 20:42)

Jonathan

My husband and I were friends of Paul and risked our lives to help him.
(Romans 16:3–4)

Priscilla

I was a friend to Paul while he was in prison.
(2 Timothy 1:16–17)

Onesiphorus

Aquila

258

Love Is . . .
Name

Look up the verses below, then write these verses of love in the hearts.

1 Peter 4:8

"Above all, love each other deeply, because love covers over a multitude of sins."

1 Corinthians 16:14

"Do everything in love."

"Whoever does not love does not know God, because God is love."

1 John 4:8

LOVE

259

Grocery Shopping
Name

Today when we go to the grocery store, we buy food that we like to eat. What kinds of food did people in biblical times eat and drink? Find out the answer to that question by reading the verses below. Write the foods mentioned in the verses on the grocery list to discover what people ate long ago.

- Numbers 11:5
- Deuteronomy 23:24
- 1 Samuel 14:25
- 2 Samuel 17:28
- Proverbs 27:18
- Proverbs 27:27
- Isaiah 17:6

Grocery List
fish
cucumbers
melons
leeks
onions
garlic
grapes
honey
wheat
barley
flour
roasted grain
beans
lentils
figs
goats' milk
olives

260

In High Places
Name

Discover the names of several mountains mentioned in the Bible. Using one of the boxed letters in the word *mountains* as the first letter in your answer, put a mountain's name in the squares. Clues are listed below.

CLUES
The mountain where Jesus prayed before he was arrested by the soldiers. (Luke 22:39–42)

The mountain where Moses died. (Deuteronomy 32:48–50)

The mountain where Noah's ark came to rest at the end of the flood. (Genesis 8:4)

The mountain where Moses received the Ten Commandments from God. (Numbers 3:1)

BIBLE

M	O	U	N	T	A	I	N	S
	L			E				I
	I			B				N
	V			O				A
	E			R				I
	S			A				
				R				
				A				
				T				

261

Answer Key

The Flood

Name_____

During the flood God stayed with Noah and kept him safe. God is always with you, too. Fill in the crossword puzzle below. The first word has been filled in to get you started.

rain   promise   animals
rainbow   Noah   flood

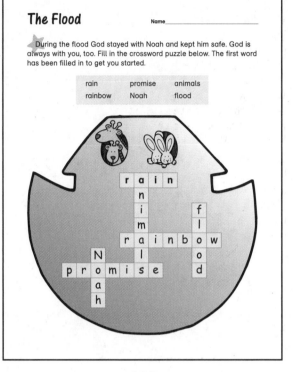

262

10 Plagues

Name_____

Pharaoh would not let Moses and the Israelites leave Egypt! So, God sent ten plagues upon the people. Find and circle the ten plagues listed below in the puzzle.

blood   frogs   gnats   flies   livestock
boils   hail   locusts   darkness   firstborn

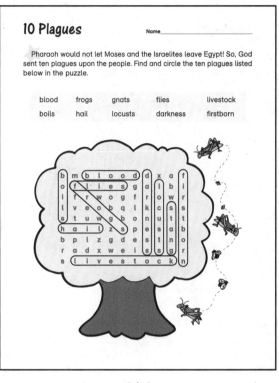

263

Praise God!

Name_____

Start with the letter P and write each letter in the spaces below as you come to them in the maze.

P R A I S E T H E
L O R D

264

3 Jews

Name_____

King Nebuchadnezzar wanted people to worship false gods. Three Jews refused because they loved God. Using the key below, decode their names. Remember to capitalize the first letter of each name.

Shadrach
Meshach
Abednego

265

Answer Key

BAPTISM

Name_____

God was very pleased with Jesus. When John baptized Jesus, something very special happened. Beginning with the letter "H", go around the dove and write every other letter on the spaces provided.

HE
SAW
THE
SPIRIT
OF
GOD
DESCENDING
LIKE
A
DOVE
MATTHEW
3:16

266

God Can Do

Name_____

Many people wonder what God can really do. What does Luke teach us about God? Using the key below, decode the message to find out what the Bible says God can do.

KEY

A 9
C 6   D 3
E 5   G 8   H 7
I 12   N 4   O 2   R 1
T 10   V 0   Y 11

G O D   C A N
8 2 3   6 9 4

D O
3 2

E V E R Y T H I N G
5 0 5 1 11 10 7 12 4 8

267

Galatians 5:22

Name_____

But the fruit of the spirit is love, joy, peace, patience, kindness, goodness, faithfulness, gentleness and self-control. Paul tells us how to live in the Spirit of God. Fill in the words from the verse above in the spaces below.

peace
patience
gentleness
kindness
self-control
joy
goodness
love
faithfulness

268

Jesus Loves Me

Name_____

This familiar song is the key to completing this crossword puzzle. Use the missing words from the song to complete the puzzle.

Jesus loves me this I __know__ (5)
For the Bible tells me __so__ (6)
Little ones to Him __belong__ (1 down)
They are weak, but He is __strong__ (7)
Yes, __Jesus__ loves me (3)
Yes, Jesus __loves__ me (2)
Yes, Jesus loves __me__ (4)
The __Bible__ tells me so (1 across)

B i b l e
J   m   o
e   e   v
s k n o w e
u   n   s o
s t r o n g

269

350

Answer Key

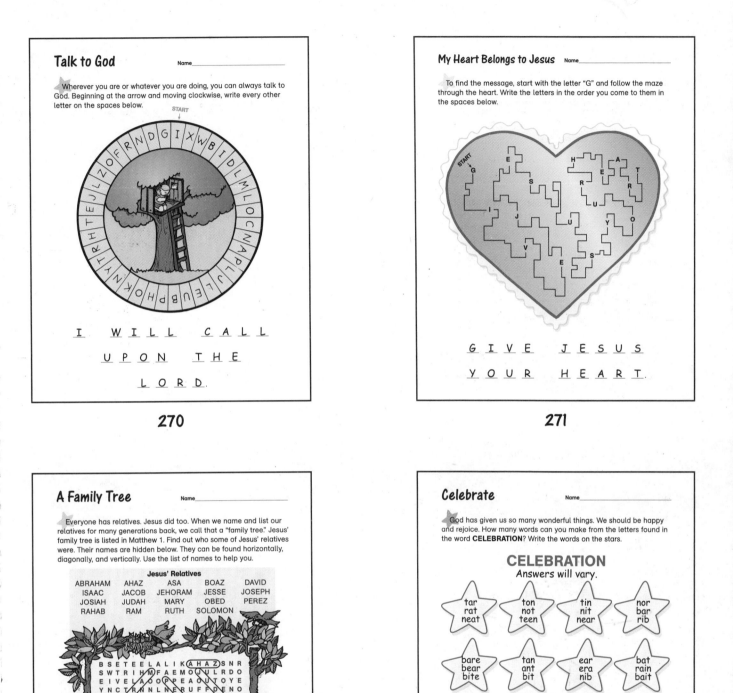

Talk to God

Name_____

Wherever you are or whatever you are doing, you can always talk to God. Beginning at the arrow and moving clockwise, write every other letter on the spaces below.

I WILL CALL

UPON THE

LORD.

270

My Heart Belongs to Jesus

Name_____

To find the message, start with the letter "G" and follow the maze through the heart. Write the letters in the order you come to them in the spaces below.

GIVE JESUS

YOUR HEART.

271

A Family Tree

Name_____

Everyone has relatives. Jesus did too. When we name and list our relatives for many generations back, we call that a "family tree." Jesus' family tree is listed in Matthew 1. Find out who some of Jesus' relatives were. Their names are hidden below. They can be found horizontally, diagonally, and vertically. Use the list of names to help you.

Jesus' Relatives

ABRAHAM	AHAZ	ASA	BOAZ	DAVID
ISAAC	JACOB	JEHORAM	JESSE	JOSEPH
JOSIAH	JUDAH	MARY	OBED	PEREZ
RAHAB	RAM	RUTH	SOLOMON	

272

Celebrate

Name_____

God has given us so many wonderful things. We should be happy and rejoice. How many words can you make from the letters found in the word **CELEBRATION**? Write the words on the stars.

CELEBRATION
Answers will vary.

tar rat neat	ton not teen	tin nit near	nor bar rib
bare bear bite	tan ant bit	ear era nib	bat rain bait
tee tie bail	lie liar bore	tone note rob	rate tear eat
beet beat ail	bee art rail	are tab lair	bet ran elation

273

351

Answer Key

Twisters

Name_____

If you enjoy challenges, this word search is for you! Hidden in the puzzle grid are the names of 12 books of the bible. The names are twisted and curved—not in a straight line. The letters in a word may be found next to each other in any direction. The letters in one word will never cross or be joined with another word. One has been done for you.

Books of the Bible

AMOS	JOB	NUMBERS
DANIEL	JOEL	PROVERBS
GENESIS	MALACHI	REVELATION
HEBREWS	MATTHEW	TITUS

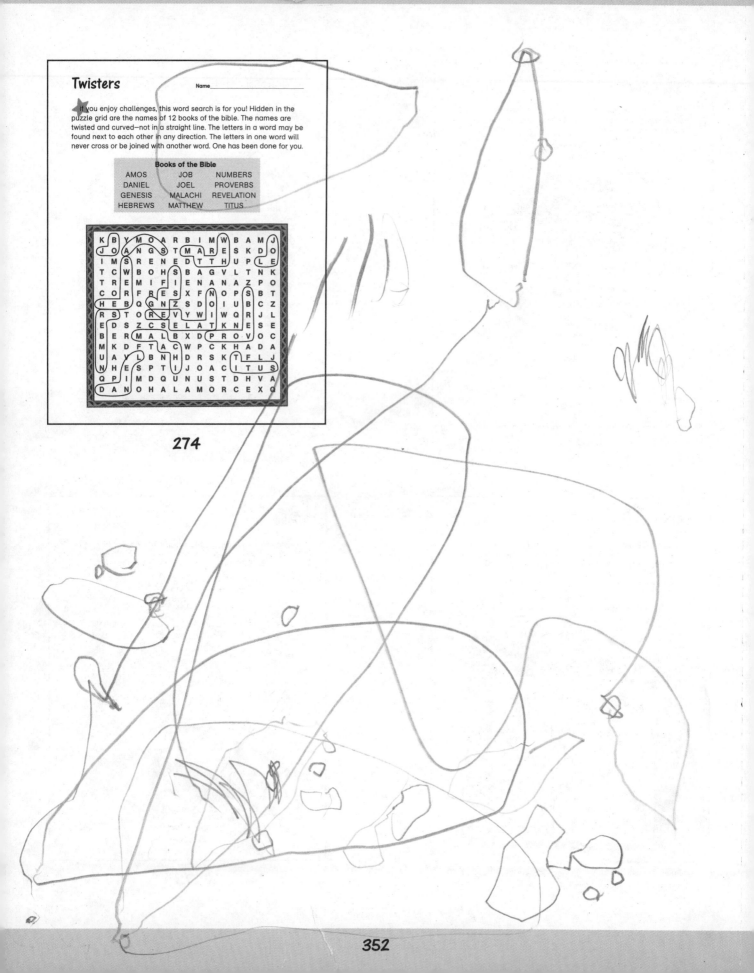

274